# Strange Journey

John R. Friedeberg Seeley and the Quest for Mental Health

**North American Jewish Studies**

**Series Editor:**
Ira Robinson (Concordia University)

# Strange Journey

John R. Friedeberg Seeley and
the Quest for Mental Health

PAUL ROBERTS BENTLEY

BOSTON
2020

**Library of Congress Cataloging-in-Publication Data**

**Names:** Bentley, Paul Roberts, 1962- author.
**Title:** Strange journey : John R. Friedeberg-Seeley and the quest for mental health / by Paul Roberts Bentley.
**Description:** Boston : Academic Studies Press, [2020] | Includes bibliographical references and index.
**Identifiers:** LCCN 2019008857 (print) | LCCN 2019011130 (ebook) | ISBN 9781644690512 (ebook) | ISBN 9781644690499 (hardcover : alk. paper) | ISBN 9781644690505 (pbk. : alk. paper)
**Subjects:** LCSH: Seeley, John R. | Seeley, John R.--Mental health. | Social reformers--Mental health--Biography. | Social reformers--Canada--Biography. | Jews--Canada--Biography. | Jews--Canada--Identity. | York University (Toronto, Ont.)--Biography.
**Classification:** LCC RC464.F74 (ebook) | LCC RC464.F74 B46 2019 (print) | DDC 362.196/8900924071--dc23
LC record available at https://lccn.loc.gov/2019008857

Copyright © 2020 Academic Studies Press
All rights reserved.

ISBN 978-1-64469-051-2 (electronic, Adobe PDF)
ISBN 978-1-64469-049-9 (hardback)
ISBN 978-1-64469-050-5 (paperback)

Book and cover design by Lapiz Digital Services.

Published by Academic Studies Press.
1577 Beacon Street
Brookline, MA 02446, USA

press@academicstudiespress.com
www.academicstudiespress.com

For my Family:

Zena, Alia, Javed, and Saara

# Contents

| | | |
|---|---|---:|
| | List of Illustrations | 1 |
| | Prologue | 3 |
| 1. | There Was a Mother in Israel | 14 |
| 2. | Home Child | 32 |
| 3. | From Civilian to Fighting Man | 39 |
| 4. | Pop Sociology | 66 |
| 5. | Mental Health for Canada | 81 |
| 6. | The Transmission of Anti-Semitism | 99 |
| 7. | The Cold White Light of Detachment | 103 |
| 8. | Free Discussion | 111 |
| 9. | Anti-Semitic Segregation | 117 |
| 10. | Film Noir | 134 |
| 11. | Unorthodox Psycho-Analysis | 147 |
| 12. | Nazi Terror | 158 |
| 13. | Floating Anxiety | 171 |
| 14. | The Unpublished Version of *Crestwood Heights* | 182 |
| 15. | Waspish Tone | 188 |
| 16. | Jewish Tempers in the Village | 205 |

| | |
|---|---:|
| 17. Protégé | 216 |
| 18. Uprising at York University | 222 |
| | |
| Epilogue | 232 |
| Endnotes | 241 |
| Bibliography | 259 |
| Index | 266 |

A slight thing, like a phrase or jest, often makes a greater revelation of character than battles where thousands fall.
—Plutarch, *Life of Alexander*

# List of Illustrations

**Cover Photo:** Dr. W. Line, OBE; Col. E. Bullis; John R. Seeley; CMHA President, Dr. J. Griffin. Centre for Addiction and Mental Health (CAMH) Archives, CMHA fonds.

1. Letter from Dr. Spock to Seeley, 1952. Seeley Papers, Los Angeles, California.
2. John R. Friedeberg Seeley, March 2007.
3. Death Notice of Else Wolff, 1922, Borchardt-Pincus-Peise, Family Website.
4. Seeley's Poetry, ca. 1952. Fischer Papers, Toronto, Ontario.
5. Lorneville JCT CNR, 1908. Courtesy of the Ross Gray Collection.
6. Dr. Clarence Meredith Hincks (1885–1964), co-founder of the Canadian National Committee for Mental Hygiene (CNCMH) in 1918, serving as its first Director General. During the 1930s Dr. Hincks was also, conjointly, head of the National Committees for Mental Hygiene in the United States. Courtesy of CAMH Archives.
7. Clarence Hincks' 1946 Macleans Article. Courtesy of CAMH Archives.
8. In 1942 Dr. Brock Chisholm was photographed in his Canadian Army General Staff uniform at National Defense Headquarter. Courtesy of CAMH Archives.
9. Memo from Seeley to Chisolm, ca. 1945. Seeley Papers, Los Angeles, California.
10. American sociologist, professor, and author David Riesman sits and reads a book, early 1950s. Photo by Pictorial Parade, Courtesy of Getty Images.
11. Flow Chart "Mental Health in Canada," 1947. Seeley Papers, Los Angeles, California.

# List of Illustrations

12. Prof. John Seeley, 1950s. Photo by Jeff Goode, *Toronto Star*, Getty Images.
13. Forest Hill Junior High School, 1948. Baldwin Collection, Toronto Reference Library.
14. The Toronto Psychiatric Hospital opened in 1925 at 2 Surrey Place. Its focus expanded to encompass all branches of psychiatry following the arrival of Dr. Aldwyn Stokes in 1947 as its director and head of psychiatry. Courtesy of CAMH Archives.
15. Exterior View of Holy Blossom Temple, Bathurst St., Toronto (ca.1956). Ontario Jewish Archives, Blankenstein Family Heritage Center, Item 932.
16. *Toronto Daily Star* coverage of School "Regrouping," October 14, 1950.
17. Forest Hill, Looking S.W. from Old Forest Hill Road, 1953. Photo by James Victor Salmon, Baldwin Collection, Courtesy of the Toronto Reference Library.
18. Beatrice Fischer and John R. Seeley in her Home, 1990s. Courtesy of Beatrice Fischer.
19. Letter from Seeley to Fischer, 1952. Fischer Papers, Toronto, Ontario.
20. Fischer's Appointment Book, Fischer Papers, Toronto, Ontario.
21. Letter from Fischer to his Brothers, March 31, 1941. Fischer Papers, Toronto, Ontario.
22. Martin Fischer with Patient, 1950s. Photo by Graham Bezant, *Toronto Star*, Getty Images.
23. Letter from Margaret Seeley to the Fischers, 1950s. Fischer Papers, Toronto, Ontario.
24. An Example of Seeley's "Time Budget," 1960s. Clara Thomas Archives, York U.
25. Aldwyn Stokes, 1957. Courtesy of CAMH Archives.
26. *Crestwood Heights* hits the front page of the *Toronto Daily Star*, May 3, 1956.
27. Clayton Ruby, ca. 1950s. Photo by Rick Eglinton, *Toronto Star*, Getty Images.
28. Murray Ross. Photo by Annette Buchowski, *Toronto Star*, Getty Images.
29. The Bentleys of Port Greville, ca. 1910 (my grandfather, "Wicks," second from left, bottom row; and his father George E. Bentley, second from right, bottom row). Courtesy of the Mariners Museum, *Newport News*, Virginia.

# Prologue

For almost twenty years I trudged down the halls of the Clarke Institute toward my psychiatrist's corner office, the very halls that Seeley once walked, hoping this time I would make the final breakthrough. In the early sessions, I rejected the medication that was recommended. In fact, I made it a condition of my participation in long-term psychotherapy that there would be "no drugs." Eventually, I came to regret this naïve pride in my freedom. I threw myself into psychotherapy, and as much as I attended my sessions dutifully, I studied the works of Freud, Jung, Kohut and other writers in the psychoanalytic tradition. Freud said that all psychoanalyses come to some form of tragic ending. My experience of this was to learn that, while the process itself was therapeutic, no particular insight or *temps retrouve* would bring an end to my suffering. My psychiatrist once applauded my efforts by saying that my success in coping with Obsessive-Compulsive Disorder (OCD) by therapeutic means alone was worthy of academic publication. But it was the hope of a final cure that drove me on. Such hope is a cruel master. It is no wonder hope was the last affliction to fly from Pandora's box.

Yet, through it all I made certain beneficial changes in my life. I abandoned the political ambitions that had once driven me from the London School of Economics to Law School at McGill University. The more self-contained career of a high school history teacher proved an effective antidote in my case of what Seeley would refer to as "floating anxiety."[1] As I settled into teaching, I became convinced that the techniques of my psychotherapist might prove useful in the classroom. Moreover, mental health in schools had become a central public policy issue during the course of my career which began in the 1990s. For example, the CBC reported on October 7, 2014 that recent studies in the field of pediatric psychiatry suggest "there may be a need for a national strategy to address the mental health needs of children in schools." In fact, mental health is now a strategic priority of the School Board where I work as head of a History Department.

Like so many people whose activism is motivated by a desire to solve the problem that besets them, at least for the sake of others if not themselves, I too set out in search of a cure for mental illness as part of my work in the field of education. I served on many character education and mental health committees. I wrote-up committee reports and spoke at professional learning conferences, but none of this satisfied me that I was making a difference. For one thing, it soon became apparent that there is no consensus about what should be done. As a Superintendent of Schools once said to me, "Character education *is* rocket science."

I turned to a more academic approach and began a doctoral program at the Ontario Institute for Studies in Education (OISE). At the time I was teaching History and Philosophy classes, so I entered the now defunct program in the History and Philosophy of Education. If my ambition to make a theoretical breakthrough in the field of mental health education was a wash-out, at least I would improve my teaching skills. When I asked my doctoral dissertation supervisor David Levine whether I should study Anna Freud and the "matchbox school" in Vienna as an exemplar of mental health pedagogy, he quickly put an end to my ambitious plans.[2] I could not speak German, he pointed out, and the financial cost of such a study would be formidable. Instead he suggested that perhaps something was going on in Toronto in the early days of psychoanalysis that would be more accessible.

I began to rummage through the archives at the Center for Addiction and Mental Health (CAMH) in Toronto and stumbled across a file entitled, "The Forest Hill Village Project." To my surprise this had been a major federally funded mental health project conducted in the schools of Toronto between 1948 and 1956. Forest Hill Village is a wealthy suburban community in north Toronto set along the crest of a ridge overlooking the city. The project was organized by the Canadian Mental Health Association (CMHA) in co-operation with the University of Toronto (U of T) Department of Psychiatry. It had introduced a version of group psychotherapy in the classroom and psychiatric clinics in schools. John R. Seeley, a sociologist with the U of T Department of Psychiatry, who also carried the title "Director of the Forest Hill Village Project," was its leader.

I was shocked to learn that there was a directly relevant history here in Canada to what has been presented in the media and institutional discourse, in my experience, as a new frontier in social policy. At the same time, however, I was relieved to discover an historical model of preventive psychiatry in Canadian schools which might lend perspective to the efforts of today's policy-makers, if not in my own practice as an educator. Then the question became whether a trail of historical documents leading back to this overlooked episode in the history of mental health in Canada could be found? This problem was solved by the rather prolix writings of the leader of the project, John R. Seeley.

When I began my search for more information about Seeley, I found that his importance as an author and educator was not to be underestimated. Many of his academic colleagues thought very highly of him. For example, Professor Leonard Duhl, M.D., of the University of California, Berkeley, wrote of his career in the following superlative terms:

> John R. Seeley is superb. He is truly a Renaissance man with deep perceptions, understanding and scholarship in vast numbers of fields ranging from philosophy to mathematics to sociology. He is a social critic and teacher with little competition. In fact, I can find nothing but superb adjectives to describe the mind, the heart and the soul of this man. Any place that gets him as a professor will be getting one of the outstanding people in the world.[3]

His protégé Clayton Ruby, a Toronto lawyer famous for his defense of Guy Paul Morin and Donald Marshal Jr., both wrongfully convicted of murder, claimed that Seeley was a "leading figure in Canadian education." Similarly, Professor Morris Schwartz, of Brandeis University in Massachusetts, wrote of Seeley: "He is the most gifted all-around social scientist I know (and I do not make such statements lightly). His book *Crestwood Heights* is the most sophisticated study of a community extant."[4]

Indeed, the scholarly consensus remains that *Crestwood Heights*, Seeley's sociological study of the community of Forest Hill where he conducted his mental health project in schools, was a significant literary achievement:

> David Riesman's *The Lonely Crowd* (1950), John R. Seeley's *Crestwood Heights* (1956) and William H. Whyte, Jr's *The Organization Man* (1956) were classics of 1950s social science that had a major impact on social

thought. Repeatedly referenced, they introduced new ways of understanding what was happening in the postwar period. This work left a lasting imprint because it helped to shape the terms of discourse about American society, not only in the 1950s but for decades to come.[5]

Lionel Trilling, a leading twentieth-century American literary critic, went so far as to suggest that these sociological works threatened to "take-over from literature one of literature's most characteristic functions, the investigation and criticism of morals and manners."[6] However, as was always the case with Seeley, high praise was mixed with some controversy.

Seeley's more famous friend and mentor from the University of Chicago (U of C) David Riesman, author of the *Lonely Crowd*, complained in his introduction to *Crestwood Heights* of an *excessive* moralism, saying that he wished Seeley "had the novelist's insouciance, as well as the novelist's sensitivity to anxiety and other forms of mental suffering among the well-to-do."[7] This sharp criticism of a book that arose out of a mental health project, and of a friend who was well-known to Riesman to be a strong proponent of psychoanalysis, calls for explanation.

Riesman also felt that the book was "not sufficiently allusive."[8] It is remarkable, for example, that Seeley's critique of the culture of the suburbs repeated, without acknowledging, many of the Lynds' observations in *Middletown;* an important community study set in Depression era Muncie, Indiana, which Riesman considered a foundational text. Seeley claimed, in a footnote to *Crestwood Heights*, that rather than "repeating in essence a type of study that had already been outstandingly well done, for example the Lynds," he adopted a "loose method," in order to "secure materials that might have a more general interest and importance."[9] Nevertheless, he returned to the same theme, first articulated by Weber in the *Protestant Ethic and the Spirit of Capitalism* that the "care for external goods" in American society has become an "iron cage."[10] We might note, however, that for Seeley the consumerism decried by the Lynds is no longer just an "American Dream" but a "North American Dream." Seeley defined this as a dream of "a material heaven in the here and now, to be entered by the successful elect through unremitting struggle and sacrifice."[11] Perhaps it is true, as Riesman suggested, that Seeley's interest in popularizing sociological theory came at the cost of academic density, but why would someone of his talent, who had won recognition for his "catholic knowledge of the social sciences," expose himself to such criticism?[12]

Riesman also noted a lack of "differentiating" or "comparative" material in *Crestwood Heights* that might have better elucidated the sociological significance of the uniquely large Jewish population living in Forest Hill in comparison to towns like Muncie.[13] Again, it is surprising that Seeley referred to the population of Forest Hill as "comparatively homogenous" even though half its population was Jewish, and in the process of integrating a large influx of Holocaust survivors.[14] But the Lynds had also overlooked the relatively large population of African Americans living in Muncie when they wrote *Middletown*. This may have been more understandable in their case because they were themselves "white" Americans, whereas Seeley's identity confusion as a non-Jewish Jew raises more questions.

Seeley's papers reveal that he in fact anticipated much of Riesman's critique in an unpublished version of *Crestwood Heights*, but chose to suppress this material because of the politics of the Forest Hill Village Project. This must also be explained. Undoubtedly, *Crestwood Heights* was as much a product of its time as of the personality of its author, but the fact that there is very little written about Seeley despite his importance as an educator, and the tantalizing questions swirling around his work, invites further study which it is the intent of this biographical history to provide. As scholar Brian J. Low wrote, "John Seeley's career is deserving of more careful scrutiny by Canadian social historians."[15]

Of course, I am not the first to raise the "Seeley Question." In fact, this was the title of a *Globe and Mail* editorial published on December 13th, 1974. That year a job offer for Seeley with the Sociology of Education Department at OISE was overturned at the highest levels of the Ontario government. The editorial concerned the lack of transparency that surrounded this decision: "Accusations are being made, darkly, that now that Dr. Seeley wants to come home again to Toronto after 10 years in California, his foes in the academic community are working behind the scenes to prevent him from getting a job."[16]

The editorial went on to question the propriety of an intervention by then Minister of Education Thomas Wells in the OISE selection process which, in effect, blocked the appointment of Seeley. It is pointed out in the editorial that the Minister acknowledged publicly in the Legislature on November 7, 1974 that he had passed on "negative information" about Seeley to the Director of OISE; and that he claimed to have done this because he received the information from "senior and respected educators in the province." Of course, the Minister refused to reveal who these "educators" were or what they said. What rumors had spread down the corridors of power in Ontario about Seeley? The editors at the *Globe and Mail* could get no farther toward an answer to "the Seeley question" than to say: "It seems agreed that sociologist John Seeley is a leading, respected but controversial figure in Canadian academic circles."[17]

Though I may not have been the first, therefore, to raise the "Seeley Question"; I am quite sure I was the last to interview "the great man himself" in search of an answer. On Levine's advice, I set out with my family for California in March 2007 to meet Seeley. Cyril Greenland and John Court at CAMH helped me to establish contact with him and supported my application for funding from the Hewton and Griffin Bursaries. This trip was the starting point for the part I was to play in his "Strange Journey."

This was the title, by the way, to a short autobiographical work Seeley read to the congregation at the Episcopalian church in Los Angeles of which he was an active member late in his life. Seeley claimed in it that, in defiance of his parents' "fashionable atheism," his grandmother inspired him with a sense of religious mission:

> From her such stories as those of David and Goliath, Joseph cast out from home and rising to full appreciation at the Pharaoh's court, or Moses set adrift in the river, only to be found and cherished by Pharaoh's daughter. It was clear to me—though never traceably said—that I was to her the possible, actually potential, David, Joseph, Moses. "Little David, he was a shepherd boy, he slew Goliath and jumped for joy, Little David, Little David, Little David, play on your harp Allelu."[18]

He did not mention in the work that his grandmother was Jewish, though perhaps it was obvious because of her focus on David and other Old Testament heroes. Like David, Seeley was a small man, described by his friend Beatrice Fischer as "fey," but he thought of himself as a conqueror, and the power of symbols to work their way through the life of a man should never be underestimated. He wrote in *Strange Journey*, "It was not just that I knew about David—I had been David once." And so, unbeknownst to me, I had set out on the "road to Damascus" to meet a man whose greatness was possibly of biblical proportions.

When I arrived at his humble bungalow just off Pico Boulevard in Los Angeles, Seeley was on his death bed at the age of 94. Despite the rather unkempt environment of his home, into and out of which roamed a few of his sons, grandsons, and Hispanic nurses, a glimmer of the charisma for which Seeley had been noted by his colleagues in Toronto in the 1950s still shone through his aging body. His skill in articulation and his intellectual versatility were an experience in themselves. We talked for hours at a time over the course of my week-long visit. Though Seeley took little interest in me, it was clear that I was to attend to his place in history with much the same level of care that his nurses were expected to pay to his social calendar.

After a few days of interviews, I was so impressed I asked Seeley if I could write his biography. He said yes. This was the pact between us though I underestimated how serious he was. In the moment, he complimented me for the way I had been able to articulate the "central direction of his career." What he meant was that he appreciated my growing recognition of the importance of his childhood and of his personal struggles with mental health to his adult projects. When I was not interviewing Seeley, I turned to the task of digging through the piles of old junk in the alleyway garage behind his house. I slowly dug through to the filing cabinets, like an archaeologist in some remote cave. Actually, I had to break into some of them because the keys had been lost.

For all the miserable searching and sorting, pushing and pulling, it was of course the very first file I came across which proved most useful. It was marked, "Crestwood Heights: Staff Memos."[19] There were some other files I felt were really interesting, like the correspondence I came across between Seeley and Canadian philosopher George Grant. I regret to say that I left them there because they did not seem chronologically relevant to my topic. The Seeley–Grant correspondence took place in the sixties, sometime after the Forest Hill Village Project, as did the letters he exchanged with Anna Freud. This was my first mistake as a novice historian. Of course, I never did return and have since learned not to be so linear in my approach to historical research. But I did make one exception, which was to keep a letter from Dr. Spock because it illustrated Seeley's presence at the epicenter of the early psychoanalytic movement.

```
                THE UNIVERSITY OF PITTSBURGH
                       SCHOOL OF MEDICINE
                WESTERN PSYCHIATRIC INSTITUTE AND CLINIC
                         3811 O'HARA STREET
                      PITTSBURGH 13, PENNSYLVANIA

                           January 3, 1952


    John R. Seeley, M. D.
    Department of Psychiatry
    University of Toronto
    Toronto 5, Canada

    Dear Dr. Seeley:-

              Thanks for your good letter. The book is "Child Life in
    School - The Study of a Seven-Year Old Group" by Biber, Murphy, Wood-
    cock, Black, published by Dutton in 1942.

              I was sorry that your report on Forest Hills Village was so
    brief. I am hoping that I can arrange to invite you to visit us some-
    time later this year to tell our group more of the details and more of
    your conclusions or hunches.

                              Sincerely,

                              Ben Spock

                              Benjamin Spock, M. D.

    BS/mvm
```

Letter from Dr. Spock to Seeley, 1952. Seeley Papers, Los Angeles, California.

When it came time to take my leave of Seeley after a week of interviews, I introduced him to my family. Despite being hooked up to the intravenous and suffering the after-effects of pneumonia, he threw out his arms in welcome to my children. He regaled them with yarns about how big the waves were, and he shared chocolates with them. He advised my wife not to be too strict with our son's potty training, no matter what the "inconvenience." Then I was subjected to the onerous tests of his son John Jr., who insisted on checking every document to be borrowed. His father suggested that I should not read too much into this last-minute search because his son was "very protective." Unsure what to make of this, I left Los Angeles with a backpack full of files which I came to refer to as the "Seeley Papers."

Not long after my return to Toronto I was surprised to be confronted with subtle threats from Seeley by phone in regard to the "Seeley Papers."

Apparently, he had expected me to maintain regular contact with him. He demanded a return of the documents and suggested that he would be forced to find another biographer to work on his materials if I failed to make faster progress. I perceived a need for reassurance that I would be loyal to my assignment. I began to make regular phone calls during which we further explored the themes we had begun to take up in Los Angeles.

Seeley's gentleness and his charm came through more clearly once we re-engaged in a conversation about his career. He confided in more honest ways about his past in what ended up being the last few months of his life. But there were features of his life-story that he did not fully develop. For example, he told me that his father's last name was Friedeberg, which suggested to me that Seeley was Jewish, but he would not say this directly. Rather, when I asked about his father's name, he said, "I am quite sure he was not Christian."

Sadly, Seeley reported to me that his father died in Germany when he was only ten years old and attending school in Heidelberg. Why were they living in Germany, I wondered? The assumption in our conversations had always been that he was English. He also said that his father had been from a family of wealthy grain merchants, and that he often boasted that Napoleon's armies had run on their supplies. But if Seeley was wealthy by birth, why were there not signs of this in his home?

His psychoanalysis was also a source of intrigue, especially in relation to his own methods as a mental health worker in schools. However, having already borne the brunt of his anger, I was afraid of becoming too intrusive. When I told him this he said, "No, I think it's lovely."[20] Finally, in a strange twist of fate during one of our telephone conversations, Seeley directed me to visit his friend Beatrice Fischer. As we were exploring the remaining unanswered questions about his past, Seeley decided that the best place to look for more information was the Fischers. He told me that Beatrice was the wife of the man who had been his analyst when he lived in Toronto, Martin Fischer. Seeley said he was still in touch with Beatrice Fischer and she would be happy to share with me what she knew. As it turned out this was our last conversation. A month later he died.

It was just after the news of Seeley's death that I first met Beatrice Fischer in her impressive north Toronto home. I was ushered by the Filipino servant Beth into the library where I found Beatrice sitting in a chair under a large poster-style photograph of Freud. The chair was draped with the same kind of blanket as one can see thrown over Freud's famous couch in Vienna. She gestured to the photograph above her head to introduce her husband, because she said she "thought of him that way."[21]

Martin Fischer was a contemporary of Freud who had also grown up in Vienna. She said that he had worshipped Freud, which I could see as I glanced at the bookshelves lined with his collected works. Beatrice recalled that her husband would sit in that chair when he was still alive and read from Freud's works and quote out loud to her from humorous passages. Martin actually met Freud one day, she told me, to sell him tickets to a show being held to raise money for a Jewish Charity. As I listened to these stories, I began to feel as though I had found my way back to *fin-de-siècle* Vienna after all.

In this, our first of many conversations, Beatrice Fischer talked fondly about Seeley both in terms of his charm and foibles. She expressed particular frustration that his sons had not contacted her at the time of his death because, "he loved me, and I loved him," she said. Eventually, she invited me to search through her basement to see if any records remained of the correspondence between her husband and Seeley. She drew a little sketch so that I could make my way through the labyrinthine cellar to where she thought such files might be found. Again, like an archaeologist descending into some long forgotten tomb, I managed to find my way to a closet-room jammed with a century full of things. Much to my amazement the first filing cabinet I opened contained a collection of files entitled, "Seeley."[22] They were full of letters, poems, articles, drafts of essays and notes which I have come to refer to as the "Fischer Papers." We had discovered a private correspondence that occurred between two friends over the course of their life-long partnership. I suddenly realized that it had been Seeley's dying wish that the truth about his life, in all of its wonderful complexity, would finally be revealed.

John R. Friedeberg Seeley, March 2007.

# There Was a Mother in Israel

There is a discrepancy in Seeley's birth records. According to the General Register Office for England and Wales "Herbert John Ronald Friedeberg," was born on February 21, 1913 in London, England. However, his birth is not recorded until June of the April-May-June Quarter of Registration. The birth of his elder brother Frank, in contrast, whose birth certificate says he was born on January 17, 1912, was recorded in the General Register Office as might be expected in March of the January-February-March Quarter of Registration. A small thing, perhaps.

Seeley was the second of four boys born to German-Jewish parents; Emil Emmanuel Friedeberg, born in Stettin Germany in 1873, and Lilly Etta Fuerst, born in Hamburg, 1890. The German origins of his family was testified to in Seeley's own lingering German accent, and his having been known to speak privately in German to members of the Fischer family. Seeley's father was absent during his formative years. As London manager for the major international grain trading interest, Bunge & Co, Seeley's rather "stout" father was accused of supplying Kaiser Willhelm's armies during World War I.[23] The British government ordered that he be interned from 1915 to 1918, before being repatriated to Germany at the end of the war. He did not finally return to London till November 1919 when Seeley was six.

Seeley's mother claimed that her husband was falsely accused of treason, and had actually worked to ensure that the British army and population were supplied with enough grain to see them through the war. She claimed that he had "stuck to his guns," presumably in the face of British governmental wartime trade restrictions and, "until the English Government itself took over the importation of grain to this country, held himself bound to do his utmost to continue the work, which he knew he was best able to perform."[24] However, it is unlikely that Emil Friedeberg was as loyal to the British Crown's interests as his wife suggested. Bunge & Co. controlled 23% of the total Argentine Grain Export Trade during the Great War. As the war progressed the Company's shipments to neutral continental countries like Holland and Denmark increased exponentially and it was likely that these increased supplies of grain were destined for Germany.[25]

Seeley's mother's deception on this question should not surprise us because she was well-known at the British Home Office for being "ready to prevaricate when it seems convenient to her."[26] This reputation was earned during the process of her application for naturalization as a British citizen which she commenced upon the untimely death of her husband in 1923 in Baden-Baden, Germany. Seeley was only 10 years old. According to her "Certificate of Release from Nationality in Prussia and the German Empire," which Seeley's mother submitted as part of her application for naturalization, her first name at birth was spelt "Lilli." The spelling may have been changed to "Lilly" as part of the overall effort to Anglicize her identity.[27] This included the unverified claim that she was "formerly British because her paternal grandfather was born and married in England."[28] It was from this supposed British grandfather that she took the name "Seeley," an Old English surname carrying the connotation of "a fortuitous place," in contrast to her maiden name, "Fuerst." According to tradition, the name Fuerst, or "prince" in German, is borne by families belonging to the tribe of Levi, indicating Levite lineage. Fuerst is documented as a Jewish family name in 1668 with Jeremias Fuerst of Hamburg, Germany.[29] These facts raise suspicion that Seeley's stories about his grandfather being a British seaman who stomped around the home in his "big blue boots," were as much family legend as memory. Perhaps he was a German master mariner, *Kapitan eines Handelsshiffes*?

When Lilly was confronted by Home Office officials about this British grandfather, she was elusive: "She is unable to state the date and place of his birth, but said the record is in an old family Bible," the minutes record.[30] On June 25, 1929 in the minutes of the exchanges between various members of the Home Office, it was suggested that Lilly back up her claim that the records regarding her grandparents' birthplace were in the family Bible: "I think that the family Bible records might be consulted by her as to dates and places of her paternal grandfather's and her father's births and marriages."[31] Lilly responded to this request as follows:

> With regard to the family Bible, this is in store with her other effects and she is unable to say which package it is in. Consequently, she is unwilling to go to the expense of having all the packages opened. She has no room for the whole of her furniture at her present address and has no intention of taking it out of storage for the present. In these circumstances if she is to be allowed to bring her application up to date, it had better be on the assumption that she was not British at birth since there is no certainty as to what might be established by the family Bible if produced.[32]

It was decided that she should be given the benefit of the doubt in regard to her claims that she intended to reside permanently in Britain. Yet, when her naturalization process was delayed at one point by her having "gone away," Home Office officials joked amongst themselves, "can we expect anything better from a woman who keeps her family Bible in cold storage?"[33]

The misrepresentation in regard to the family Bible was not the only one to befuddle Home Office bureaucrats. She is recorded by the Home Office Minutes as having, "on two or three occasions made misleading statements as to her birthplace to Home Office and Police."[34] The following statement was particularly misleading, "This lady is very English in speech and appearance: she has been in U.K. since she was a baby, has never been to Germany, and does not intend ever to go there."[35] Of course, she was born in Germany and traveled there frequently, but her "prevarications" on this matter may have been as much out of necessity as dishonesty; that is, the necessity of protecting her family from the prejudice they would likely suffer, and did suffer, as Germans and Jews living in England at the time.

There is no doubt, however, that by the age of two Lilly had moved to Hampstead where she was educated at the local synagogue. Moreover, in the words of Seeley himself, written at the age of 15 in defense of his mamma's naturalization application, it was true that she presented as more English than the English:

> My mother is a thousand times more English, having lived and been educated here since babyhood in the same district, in the same town, than hundreds of people who can call themselves English owing to having married

Englishmen or through some other fortunate chance—without their actual feelings or accent having to come up for consideration.[36]

This Englishness was certainly an advantage in her attempts to escape the social dangers posed by German-Jewish heritage, as was her wealth. The white walls and garden groves of Hampstead, still the most expensive neighborhood in London where Freud himself spent the last year of his life, attest to this. Moreover, the frequent reference in letters to the "servants" and "chauffeur" suggest that the Fuerst and Friedeberg families were rather well-to-do. International travel, like Lilly's trip to New York in 1909 to stay with relatives, was probably quite common for residents of Hampstead. She continued to live this lifestyle once married to Emil Friedeberg in London in 1911, though Seeley remembered that she would sometimes "refuse to follow him to Italy or the Argentine."[37]

Indeed, at the time of Seeley's father's death in 1923, he left his wife and children a considerable inheritance. According to the Home Office records:

> Memorialist is in receipt of an annual income of about 500 pounds sterling, from money left by her late husband. Her four children are in receipt of a similar sum, from money left in trust by their father. All the money is invested in British securities. The house where the applicant resides is the property of her children.[38]

Taking inflation rates into consideration, the equivalent today of five hundred pounds sterling in the 1920s would be approximately $100,000. If we add to this the value of one-quarter ownership in an expensive house in Hampstead, we can see more clearly just how much money was involved. But, as is so often the case when there is money at stake, tensions within the family were intensified by the "great matter" of the inheritance of the estate. In fact, Seeley was eventually disinherited by his mother which wounded him deeply. Seeley alluded to these tensions in a letter to his friend Martin Fischer dated December 12th, 1954:

> My dear Martin,
> I thought you might be interested in the attached letter to my beloved mother. It is in reply to one written to me in spite of my request that she not write, asking what had become of her precious $700. I recognize her claims, but for the first time in my life I make some claims of my own.[39]

In a letter to his brother Frank, dated to Easter Monday, 1953 Seeley introduces his mamma's shocking "origin-story," on the basis of which his claims to Emil's estate were denied by his mother:

> If her origin story is true—her conduct becomes more rather than less monstrous. To protect herself—and Emil—she accepts an infant into her arm, raises it materially and emotionally a Cinderella, and then flings in its face at adolescence a claim to magnanimity and a disinheritance, again emotional and material, that is to be ended in one respect (though not the other) when it has mined its every resource into a career of suitable respectability.[40]

If the "origin story" does follow the pattern of Cinderella, then we might assume that the father had a child by some other woman and Lilly felt pressured to adopt the child in order to protect her marital status. Once the child's father was dead, the evil step-mother took advantage of her trusteeship of the will to disinherit the adopted child. However, in a letter to his mother, Seeley adds a further complication to this picture:

> You told me a story of my origin (in 1929) which in my naiveté and fear I accepted and upon which I further accepted your view of your own magnanimity and my claimlessness vis-à-vis the family, both financial and affectional. May I now know—in order to assess what claims I have: a) whether there is anywhere any shred of evidence for the account b) if so, may I see it, or copies of it c) whether a burial certificate is available for the alleged Wolff child d) whether Pappa, if he was told, and if he believed it uttered any views as to how the matter should be handled, particularly as to the continued recognition of me as his son, with all the implicit claims for equality and justice that he, as a just man would take that to connote.[41]

The curious reference to a burial certificate for the "Wolff child," suggests that in some way Seeley was a changeling! This may be confirmed by his elfin stature, and the twinkle in his eyes; but, if we set aside the supernatural, the historical explanation must still be that, for some reason, Seeley was adopted under false pretenses. A clue to this mystery may be found in the death notice of Emil Friedeberg's sister Else Wolff.[42]

Death Notice of Else Wolff, 1922, Borchardt-Pincus-Peise, Family Website.

If Seeley was the illegitimate child of Emil's sister Else, whose husband was "unknown," then Lilly's claim to "magnanimity" was based on the fact that she adopted this unwanted child to protect the family's reputation. The fact that according to family legend the father came from a family of lower social status to that of the Friedebergs, may also have justified her self-righteous claim. One of Lilly's dismissive remarks, which stung Seeley so deeply that he remembered it till his dying days, was that since he was of the lower orders, he would have to learn to "work with his hands."[43]

The "origin story," would also explain why, in his letter to the Home Office, Seeley was able to claim perfect health, "unlike the other boys." According to Lilly's letters to the Home Office, in which she attempted to explain her absences from England during the process of naturalization, the other boys were riddled with ill-health from childhood. As had been the case with their father, their illnesses had required frequent visits to Europe for operations and recuperations:

> I was obliged to proceed to the South of France with my mother and my eldest son, also my third son, in account of their health. . . . We were unable to return until August of last year for my son was in a nursing home, after suffering a most serious operation, and the best part of eighteen months his life was in very great danger. My third son, after an operation the same year was also unable to return to the rigors of an English winter, and for the first time in his life, at the age of thirteen years is now able to attend a day school.[44]

Assumedly, she kept her first and third born sons at home with her while they were being raised because of their ill health. Seeley, being in good health, was able to attend boarding schools in Heidelberg and Henfield far away from home.

Despite Seeley's own doubts, the "origin story" may also be confirmed by the evidence of Lilly's harsh, step-motherly relationship with Seeley, in contrast to her coddling of Frank and the other boys. Seeley went so far in his letters as to accuse his brother of a "near-incestuous" relationship with their mamma. He warned Frank of dire mental health consequences if, "you do not in some sense come away from out of this deadly embrace and entanglement now." From Seeley's perspective, Lilly's indulgence of Frank was as abusive as her physical and emotional violence towards himself.

In a letter to Frank, he complained of, "the earliness, totality and persistence of her destructiveness":

> Memories literal and symbolic in very nearly all areas of life crowd close and return vivid and easy—even down to the recapture and re-enactment of attendant bodily phenomena e.g., the squirming muscles under mamma's "dutiful whipping"; the persistent pain of a torn eye-lid corner from a misplaced slap, even the peculiar sensations in the lip from a kiss refused.[45]

Seeley explained to Fischer that his mother's beatings, "by whip or by tongue," were unequally damaging.[46] It was the verbal abuse that hurt the most:

> As I look back my mother's beatings were trivial—other beatings didn't bother me deeply at all. But the endless accusations, the constant teaching that I was no good; that those who loved me were simply "taken in," "fooled" that I didn't know what they said or thought in private, that I was bad or incompetent and doomed and hopeless—that was what all but destroyed me.[47]

Perhaps the greatest insight into the nature of the abuse comes to us in Seeley's "Easter" poems of 1953, which ironically focus on Jewish themes:

> There was a Mother in Israel, shame be upon her!—
> That was farrowed of five and they went all for naught—but me
> Where here people's pride had set an aureate flame upon her
> And shines none
> In the dark of her inmost room—say a darker darkness
> Wherein no breath or shadow of light may light or love
> She yearned on her first

> ~

> Sit shiva with me O my heart that she is dead that liveth
> In the flesh yet—but long since dead;
> To the grey, grey ash that life lived asks and giveth
> Bow down my head . . .[48]

Seeley's Poetry, ca. 1952. Fischer Papers, Toronto, Ontario.

The ancient "darkness" with which he enshrouds his mother's memory conveys his sense that she was dead to him from the beginning. The poems imply that the author wished her dead in retaliation for her "shameful" neglect. They may even be read as a wish to murder his mother, for her death presupposes this. The emphasis on her being a Jewish mother who has failed in her duty to protect her children is flung in her face because, it is assumed, this makes her failure all that much worse.

Seeley felt himself strangled and bloodied by the loss of his mother. Again, in another set of untitled poems, Seeley uses biblical imagery to express his feelings:

> How shall I limn her now, this mother of boys, this infant hater
> This thrice-fanged asp with poison in her soul?
> How shall I paint her now, destroyer and eater
> One hole agape to swallow alike with love or hatred
> Friend and lover or husband or mother or child;
> Fanged for enemy, baited and barbed for the fated
> Cloyed and sweet and suffocate for the loved
> For pure she was with a purity lewd and burning
> A purity fetched of the cesspool and got of the slime
> Fetid, corrupt and corrupting, purist of poison
> Quintessent crime
> How shall I sing of her now who made song songless,
> Who strangled at birth the unlaughed laugh with the unsung song?[49]

The poems may reflect Seeley's feeling, from the very earliest memories of childhood, that Lilly was not really his mother. He makes this ancient memory of estrangement most explicit in a poem written in German, in which he says that he can see in his mother's eyes that he was "not one of hers":

> In dein auge sie nur blitzen
> In dein herzen find nur werth
> Dein gesicht nur besetzen
> Hass und auf dein hande blut.[50]

We might consider the objection raised by Frank that Seeley failed to remember the kindnesses their mother had showed him. This was Seeley's response:

Not balanced? I remember she once showed concern and wrapped me in a warm Turkish towel when I had a bellyache. And once she melted, and kissed me as I pled and apologized.[51]

In other places, Seeley makes vague references to his mother's behavior being excusable because it was caused by some form of illness. In a letter to Frank, Seeley notes the claims of others that her, "behavior was naturally caused, blame-free and, at worst, mistaken."[52] Eventually, the implication that the exculpatory circumstance related to mental illness comes into focus, "And then I didn't know that my mother was sick. I took all this for real. I confirmed her prophecies and was punished and self-tortured accordingly," Seeley wrote to Fischer.[53] In the obituary written for John R. Seeley in the *Globe and Mail* based on interviews with family and friends, it is claimed that she "may have been mentally ill."[54]

But what kind of mental illness might have led to such an inversion of the maternal instinct in Lilly Friedeberg-Seeley? The poems reveal one other clue to the mystery of the Wolff Child which we might take into consideration; namely, that Lilly was "farrowed of five." But according to birth records, and the family oral tradition, she only had four children, all sons. The possibility that there was an additional, dead child, for whom Seeley served as a substitute or replacement baby, might further explain Lilly's motivation to go so far as to arrange the forging of birth and death records, and her need to protect "hers—and Emil's" reputation, in the adoption of the "Wolff child." Does the poet "sits shiva" for the loss of his mother alone, or also for the loss of the fifth child, perhaps a potentially sympathetic sister?

It may sound fantastical, but perhaps Lilly's frequent travel for the sake of the ill health of her children; the operations that kept her out of the country and interrupted her applications for naturalization in 1924 and 1929; the mysterious drowning of her third son Cyril as a young teenager; and last, but not least, the evidence of child abuse in her relations with Seeley; were all part of a larger pattern of inducing illness in her children, commonly known as Munchausen Syndrome. The termination of pregnancies and the death of children are frequently associated with woman suffering from this syndrome. In addition, we have already seen a pattern of deviousness and lies in Lilly Etta Friedeberg-Seeley's behavior which are the means by which the Munchausen mother operates. Add to this list the loneliness and depression of a woman whose husband's work frequently took him away from home, and finally put him away for years in a British Prisoner of War camp, and the constellation of contributing factors to a case of Munchausen Syndrome becomes complete. Indeed, the life of the historical Baron Von Munchausen himself, after whom the syndrome is named, seems quite familiar in the context of the Friedeberg-Seeley family history. Like them, he was a Prussian aristocrat born near Hamburg Germany who traveled far and wide. And, like them he suffered from *pseudologia phantastica*, or the practice of spinning grandiose tales out of a smidgeon of truth.

At any rate, the "origin story" is strong evidence that, at the core of his personality, Seeley really did not know who he was. Until he was an adult, he did not know who his parents were, nor whether he was an Englishman or a German, a Christian or a Jew. As an adult living in Canada during the fifties, Seeley dropped the use of the name Friedeberg, which the other members of his family retained, and chose to identify as a man of English and Anglican cultural heritage. Beatrice Fischer, with whom he was quite close, told me that she had always joked with him that he had a Yiddishe Kopf, a Jewish sensibility, even though as far as she knew he was not Jewish.[55] She said that he always laughed these comments off.

Yet, already in his poetry we can see that he was more than dimly aware of the question of his Jewish ancestry. In fact, in his letters with Frank, he was determined to expose the pattern of denial, or "de-Judaization," to which he was subjected during his childhood. "The whole question of Jewishness is of immense significance," he wrote:

> On matters Jewish there is a deep and terror-laden secrecy . . . What was Grandma's open position? What was her hidden agenda? What was Mamma's. . . .Where did Grandpa go in a topper—or did he—on Sunday mornings? What was on Finchley road near Mamma's bank and on the same side, but closer to the metro station that I could have understood to be Grandpa's church or Papa's? What motivated the episode in which Grandma came to the Abbey Road R. C. Church near Kilburn and sat still and disapproving all through the mass? What does it tell us about her relation to Mamma in this matter? Why on earth did Mamma keep her promise about your learning Hebrew—the real reason—not the romantic one about keeping faith with her pledge? How did other members of the family, Friedebergs and Fuersts, view this de-Judaization and what efforts

did they make to save us? Why was I not confirmed at Henfield—it would have been natural—and what did Mamma explain to Mr. Churcher? How did we know enough to use German words and avoid Yiddish ones in Grandma's mixed vocabulary?[56]

Despite the depth of Seeley's concerns about his Jewish identity, Frank dismissed these as a sign of his mental difficulties. An example of the counter-arguments that Frank offered was the following: "Sunday morning would suggest the zoo (of which Max was a fellow) rather than the synagogue."

Unfortunately, Seeley's second childhood homes in Heidelberg and Henfield were Christian schools that had long before secured against any hope that Seeley might be reconciled to his Jewish identity. He was sent to Heidelberg while his father lay dying. He only heard the news of his father's death by letter. The way that Seeley displaced his emotion about this loss is captured in the following scene he describes in a short "Educational Autobiography," submitted for his course work at the U of C in 1940:

> The year was 1923, the year of the greatest and worst inflation. Men fought in the streets. Women wept. Children died. The French invaded the Ruhr. They saw fit to bring in colored troops. There were the usual rapes, the usual atrocities. A proud people writhed in the agony of its humiliation. In the classroom we had Diktat, Geschichte, Handschriftsubungen. I don't remember a detail we learned. But there remains with me a sense, almost a physical feeling, of Germany's darkest hour. The school matron told me what had happened in her home town. She wept and though boys don't cry, I wept with her.[57]

One can easily imagine the German matron with whom he wept as a substitute for his missing mother, and the sadness for Germany standing in for his feelings about the loss of his father. This transference was obviously not unique to Seeley at this time, and neither was the tendency, suggested in his reference to "colored troops," to racialize the problem. The hyperinflation of 1923 sparked Anti-Semitic pogroms, and outrage at the use of Senegalese troops as part of the occupation force, the "black horror on the Rhine," that shook the Germany of Seeley's youth. But it is clear that at this early point in his life, despite his confusion about his family's Jewish heritage, he identified more strongly with the "Aryan" majority, than with marginalized peoples. Perhaps bearing witness to violence toward Jewish boys in Heidelberg during his school days there taught him the life lesson that it was safer to conceal his private doubts about his heritage.[58]

Before long Seeley was torn away from his friends at Heidelberg and, "sent off to a poor, hence cheap, boarding—school in the English countryside." Henfield, now called the Lucton School, was "near the beautiful South Downs in sea-washed Sussex."[59] It was actually a relief for Seeley to be away from his mother and to find a substitute father figure in the headmaster Edwin C. Churcher, "By direction and indirection he became my earthly father."[60] He had fond memories of his early indoctrination in the Church of England under the "booming voice" of the Headmaster father-figure. It was there at Henfield that Seeley learned all of the Anglican hymns and prayers, to which he makes constant reference throughout his career: "My inner life was largely a life of song, 'Abide with me, fast falls the eventide . . . when other helpers fail and comfort flee . . . oh, abide with me.'"[61]

The hint at "indirection," however, may have been an allusion to the darker side of school life at Henfield. A second teacher father-figure, who had "been sent down from Oxford" took an interest in Seeley. Seeley went so far as to inform me in our interviews that he had "been subjected to child abuse" by this man. Seeley's recollections of his attachment to this teacher must be understood in the context of the sexually intimidating atmosphere in so-called "elite" British Public Schools. This was created by the "fagging system"; whereby, amongst other displays of dominance, pedophilic advantage was sometimes taken by Masters of students, and by the elder "prefects" of younger boys. The problem for the younger boys was to avoid the risk of exposing themselves and their friends to flogging.[62] The incomprehensibility to a young boy of such power games makes him vulnerable to assault; moreover, it seems that the adolescent male's desire not to let down one's mates; especially one as lonely as Seeley was at the time; outweighs his fears.

Such rituals of initiation into the culture of hierarchy and exploitation persist to this day in Anglican "private schools" throughout the ruins of the British Empire. For example, a Housemaster named David Panter, who taught English and History at the Lucton School between 1971 and 1980, was jailed in 2016 for sexual exploitation of students. He "targeted pupils and often became a father-figure to them," according to the *Hereford Times*.[63] Like most graduates of such schools, Seeley participated in the cover-up of the lurid realities of the "fagging system." Indeed, the nature of his relationship with his "father figure" at Henfield is portrayed quite rhapsodically in his "Educational Autobiography":

> In the second year I had the good fortune to be in the class of a man to whom the intellectual life was important. He seemed to us a tyrant; his standards were unreasonably high and unconscionably strict—by our measure.... He taught me the whole of Euclid in his own spare time and mine. We did it in less than one term, and started on analytic geometry. At the end of the term he left. I don't even remember his name. I remember his manner, his clarity of reasoning, his insistence on accuracy, his contempt for the sloppy, his love of learning. These things abide.[64]

Viewed through a Freudian lens, however, the punctilious qualities of this man, his "volunteering" for extra private tutorials and his sudden departure, are at least an occasion for raised eyebrows.

Seeley returned home from Henfield at the age of fifteen, a time when many boys are eager to strike out on their own. The resumption of his struggles with his mamma led him to contemplate running away from home. The turning point, Seeley claimed, came when he was asked by his mother to go and pick up anti-constipation medicine for her at the chemist. They were living at the Tudor Hotel near Lancaster Gate in London at the time. Lilly demanded of John that he "be careful with the change." He found this hypocritical because she "always spent lavishly." When he returned with the medicine, she held it up to the light and said, "This bottle is a little empty. The chemist is cheating you. You should not have brought home a half empty bottle. Go back." When Seeley went back, the chemist took offence at this suggestion and said that the bottles were sealed by the manufacturers. When Seeley returned again with the same bottle, his mother was livid and raised her voice, "You are taking the word of a tradesman against mine? Go back." When he was sent back empty handed again by the chemist, his mother went too far, "I can still take your trousers down," she said.[65]

In addition to being too old to take a beating, Seeley claimed he wanted to leave home because his mother would not let him enroll at the London School of Economics (LSE), "to study economics under Keynes." In fact, Keynes did not teach at the LSE. He also said that his mother refused to allow him to accept a scholarship offer to attend Sandhurst Royal Military Academy, because his "becoming a common soldier," might have interfered with "Frank's chance to become Head of the Foreign Office." Feeling belittled, Seeley began to look for opportunities to break out of his perceived domestic prison. Unlike most adolescent acts of rebellion, however, Seeley was ready to take his quite far.

The following excerpt from Kenneth Bagnell's *The Little Immigrants* describes the scene of Seeley's departure from England in the following way:

> His childhood was filled with great affluence and deep deprivation, an experience that would best be described as a gothic tragedy. When he was fourteen, a very lonely, unhappy boy, he set out walking through a London Street and caught sight of a poster that showed a smiling youth, stripped to the waist, astride a load of hay, and beneath, in large letters, the words, "Come to Canada, Be Your Own Boss at 21." He went to Canada House, where a clerk told him that his passage would be paid, in steerage of course, provided that he accepted the farm job given him—which he knew from the shiny poster to be a ripe, golden opportunity—and stayed with farming for four years. Within a few weeks he had parted company with his mother forever, trying as much as he could to put the past behind him, and that August he landed in Quebec, not as others did, with a group of similar children destined for a common experience, but by himself, alone and penniless.[66]

According to Lilly Friedeberg-Seeley's letters to the Home Office, on the other hand, the situation was not at all one of voluntary and heroic escape from abuse as her son claimed. Rather to protect her son, she said she sent him to "the colonies" rather than allow him to return to Germany to be with his father's family. The implication of the felt danger on Seeley's mother's part was that she was trying to find a way to allow him to leave home as safely as possible, or at least in a manner that was commensurate with her own interests in completing her application for naturalization. According to Seeley, his mother was quite litigious by nature. He recalled her shouting from the back seat of her chauffeur-driven motor vehicle as she sped-off after some quarrel, "You will hear from our Solicitors!"

There was one other alternative that Seeley and his mother had hoped for. This was that he would be admitted to the British Armed Forces. The problem was that neither of his parents were naturalized British Citizens. Lilly wrote to the Home Office with reference to her son's applications for admission to the British Armed Forces:

> I might add that the latter has tried unsuccessfully to enter the army and the Air Force lately, and this owing to the fact that his remaining parent is un-naturalized; and I am therefore obliged to send him to the Colonies rather than let him go to his late Father's relatives abroad.[67]

It appears that Seeley's claim that he had been offered a scholarship to Sandhurst Military Academy was a typical exaggeration. There is, in fact, a letter from the Air Ministry rejecting Seeley's application for the "Aircraft Apprentices, Royal Air Force, Limited Competition, June 1929," on the grounds that "candidates must be not only British subjects, but sons of natural born or naturalized British subjects."[68] In a precociously worded letter of his own to the Home Office pinning his hopes for entry in the Air Force on the success of his mother's naturalization application, the young Seeley makes no mention of any scholarship. Instead, Seeley pleads in surprisingly familial tones of his own great promise:

> If you could possibly manage to see your way to help us promptly, not only would the privilege of naturalization be acclaimed with utmost joy by my Mother and her little family, but I personally should be able once more to apply for entry to one of His Majesty's Forces, and I am convinced I should do very well, for my School Record is A1, I am physically fit as a fiddle, and have always been so, unlike the other boys, and my brains though I say this myself, are well above the average having passed the College of Preceptors Exam in the Senior Grade at the age of fourteen.[69]

Yet, it would seem that the efforts of mother and son were to no avail. Even a few days before her son was scheduled to depart in July of 1929 for Canada, Lilly wrote the Home Office begging them to expedite her papers so she could cancel his trip:

> Sir,
> I hope that you will be able to let me know something definite before the end of next week as my Son is due to sail on the 27th with the Megantic, and I should then be able to cancel his sailing instructions. I may add that it is doubly important for me to keep my boys together and in England, for no one, perhaps, has appreciated in all its bitterness, as I have, the misery—mental and moral—that can be brought about in the most united of relations, given a touchstone such as the Great War, and circumstances such as prevailed in my late husband's family, where each brother lived in another country long years, and considered that country where his children

were born as his! If I have to send one of my boys away, be it even to a British Dominion what absolute guarantee can I have that he stay there—and how can I be assured that his relatives on his Father's side, with whom I have almost entirely broken (the Grandparents having died years ago) may not approach him?[70]

Is this the heartfelt sentiment of a mother to "keep my boys together and in England"? A woman whom, we might note, has been forced to raise four sons without a father because of his internment; who was "without nationality" after being de-naturalized from Germany; and who finally lost her husband forever when she was only thirty—three? Or, was this a ploy to use the circumstances of her unhappy son's demands to leave home to her advantage, making it sound as though the British Empire might suffer by his flight, but gain from her naturalization.

The fact that Seeley made the voyage to Canada with no more than a single pound note in his pocket, seems to cast doubt on his mother's motives. As he put it, she gave him "one pound or five pounds—to leave England with, because the law required it, and even that she threatened to withhold." Moreover, to have told him the "origin story" about the "Wolff child" on the dock seems rather cruel. On the other hand, perhaps she was just as angry with him for leaving her, as he was that she had abandoned him in so many ways, not the least of which was with the "origin story." In a letter to Frank, Seeley recalls his terror upon hearing the story:

> I was angry because you defend Mamma, or at least push the claim of "context" and, therefore, in effect, plead mitigating, if not exculpating circumstance. When in 1929 Mamma told me in the way she did—in hate and anger and intent to do maximum damage of my origin, she opened up floodgates of terror and hate beyond my capacity to manage. I swore accordingly (all this in the first few months of 1929) that I would do everything possible to ensure that such a thing could never happen again. That gave me a program: a) to understand what had happened b) to help others to 'understand' c) to fight conditions of inequity, ignorance, or cruelty ie., to learn, teach, to fight.[71]

Seeley traced his career long dedication to working on the problem of mental illness to the traumatic events of his childhood. In the end, however, Seeley came to accept the truth of the "origin story," as he wrote to Frank:

Thanks for the enquiry on "origin" and the report of it. Here Mamma's casualness in my mind adds to the plausibility of the story. Unless she is tired or now indifferent, I should have expected a spirited defense of an untrue story. Actually, now, I would prefer to have it so. I do not think it exculpates her one whit—in fact, to me, it makes many things more heinous; but it does add to intelligibility.[72]

# Home Child

According to the Canadian Immigration Service Records, Herbert John Ronald Friedeberg-Seeley disembarked from the S.S. *Calgaric* (not the *Megantic*), sailing from Southampton to Quebec City on August 19, 1929. He was just sixteen years old. The "money in possession belonging to the passenger" according to the Immigration service records was listed as, "1 pound." His passage is listed as having been paid for by the "Gov't," which was the case for all the other young boys aged 15–18 listed alongside him as members of the "B.I.C.A. Party," all traveling "Third Class."

The British Immigration and Colonization Association (B.I.C.A.) was a philanthropical organization founded in November 1920 by a group of Anglophone clergy and professional men in Montreal concerned that the supply of good "British stock" to Canada be sustained.[73] Seeley was therefore not a "Barnardo Child," as Kenneth Bagnell had claimed, whose emigration to Canada was organized by one of Dr. Barnardo's Homes for destitute or orphaned children in England. Nevertheless, in a harsh twist of fate Seeley suddenly found himself without money or family in a strange land. It was perhaps a reference back to this moment in his life when Seeley later complained to Fischer of the "terror of an empty pocket."[74]

The information listed about the Friedeberg-Seeley boy was typical of all the other members of his party. He was born in England. He was coming to Canada to follow the "farming" trade. He spoke English. However, in some respects his information was quite unique. Friedeberg-Seeley was the only boy listed under "Race or People" as not being English, Scotch, or Welsh. He was listed as "German," which in the interregnum between the two world wars must have made the other boys and officials suspicious of this lad.[75]

Though he may have easily hidden his German origins from the other boys simply because of his English upbringing, it may have not been quite so easy to hide the fact that he was one of the few who had been to school. Most of the other boys had already had working-class jobs of one sort or another. One boy had been a factory hand, quite a few of the others had already worked in farming, and there was a pot-maker, a decker, and a "laborer" listed. Seeley, meanwhile, had been studying Euclid at Henfield.

All the boys were taken by CN Rail promptly on arrival in Quebec City to Montreal. There they registered at the BICA headquarters before continuing their train ride to the location of their new farmstead homes throughout rural Canada. Seeley was destined for a small railway stop in farm country just east of Lake Simcoe, appropriately named "Lorneville," one-hundred kilometers north of Toronto. As Seeley described it, he found himself, "a farm boy in a far-away (and far-out) lost and lorn little village, Lorneville."[76]

Lorneville JCT CNR, 1908. Courtesy of the Ross Gray Collection.

The philanthropists who led B.I.C.A. might have been quite pleased about John Friedeberg-Seeley's presence amongst the newly imported youth of Canada; that is, assuming they were unaware he was Jewish. Their interest in child immigration programs lay in the contribution these might make toward, "distributing the white population of the Empire in the manner most conducive to the development, stability and strength of the whole."[77]

As a public school educated lad, Friedeberg-Seeley was just the "right class of boy" that the leaders of the B.I.C.A. were looking for.

Unfortunately, Seeley and many others of the up to 5,400 boys brought to Canada under this imperial scheme, would prove disappointing to their sponsors in the Canadian Department of Immigration and B.I.C.A. Perhaps because of their age, and certainly because of the harsh working conditions on the farms, these boys tended to be drawn to the more exciting lifestyle in expanding cities like Montreal and Toronto. Hence they often failed to materialize as a new generation of farmers who would build the Canadian economic base which was still at the time thought to require agricultural development. F.C. Blair, the infamous Deputy Minister of Immigration for the Federal Government responsible for the Voyage of the St. Louis Affair, said that the "boy immigration" movement "seems to have totally failed."[78] Seeley's case was the perfect illustration of Blair's concern. Not only was he in fact Jewish rather than "white"; within two years of arriving in Canada Seeley had drifted to the city, despite having pledged himself to at least four or five years on the farm.

The exploitation Seeley was subjected to on the farm was certainly no incentive for him to stay there. The main interest of the Smith family of Eldon County who hired Seeley was cheap labor, not preservation of the racial pedigree of the British Empire. After all, the empire had done nothing for them. They had, "all originated in Islay, most in the Kilmenny Parish, and came early to Eldon, in the 1830s and 1840s."[79] They were likely crofters used to the harsh conditions for farming on the Scottish Isles, who were forced off their land during the clearances of the early nineteenth century to make room for sheep.

Seeley's new master Donald A. Smith, whom Seeley referred to with an air of condescension as "Donny," was one of a family of eight who had established a farmstead near the Lorneville railway station and general store. The rolling hills around Lake Simcoe, and the relatively rocky farmland of that region, may have reminded the Scottish pioneers of their homeland. Though Donny was able in this way to continue the way of life that had been stolen from his ancestors in Scotland, he might have laid claim to greater success in the New World but for the frugality of his relatives. Donny, it turns out, was related to the Reverend William A. Cameron, his cousin, who became Moderator of the Presbyterian Church of Canada. He was also named after his famous relative Sir Donald Smith, who was a key financier of the Canadian Pacific Railroad and President of the Bank of

Montreal. However, Donny reported of his famous namesake, "He didn't leave me a cent."[80]

According to Seeley's memories, Donny was a poor farmer who lived in a dilapidated old pioneer log cabin with his mother. This pair demonstrated stereotypical Scots-Presbyterian frugality themselves in their dealings with the "new lad." Seeley remembers when he first arrived at the farm that Mrs. Smith asked him whether he would like some apple pie but "without the cream." She also made fun of Seeley's request for a bath at the end of the week, "My man, the baths he had in his life you could count on one hand, and he's a better man than you'll ever be."[81] We might well imagine how disappointed the young Seeley was to discover that his attempt to escape an abusive family of origin had only led him into the clutches of another nasty step-mother figure. What must have been even harder to bear was that he also lost the creature comforts to which he had become accustomed in Hampstead, England.

Seeley's only fond memories from his time in Lorneville were of the local Presbyterian "Kirk." This plain old stone church, without a steeple, is still there in Woodville, Ontario, just down the road from the farms around the Lorneville crossroads where Seeley lived with the Smiths. As Seeley recounts in *Strange Journey*:

> This was the church of Donny and his mother and two thirds or more of the surrounding community. To this every Sunday morning Donny drove us both by car or cutter, and every Sunday evening repaired, by horse and buggy or horse and cutter as the primitive roads and the weather allowed or dictated.[82]

In particular, Seeley remembered the pipe bandleader, a Mr. Macdonald, and how he would "dance and swill his kilt at the lasses and weren't they shocked by that." The local "Meenister," as he was referred to by Seeley, also took an interest in the intelligent young boy. Seeley describes this Presbyterian Minister, Robert Simpson, quite fondly:

> This Meenister . . . was a Scottish-born, University of Edinburgh educated, Presbyterian Minister, the father of two beautiful young ladies, and a generous and justice-and-reason-and-mercy Preacher and exemplar. He had been many years before, a missionary, to the Indians in the Peace River Country of Canada where he and his good wife lost their first born—a son—to the ravages of time and place, and the paucity of medical aid. The framework

of Abraham and Isaac comes to mind, but this time the Lord, blessed be he, did not provide the Ram in the Thicket, as an adequate substitute. This experience saddened him forever, but enhanced the tender side of him.[83]

Another father-figure bond was formed between Simpson and Seeley, and it was through this relationship that Seeley was able to make his escape from the Smiths' farm.

According to the Juvenile Inspection Reports kept by immigration officials with the Canadian government on Home Children, "Herbert Friedeberg-Seeley left the employ of J. G. Smith," in Lorneville in July of 1931, within a year of his arrival. The report states that he was being paid $120 per year. The inspection report further records that with the help of Reverend Simpson, Herbert Friedeberg-Seeley moved to another farm in Brooklin, Ontario, just north of Oshawa, and nearer Toronto, where he served in the employ of R. Ratcliffe. Not long afterward, according to the inspection report, Seeley also left Brooklin and found himself "employed at a Printing Co." in downtown Toronto in March of 1932. This was a promotion from Seeley's point of view, not only because the literary and administrative demands of work at a printing company were far more suited to his talents than farming, but also because his pay went up from $10 per month, to roughly $8 per week.

Reading the inspection report, one might think that Seeley had been a favorite of his first employers in the New World. In all categories of behavior, including, health, satisfaction given, and character, Seeley's inspector marked "g" for good. The inspector even made the extra effort at the end of the report to record his impression of Seeley as "A Splendid Chap."[84] How is it possible that Seeley could receive such a positive report on paper when, in reality, he had violated the terms of his emigration contract with B.I.C.A. and the Federal Government, and had also left the farmsteads of both Smith and Ratcliffe before there would have been much chance for either of them to reap benefit from his labor power? Seeley may not have been a very useful farmhand, but there were early signs in his career in Canada that he had a talent for reinventing himself.

Seeley admitted that had he not managed to eke out a living for himself in depression era Toronto, he would have been forced to go back to the farm to fulfill the terms of his contact. Luckily, it was not long before he found a donut business in the city that was willing to employ him in exchange for a room in a cellar and "all the donuts he could eat."[85] Like his work at the farm, selling donuts was just a transitional job in the city for Seeley while he searched out somewhere he could fit in more happily.

This he did find as a result of his volunteer work as the leader of a cub-scout pack at Kimbourne Park United Church in East Toronto. This church was a humble brown-brick building much like many other Churches across Ontario. The use of its adjoining gymnasium and meeting rooms for community activities like cub scouts formed as important a part of church life as the sanctuary. According to Seeley, he had come within an inch of having to return to the farm, when a member of the congregation named Mr. Robertson offered to take him in while he looked for a new job so that he could continue his work with the cub pack.

It was this Mr. Robertson, the father of Seeley's second new family in Canada, who would land Seeley the job as an apprentice with the reputable east end lithograph and printing firm named Rolph–Clarke–Stone. Not only did this volunteer work lead to his winning this very satisfactory position, it also enabled him to slide out of the working class environment into which he was thrown upon arrival in Canada, and into a middle class setting where he felt more comfortable.

The cubs also gave Seeley a start in what was to become his lifelong calling as an educator. Seeley was very dedicated to his work with the cub pack as was suggested by the continuity of his attachment to them over several years from the time he arrived in Toronto in 1931 to the time of his leaving for the University of Chicago in 1940. It was very upsetting for him when one of the cubs in his pack died at the age of twelve and was buried in his cub uniform.[86]

But Seeley's work with the cubs did cause some parental concerns. According to Seeley, the parents of the cubs raised questions about the fact that Seeley would often take the boys swimming in the nude. Seeley remembered that he would take the boys swimming at the YMCA up to three nights a week. The local YMCAs of the time believed that infections were passed by dirty bathing suits, so the boys were in fact required to swim in the nude. The parents nonetheless would ask Seeley if this might lead to homosexuality. He reassured them that it would not. He highlighted this episode in my interviews with him as his first experience in the field of mental health education.

The Robertsons had only promised to let Seeley stay with them until he found a job, so once he started at Rolph-Clark-Stone he needed to find a new place to live. Luckily, he was welcomed into the home of another family from the Kimbourne Park United Church Community, the McReynolds. Seeley stayed with the McReynolds for the next eight years. With great pleasure, he told me the story of how the McReynolds children had asked him if he would "come and be our brother." He prided himself on how much he had done to influence the younger McReynolds boys who were also members of his cub pack. He remembered, in addition, how he had been treated like a son by Mr. McReynolds who was a Telegrapher with the Canadian Imperial Bank of Commerce.

Mr. McReynolds once scolded Seeley, in a fatherly way, for buying a 1922 Oldsmobile with the money he had made at the printing company. He bought the car so that he could take his new girlfriend, Margaret, out on dates. Seeley met Margaret at Rolph-Clark-Stone where they both worked in the Hispanic Affairs Department. McReynolds senior felt that he would have been better to put the money into savings for college.

In addition to this advice from Mr. McReynolds, Seeley's academic ambitions were kindled by a fortuitous event at the YMCA. During one of his many visits there he attended a meeting held by an ambitious young social worker from Cape Breton, Murray Ross. Seeley's questions during the meeting so impressed Ross that he invited the wispy youngster to take an IQ test. Seeley did, and the results were off-the-charts. Seeley was gifted with an extraordinarily high native intelligence. Ross, who would go on to become the first President of York University, encouraged Seeley to attend University, and remained his friend for many years.

As for the car, it turned-out to be money well-spent. Seeley soon married Margaret. He said that it was love at first sight the day she walked into the office looking for the job of Secretary. He remembered "the exact color of blue that she wore and a feather in her hat."[87] Meanwhile, the storm clouds of war were gathering on the horizon.

# From Civilian to Fighting Man

Seeley's applications to serve were at first rejected by the Canadian Forces on the basis of rather arbitrary height requirements. Seeley was just short of the five foot three inch medical standard for enlistment. When the war began, these medical standards, which hailed back to World War I, had not yet been adjusted to allow for recruits who "fell short" to be placed in some other useful capacity.[88] Not to be deterred, Seeley took advantage of the space created by declining enrollment at the University of Chicago during the first few years of the war to win a scholarship and pursue his bachelor's degree. Seeley started at U of C in 1940, and completed the required comprehensive exams in general arts two years later.

The timing of his graduation was fortuitous since a newly formed Directorate of Personnel Selection (DPS) was up and running within the Canadian Department of National Defense (DND). This unit was determined to overturn the archaic recruitment standards that had barred Seeley from active duty. Ironically, Seeley was recruited by the DPS to conduct the very kinds of testing that originally led to his being declared ineligible for military service. He received a telegram from Dr. William Line, the new Director of Personnel Selection (formerly a Professor of Psychology at the U of T) saying in response to his repeated letters of application: "Of course Canada needs you! Report to the Officer Training Center in Toronto immediately."[89] Seeley enlisted with the Canadian Army (Active) as a second Lieutenant on October 29, 1942 in Toronto, Ontario. He was employed first as an Army Examiner with the Personnel Selection Office and rose to the permanent rank of Captain.[90]

As a recent university graduate, Seeley was typical of the kinds of recruits allocated to the Directorate of Personnel Selection, more than half of whom had degrees. According to Carver's study of the DPS commissioned by the DND, 41% of the army examiners assigned to Personnel Selection had BAs, 10% had MAs, and 5% had PhDs. Carver also pointed out that of the first 50 members of the Directorate's Staff who formed the core of the unit for the duration of the war, a full 46 of them were university educated and most of these were professional teachers at the university or secondary school level. Carver suggested that the emphasis in recruiting teachers was justified because of their particular aptitudes: "The teaching profession supplied the largest proportion of Army Examiners because their training and attitudes were found to correspond with the requirements more closely than that of any other group."[91] According to Carver it was found that:

> Practical experience has made it apparent that no other occupation or profession has been able to produce in any comparable degree the type of person who can make objective and unprejudiced appraisals of other men. A keen interest in the personal development of human beings, a quick comprehension of their foibles, capacities and impediments, is an essential part of every teacher's training and he has had to cultivate an impartial attitude towards the many varieties of human character with which he comes in contact.[92]

Some other historians have not commented as favorably on the qualifications of those who staffed the new Personnel Directorate. For example, Copp and McAndrew, in their study of psychiatry in the Canadian Army during World War II entitled *Battle Exhaustion: Soldiers and Psychiatrists in the Canadian Army*, sided with the more critical view that these white-collar soldiers were unqualified not only as soldiers without any battle experience, but also as pseudo-psychologists who tended more toward psycho-babble than professional evaluation in their determinations of whether recruits were "unfit."[93] Copp and McAndrew noted that already by January 1942, Line had prepared a memorandum for the personnel selection staff asking them to avoid using psychiatric diagnostic terminology, "in a casual way," and to avoid the misuse of slang expressions:

> Popular phrases like 'ignorant hobo', 'needs a good thrashing', 'should be put through the mill', were, Line wrote, "expressive of the feelings of the examiner" but of no other value. "Even when the soldier's limitations

are such that he is not likely to respond to training," he warned, "it is still desirable to state his case without diagnostic reference or recommendations for discharge."⁹⁴

For his part, Seeley said that corruption in the military enlistment process during the War was more the effect of a "class-ridden and undemocratic process," than of professional incompetence.⁹⁵

In Seeley's role as staff captain under Line's supervision responsible for, "planning and development of the testing and interviewing procedures and with the statistical analysis of the records obtained"; he was the administrative counterpart to Lieutenant Colonel John Griffin (M.D.), the lead psychiatric consultant to the Director.⁹⁶ In turn, Line reported to his predecessor as Director of the DPS, Brock Chisolm, who had been promoted to the position of Director-General of Medical Services for DND. All of these men, with whom Seeley would work so closely during World War II and the early phase of the Cold War, had been associated prior to the war as students and colleagues of Clarence Hincks, head of the Canadian National Committee on Mental Hygiene (CNCMH). The relationship Seeley was to build with this tight-knit circle of elite Upper Canadian medical professionals was the key to the development of his career. Ironically, however, if they had any idea that he was a Jew, this might not have happened; for, they were leaders of the eugenics movement in Canada. In order to fully understand Seeley's complex relationship with eugenics, we must digress from the central narrative at this point, and tell their story.

The CNCMH was formed in 1918, on the instruction of C. K. Clarke, then Chair of the Department of Psychiatry at U of T, as a political action committee to lobby for the interests of mental health professionals. Originally, the CNCMH focused on eugenicist measures to prevent mental disease, as treatments were few and ineffectual. It is quite important to stress that in this early stage of the mental health movement it was indistinguishable from that of eugenics. In the eyes of Clarke, there really were no alternatives to population control as a way to "cure" mental illness. Psychoanalysis was only beginning to be understood, and pharmaceutical agents were in a very primitive state of development. The CNCMH thus advocated for, amongst other things, immigration policies to stem the tide of what it saw as the overflow into Canada of the "feeble-minded" and "degenerate" of European society, who might "infect the race as a whole." For example, the CNCMH opposed immigration schemes for "home children" that brought thousands of "defective" British orphans to work on Canadian farms, including Seeley.[97]

Clarke turned to Dr. Clarence Hincks, with whom he had worked to establish a psychiatric out-patients clinic from 1914–18 at the Toronto General Hospital, as his operative for advancing such anti-immigrant campaigns through the CNCMH. Despite his personal struggles with mental illness, Hincks was quite successful in his role as a fundraiser and project coordinator. This work required frenzied periods of busy-work, which Hincks performed during his manic episodes, only to be followed by periods of deep depression during which he withdrew to his Muskoka cottage. Seeley would get his first post-war job with the CNCMH as Executive-Assistant to Hincks in which capacity, he explained to me, he was to "keep an eye" on his unpredictable behavior. Hincks was particularly successful in marshalling Ontario's family compact behind the work of the CNCMH. Indeed, there is no better evidence of the importance of class in shaping the agenda for eugenics and mental health than the success of Hincks in winning grant after grant from wealthy local philanthropies like the Rockefeller Foundation of Cleveland, Ohio: "Hincks recruited to the board of the CNCMH Lord Shaunessy, President of the CPR, E. W. Beatty, Vice-President of the CPR, Sir Vincent Meredith, President of the Bank of Montreal, and F. W. Molson, of Molson's Brewery."[98]

Historian Ian Dowbiggin in, *Keeping America Sane*, has argued that: "The standard political interpretation that eugenics was a ruling class, reactionary, or conservative phenomenon is no longer tenable." He suggests that populist backing for eugenics and the support of proto-feminists like Agnes McPhail, "undermines the customary notion that it was a pet theory of the elite."[99] However, the fact that McPhail and socialist leaders like Tommy Douglas were proponents of the use of eugenics in the interest of their class, does not mitigate the reality that the Canadian elite also saw advantages in its methods; principally by naturalizing social hierarchies in racial terms, and by legitimizing population control strategies designed to reduce tax rates and eliminate competition.

Dr. Clarence Meredith Hincks (1885–1964), co-founder of the Canadian National Committee for Mental Hygiene (CNCMH) in 1918, serving as its first Director General. During the 1930s Dr. Hincks was also, conjointly, head of the National Committees for Mental Hygiene in the United States. Courtesy of CAMH Archives.

Hincks is most famous for his determination to add sterilization policy to the list of eugenics measures used in Canada to fight mental disease. This is nowhere more evident than in an article he published in *Maclean's* magazine. This article, boldly entitled "Sterilize the Unfit," is especially shocking in light of the timing of its publication. He wrote it within a year of the end of the World War II, a time when the public was first being forced to face the horrors of the Holocaust. It makes clear that in the minds of the leaders of the mental hygiene movement in Canada, educational means by which to prevent the spread of mental illness were seen as complementary, rather than as alternative, to eugenics:

> Common sense and scientific judgment dictate a combined attack on mental health problems aimed at both constitutional and hereditary factors and environment. And this means amongst other things, selective eugenical sterilization.[100]

The continued adherence long after World War I to eugenics by the Canadian mental hygiene movement, as evidenced by Hincks' article, distinguishes it from its counterparts in the USA. American author Sol Cohen wrote in an influential article entitled *The Medicalization of Education* that: "After a brief' flirtation with eugenics, hygienists in the post-War period rejected the pessimistic hereditarianism of the eugenicists and the intelligence testers."[101] According to Cohen, it was this rejection of eugenics that turned the attention of the mental health movement toward the schools. While on the one hand, it is certainly true that the Canadian mental hygiene movement also favored intervention in schools, and Seeley's Forest Hill Village Project was a primary instance of what Cohen referred to as the "medicalization of education"; on the other hand, as Canadian historian G. E. Thomson noted; "The Canadian situation was somewhat different from the American as it involved a strong connection between the medical profession and the active promotion of a eugenically-based form of mental hygiene."[102] This was due to closer ties between the Canadian and British medical elite: "Canada, like Great Britain, continued to emphasize race degeneration well into the late 1930s through its own mental hygiene movement as led by prominent medical doctors."[103] Moreover, according to McLaren's book, *Our Own Master Race: Eugenics in Canada*, our doctors saw no incompatibility between eugenics and education: "It is important not to exaggerate the gap that separated the eugenicists and the environmentalists. Although their methods differed, their goals of efficient social management were similar."[104]

This depth of commitment to eugenics in Canada is important to note because it was an important factor in Seeley's marginalization as an active player in the field of mental hygiene. Given his sensitivity to Jewish issues and associated preference for psychoanalytic method, Seeley's horror at the eugenicist tendencies of his colleagues set him up for conflict from the outset. Indeed, in the following paragraphs we shall learn how deeply implicated his superiors and colleagues in the military, not just Hincks but also Griffin, Line, Chisolm, Bott and Blatz, were with the eugenics movement.

Jack Griffin, who had assumed the role of medical consultant and principal assistant to Hincks at the CNCMH prior to the war, and who after the war would succeed him as President of the Committee, was necessarily complicit with his mentor's campaign to drum-up support for eugenics. Griffin is recorded as having promoted the same arguments that Hincks was parading around the country about the dangers of the "rising tide" of mental illness. In a radio broadcast on the CBC of May 23, 1938 Griffin warned that "if we are ever to achieve a mentally healthy race" we must attend to the dangers of mental illness:

Clarence Hincks' 1946 Macleans Article. Courtesy of CAMH Archives.

> Do you know that occupied beds in our mental institutions outnumber those in all other hospitals combined? At this moment over 35,000 of our fellow citizens are being treated for crippling forms of mental disease in mental hospitals throughout the country. Furthermore, we must take into account a veritable army of mental defectives, epileptics, neurotics and other abnormal types.[105]

Griffin carried this alarmist message to a meeting of the Mental Hygiene Group of the University Women's Club in Hamilton on January 21, 1938 at the invitation of Elizabeth Bagshaw, the eugenicist doctor who served as the head of the Birth Control Society of Hamilton's (BCHS) clinic. According to the *Hamilton Spectator*, Griffin said:

> The fact that there are some 40, 000 Canadian citizens in mental hospitals, a number far exceeding the number enrolled in all the Canadian universities, illustrates the immensity of the problem from an economic as well as from a social standpoint. He stressed the importance of the teacher's part in maintaining the mental balance of the child. Dr. Elizabeth Bagshaw, leader of the mental hygiene group of the club, moved a vote of thanks to Dr. Griffith [*sic*].[106]

While this report might suggest that Griffin preferred educational methods to eugenics, his emphasis on the "economic and social" costs of mental illness were exactly the kind of claims Bagshaw relied upon to justify the eugenicist goals of her birth control clinic. According to historian Catherine Annau's study, *Eager Eugenicists*, Bagshaw consistently stated publicly, even during her unsuccessful campaign for alderman in 1934; that the goals of her clinic were to, "reduce maternal mortality," "put an end to the breeding of the unfit"; and "reduce the city's expenditures on the poor."[107]

As a man of his times, Griffin sought to emphasize the need for physiological interventions to address those mental diseases rooted in "constitutional inadequacy," rather than indulge in what he referred to as "psychoanalytic mysticism."[108] In a speech entitled, *Mental Hygiene—The Extent of the Problem*, dated February 21, 1939, Griffin himself reported, approvingly, about experimentation with sexual sterilization in Alberta alongside his advocacy for the horrifically painful "insulin and metrasol shock" therapies and "electro-encephalography" being tested in other provinces:

> Many of the mental hospitals in Canada are devoting time to research into the problem of mental disease. Under the able guidance of Sir Frederick Banting, the Department of Medical Research in the Banting Institute is co-operating with the Provincial Department of Health and the Toronto Psychiatric Hospital in investigations into the physiological and biochemical mechanisms underlying the beneficial results of insulin and metrasol shock. Other centres in Canada are tackling other problems. In Alberta the programme of sexual sterilization has been continued and the results carefully tabulated.[109]

Like Hincks, Griffin also uncritically acknowledged the widespread *de facto* use of sterilization by medical doctors in Ontario without legislative authorization. In an article published in 1940 in the *Canadian Public Health Journal* he said: "It is probable that sexual sterilization is occasionally performed in many centers in cases where medical or social reasons warrant it."[110]

But we must not restrict our view of the leadership of the CNCMH to its titular heads Hincks and Griffin. Even after the death of Clarke in 1924, the real power behind the Committee remained in the hands of the U of T Department of Psychiatry well into the post-World War II period. Successors to Clarke's position as Head of the Department of Psychiatry, have always been cross-appointed as head of the Toronto Psychiatric Hospital thus giving them more than merely academic influence. C. B. Farrar, who followed Clarke as Head of the U of T Department of Psychiatry, was also appointed Director of the Toronto Psychiatric Hospital, as was his successor Aldwyn Stokes.

The fact that Farrar had been trained in Heidelburg, Germany at Emil Kraeplin's psychiatric clinic only reinforced the importance of eugenics in Ontario in the 1930s and 1940s. Representing the generally biological orientation of German psychiatry at the turn of the century, Kraeplin was opposed to Freud's theories, as was his student Farrar. In fact, Farrar is quoted as having said that "the shadows of Freud linger as the last touch of mysticism in medicine."[111] Instead Kraeplin's clinic was committed to the view that all mental health issues had physiological causes. Unfortunately, this biochemical orientation in German psychiatry led to an interest in the genetic origins of mental illness which in turn translated into support from psychiatrists on both sides of the Atlantic for eugenicist programs. In fact, another of Kraeplin's pupils, Ernst Rudin, became a leading figure in Nazi sterilization programs as the author of the official commentary on the implementation in Germany of the 1933 "Law for Prevention of Hereditary Diseased Offspring." For his part, Farrar brought this prejudice in favor of biological psychiatry back with him to Toronto in his calls for, "sterilization to prevent procreation of mental defectives."[112]

No wonder Farrar, like Hincks, was so quick to join the Eugenics Society of Canada (ESC) when it was formed in 1930. According to McLaren, Farrar had, "declared himself willing to lose one potential genius if ninety-nine defectives were also eliminated" through sterilization programs. Farrar also believed that sterilization could be justified on economic grounds citing the example of "impoverished parents of an already considerable family, particularly if of inferior stock, who must constantly depend upon charity, and with whom birth control technique is impracticable."[113]

Just as we should not overlook the involvement of the U of T Department of Psychiatry in the eugenics movement in Ontario, neither should we disregard the power of the rival Department of Psychology; for the tentacles of eugenics spread quite deeply within the medical establishment in Ontario. Indeed, "Ned" Bott, as Head of the U of T Department of Psychology, was also a founding member of the CNCMH along with Clarke and Hincks. In fact, Bott "was affiliated with every major mental hygiene activity which operated out of U of T until 1957," according to McLaren.[114] Bott's colleague and friend William Blatz too, was an active member of the CNCMH. According to Gleason, Bott and Blatz were financially dependent on the CNCMH: "Since several members of the Department, including William Blatz, received half their salary from CNCMH monies, many felt they had little choice but to conform to the desires of the committee."[115] In fact, it was Hincks in his role as leader of the organization who had arranged Rockefeller funding for the appointment of Blatz as head of the St. George's Nursery School, in which capacity he became infamous in the thirties as the supervisor of the Dionne Quintuplets.[116]

The clinical conditions organized by Blatz for the education of the Quintuplets, not to mention the one way mirror through which millions of tourists observed them, were traumatic. As adults they successfully sued the Government of Ontario for this exploitation. Freudian psychologist Alfred Adler issued a prescient warning in the March 1936 edition of *Cosmopolitan* Magazine:

> Psychologically, the separation from their family is not an asset for the Quintuplets. The Quintuplets live like the inmates of a model orphanage,

and a certain emotional starvation is inseparable from institutional life. Life in a glass house is not conducive to normal human development. Five little guppies living in a fish bowl may not be distracted by constant exposure. But babies are not fishes. There is danger ahead.[117]

Perhaps we should not be surprised to find such aggressive clinical practices amongst psychologists associated with the eugenicist agenda of the CNCMH. Our surprise is further mitigated when we briefly consider the personal backgrounds of Bott and Blatz. Bott was the descendent of Scottish, "white slavers" from the British Virgin Islands who immigrated to Ontario to escape the consequences of emancipation in the mid-nineteenth century. Blatz was a descendent of the great Franz Anton Mesmer, father of European psychotherapy, from Alsace-Lorraine in France. It appears that Blatz not only inherited the personal "magnetism" of his ancestors, but also their anti-Semitic tendencies.

This quickly became apparent to Reva Gerstein when Blatz stood in as supervisor of her PhD program because William Line, as we have already seen, had assumed a wartime position in Ottawa. For example, when she appeared in the Senate to defend her thesis on psychological testing, Blatz asked her, "Do you think the Jews are a superior race"?[118] She was taken aback, and did not know exactly what to say. She merely answered "No" with a slight tone of surprise. Upon reflection, however, Gerstein suggested that she should not have been surprised. During her academic studies at the U of T she had often been confronted with obstacles based on her Jewish heritage such as not being allowed to take calculus, or being forced to attend University College as the only U of T College that admitted Jews. She also remembered that her marks were deliberately lowered from an earned A average to a B because she was a Jew, and that she had had difficulty in arranging an internship at a local hospital for research purposes because it was government policy not to allow Jewish interns in the 1930s.

It was through his connections with Hincks, Bott and Blatz that William Line, who was Seeley's direct supervisor at the DPS, made his way into the inner circle of Ontario's medical elite. Line was born in England and his service as Second Lieutenant during World War I with the "Oxford and Bucks" light infantry suggests upper class origins. After the war Line completed his PhD in Psychology, and "accepted an invitation from E. A. Bott to join the faculty at the U of T," where he soon, "succumbed to the applied mental hygiene atmosphere of the Department."[119] With the financial and organizational backing of Hincks; Line and Griffin first had the opportunity to work together under the mentorship of Blatz on the Regal Road School's Project. As Griffin remembered in an interview published in 1989:

> By this time, September 1936, I had decided to accept a position with Dr. Hincks. Bill Line was back in Toronto and had talked to Hincks. He told him, "You've got to get Jack Griffin back. He and I will set up a program of mental hygiene in the schools, doing preventive mental health work with kids." I accepted the post and I hurried back, took an early return from my scholarship which the Rockefeller people didn't think too well of, but I got started around September 1, 1936 with the National Committee for Mental Hygiene. I had a title; I was Director of Mental Hygiene Education and Bill Line and I started to work in that field.[120]

In a personal interview, Ontario historian of psychiatry Cyril Greenland labelled the Regal Road Project a "poor man's version of the Forest Hill Village Project." It did not have the same extensive backing in terms of private or intergovernmental funding as would the Forest Hill Village Project, nor did it have as extensive University of Toronto academic resources available to it. Nevertheless, under the supervision of Blatz, the Regal Road Project sought to "make a longitudinal study of conduct deviations and adjustment of school children, primarily by way of observation; and to work out, through a testing program, the classification of the causes and possible treatment for maladjustments."[121] These were also the main goals of the Forest Hill Village Project. In fact, it was during their work together on the Regal Road Project that Griffin and Line first articulated the concept of "human relations classes"; a therapeutic technique in which students were engaged in free associative discussions as part of their school program. This technique would become a central focus of the Forest Hill Village Project.

Finally, we come to the important figure of Brock Chisolm, the founder and original Director of the DPS, who appointed his friends Hincks, Griffin, Line and Seeley to various military posts during the war. Chisolm was a U of T educated medical psychiatrist in private practice in Oakville, Ontario. Chisolm studied under Clarke and Hincks at the University and became an active participant in their eugenicist campaigns. Historian Ian Dowbiggin observed that Chisolm consistently, "revealed his inveterate fondness for broad schemes of social engineering, a taste that dated back to his early years in the mental hygiene movement when he was surrounded by other physicians with pro-eugenic opinions."[122]

But it was not his psychiatric connections that propelled Chisolm into a prominent staff position with the military during the war. Like others amongst the high staff of the Canadian military during World War II, Chisolm was a decorated soldier during World War I and had remained involved with the military between the wars. Indeed, it would seem that the personal friendship between Chisolm and Harry Letson, Deputy Adjutant—General, was a significant factor in Chisolm's appointment to start-up a Personnel Directorate with the Canadian Forces in 1941.[123]

Unfortunately, Copp and McAndrew do not trace the source of the connection between Chisolm and Letson, but a brief comparison of their careers would suggest that they would have had multiple opportunities to make contact, and much in common. Both men were wounded terribly during World War I. Letson had lost the use of his leg while Chisolm was once removed from the front lines because of shell shock and again, late in the war, "received a deep, dirty and offensive gutter flesh wound from a piece of German shell in his left thigh."[124] Both men received the Military Cross for their valor in battle. After the war, both became academic types who, like typical Canadian scholars of the time, pursued post-doctoral studies in London, England. Though academically inclined, both men kept their hands in the more practical worlds of business and the military. While Chisolm was establishing a successful medical practice; Letson found time away from his teaching duties at the University of British Columbia to transform the engineering firm he inherited from his father into a ship-building giant that "proved to be of vital importance during the Second World War."[125] The determination of both men to forge connections between their work in private business and military affairs foretold of the emerging "military-industrial complex."

It might seem strange that men so badly mangled in combat would want to return to the scene of the crime, but these men wanted to redeem their suffering. Though their efforts to make the Canadian Forces more humane during the war were undoubtedly sincere, it would seem that they carried within them the scars of ancient battles. This can be seen in the extent to which Chisolm, in particular, advocated the use of psychiatric insight for sadistic purposes in war, and for social control purposes in peacetime. For example, Chisolm blamed problems of battle exhaustion, formerly known as shell-shock, on the ways in which western culture makes men soft. Chisolm even went so far, according to his biographer Alan Irving, as to define the mental health of a good soldier in the following shocking terms, "He must be able to hate and kill without crippling degrees of guilt."[126]

In addition to utilizing his personal connection to Letson, and his military fervor, to win a senior command during the war; there is evidence that Chisolm sought to influence army administration through other channels including the ESC and the newly founded Canadian Psychological Association (CPA). In an exchange between the G. Radcliffe, secretary of the Eugenics Society and the Adjutant General's Office during the winter of 1939, DND is shown to have been cooperative in providing the ESC with, "the number and percentage of recruits rejected on account of mental disabilities." This was obviously highly useful information to eugenicists eager to show that mental defectiveness was not only a matter of medical interest but also a national security concern.

In 1942 Dr. Brock Chisholm was photographed in his Canadian Army General Staff uniform at National Defense Headquarters. Courtesy of CAMH Archives.

Moreover, the Eugenics Society would also have an interest in gathering statistics that might bolster their claims in regard to the high numbers of mental defectives in the population. The Eugenics Society was provided information by the Department of Defense showing that, during the year in question "6,000 troops out of 61,000" recruits were rejected on the basis of mental defectiveness. The Eugenics Society used this statistic to justify their call, in the fall of 1939, for the Department of Defense to establish a psychological directorate, "in order to see to it that no round pegs are placed in square holes."[127]

The Secretary to the Eugenics Society, G. Radcliffe wrote approvingly to the Minister of National Defense that: "The Eugenics Society notes that Canadian psychologists have offered to co-operate with the Department of Defense."[128] The CPA, meanwhile, had been established just a few months prior to this letter from the Eugenics Society to the Minister of Defense. In April of 1939, Line, Griffin and others met in Toronto to establish this additional form of association. They met to set up a "War Committee," otherwise known as the Test Construction Committee, of the CPA. The goal of this Committee was to "construct a test for use in the Canadian Army."[129] This was two years before the need for such a test was officially sanctioned by the DND. As it turned out, however, their effort was not wasted. Once the DND established its Personnel Directorate under Chisolm, Line and Griffin in 1941, the test that was developed by the "War Committee" of the CPA, which came to be known as the "M test," became the mainstay instrument used by the military for personnel selection and classification for the duration of World War II.

The ideology behind this test, which reflected the links of the members of the CPA "War Committee" with the leadership of the CNCMH and the ESC, is apparent in the "Preliminary Memorandum on the Use of Psychological Methods in Wartime," submitted by the CPA to the National Research Council in September of 1939. This memorandum states that the major contribution which psychology could make to military operations at that time was in regard to "Methods for the Classification of Personnel." Eugenicist jargon slips into the discussion of such methods in this memorandum most clearly in part (1) C where it is suggested that: "Recruits who by reason of inferior intelligence are unfitted for work in the field may be segregated at the outset."[130]

Thus, by the fall of 1941 the combined efforts of Toronto mental health professionals to work through a series of personal connections and lobby groups for the establishment of an institutional base within the Army had paid off. At that time, General Ralston, then Minister of National Defense, authorized the establishment of a Canadian Directorate of Personnel Selection under the command of Brock Chisolm. The terms of reference for the new Directorate were sufficiently broad that it was assured of far more influence than merely the administration of IQ tests. The Adjutant-General R. W. Browne stated in a letter to all branches of National Defense Headquarters in October 1941 that the purpose of the new Directorate would include: "the handling of personality problems which arise and which may adversely affect training, discipline, morale, efficiency and advancement at military establishments throughout Canada."[131]

Under Chisolm's leadership, it was to be Line's job to supervise the testing aspect of the Directorate's responsibilities, and to recruit promising staff for the Directorate, including Seeley. It was to be Griffin, as a psychiatrist and protégé of Hincks, who was to oversee shell shock and other discipline cases within the army medical corps. By way of summary of the process by which this group of soldier psychologists managed to reach the highest level of the Canadian Military during World War II, we should review it in Griffin's own words:

> Brock came down to see Dr. Hincks and said, "What do we do about personnel selection?" Bill Line and I were there at the time and he said, "Well, here you are. These are my right and left hands. You can take them both and build a department." So Bill Line went in as his deputy and I went in as liaison between the Royal Canadian Army Medical Corps (RCAMC) and personnel selection. The three of us started building a Personnel Selection Directorate."[132]

The battle to legitimize the usefulness of psychiatry to the military had only just begun once Chisolm, Line and Griffin achieved an administrative base within DND. They still had to deal with stigmatization issues which have perennially plagued issues of mental illness. According to Copp and McAndrew's account, Jack Griffin met with open defiance as the new psychiatric consultant with the Directorate of Personnel Selection:

> When he arrived in Ottawa in the fall of 1941 Griffin was met with open hostility by senior RCAMC officers. Brigadier Gorslinne, Director General of Medical Services (DGMS) had rejected Griffin's offer of assistance in developing mental hygiene services in 1939 and he had not changed his mind in the interval. "He said to me," Griffin recalled, "Well, you got in eh? . . . [R]emember under no circumstances will you treat anybody in the army for a psychiatric condition."[133]

In this context, the DPS was inclined to look for an issue to hang their hat on. According to Seeley's recollections, the rising rates of suicide during the war proved useful in this regard. It should be highlighted at this point, that it is in relation to this issue that Seeley returns, invisibly at first, to play an important role in events. Line had plucked Seeley out from amongst the many Personnel Selection Officers (SPOs) across the country for assignment to the Headquarters of the DPS because he had been "impressed" with the quality of Seeley's write-ups of interviews. Seeley was assigned to the suicide file once he arrived in Ottawa. He remembered himself having been quickly

> placed in training camps with psychologists trained to interview soldiers and to advise commanding officers in regard to their methods. In the penal camps where soldiers were sent, the generals who ran them had been advised by the psychologists to discontinue beating up prisoners who had been slacking.[134]

Seeley continued in his interview with me to describe the fact that the DPS had been compiling reports on suicide cases in the hope that they would be able to accumulate evidence of a link to the mistreatment of prisoners in wartime detention barracks. With this evidence in hand, Seeley said, the DPS wanted to argue for a change in the policy of the army toward more humane methods of discipline. Seeley even went so far as to claim that because of the success of the DPS in showing that suicide was a problem, and that it was the cause of a great loss of manpower for the Canadian army; Chisolm, Griffin, Line and Seeley were invited to meet with the General Staff on the question. The result of this meeting, Seeley claimed, was that, "some of the generals were fired."[135]

A memorandum to various high officials in the DND dated January 26, 1945, from Colonel Griffin provides evidence of Seeley's claims. The memo gave an opinion on a "Suicide Case" in which Griffin outlined his arguments for greater psychiatric involvement in the screening and treatment of soldiers at risk of becoming, "a liability to themselves and to the army if not given the appropriate help."[136] He begins the memo by noting that:

> Over 170 cases of suicide have occurred in the Canadian Army since the beginning of this war. The importance of this does not lie in the number of such cases alone but also in the fact that for every case of completed suicide there are many cases of emotional upset who almost commit suicide.[137]

Griffin's argument in the Memorandum is that these suicides might have been prevented because, soldiers like those whose "completed suicide" was in question were often already identified as having problems. In fact, the soldier in question, who was not named, was "on the staff of a recruiting officer," which Griffin found noteworthy because, "some recruiting officers are particularly vocal in their opinions that some medical specialists find mental or emotional deviations without justification." In other words, Griffin is suggesting that the stigmatization of mental health issues within the army was in part to blame for the failure to recognize and prevent potential cases of suicide. Griffin pointed out that 75% of all recorded suicide cases in the Canadian Army during World War II had come to the attention of medical or administrative officers but had not been referred to psychiatric specialists. According to Griffin, these men had either presented in military hospitals with acute somatic complaints or in detention barracks, "for offenses such as A.W.L, for example, because of requests for compassionate leave or for investigation of conjugal difficulties, or because of nervousness in training." Griffin concludes the memorandum saying that "suicides have occurred in individuals who have been problem cases to both Meds and Admin and that insufficient attention had been given to considering the individual."

It would seem that Griffin did succeed in making a breakthrough for the psychiatric function in the military with this memo. Within a month of its receipt the Department of Defense had distributed a new policy to all commanding officers and administrators on the subject of "Discipline, Soldiers Suffering from Mental Disorders." This Memo recounted Griffin's argument that "soldiers suffering from mental disorders or extreme emotional disturbances have not received proper medical attention." It gives the order that that any soldier presenting with "emotional difficulties" should be "promptly referred to the nearest Medical Officer." It is remarkable as well that the memo stipulates that such referral should be made even if there are doubts about the sincerity of the complaints. More significantly in terms of Seeley's claim that the underlying aim of the DPS on this issue was to make punishment in Detention Centers more humane, the memo stipulates, "under no circumstances will an examination by the nearest Medical Officer be delayed on the grounds that the soldier should be held pending completion of some disciplinary or administrative action."[138]

In a follow up memo on the new "Suicide Policy" distributed to medical offices throughout the Canadian Military, the Director of Medical

Services, C. P. Fenwick, outlined the symptoms of suicidal behavior and stressed that:

> It is important that all medical officers make sure that seriously disturbed individuals are not treated casually or harshly. Adequate time must be taken to obtain a complete history in order that an immediate decision may be made as to the need for special disposal including referral to a psychiatric specialist.[139]

Here Griffin had killed two birds with one stone. He achieved a reform of the punitive regime in the Detention Barracks, and he assured a steady supply of psychiatric referrals within the army. The significance of this episode derives from the light it sheds on the meaning of Seeley's oft-repeated claim that, perhaps acting as the ghost-writer on Griffin's memoranda, he had helped to make the army more humane. It would appear that what he was referring to was the attempt to move the army away from traditional methods of punishment that may have been psychologically debilitating, if not also dangerous and unfair. The issue of punishment, which was to dominate Seeley's career as an educational activist, first surfaces in this context. It is not hard to see the connection between his activism on this issue and his suffering as a child. Ironically, like the soldiers he was trying to help, we know from his letters to Fischer that he himself sometimes contemplated, "infantile threats, or fantasies of suicide."[140]

To this point we were forced to infer Seeley's presence behind the scenes in the work of Griffin and the DPS on suicide policy, but his name re-surfaces in the records of the Library and Archives of Canada for the first time since his arrival as a Home Child on the SS Calgaric in 1929, as a representative of the DND on a Civilian Advisory Committee in 1944. This committee had originally been established in 1941 alongside the new Directorate of Personnel Selection, but it never actually met until the spring of 1944. Line's "Summary of Minutes" states the ostensible purpose of reconvening of the Civilian Advisory Committee:

> The deliberations of this first meeting of the Civilian Advisory Committee culminated in one major interest and recommendation, namely, that the needs of the soldier must be taken care of from the moment of cease-fire in Europe until he has settled down and become re-established as a citizen. Beyond this, it was felt that considerations should be given to the psychological issues to be taken into account in considering the roles of 1) an army of Occupation and ii) a force engaged in the Pacific Theatre. As

the Army had hitherto concentrated on making sound provisions for the soldier in his progress in training from civilian to fighting man, it was to be expected that similar attention would be paid to the handling of problems of readjustment both for the immediate post-war phase with its emotional disorientation and to the problems of post-war civilian life.[141]

What is interesting about the general perspective revealed in this document is the ambitious scope in terms of which these psychiatric experts envisioned their role in engineering the peace. For example, they suggest that the Medical Services organization of the Army be re-organized to include "all medical and related non-medical services," under the new title of a "Royal Canadian Army Health Corps." They justified such a move in terms of its achieving a new concept of health as a "concern and function of the whole of the Army community." Moreover, the Civilian Advisory Committee suggested that if the Army would adopt such a holistic view of health, then perhaps Canadian society in general would follow this model, "It was also felt that such a concept might have far reaching implications for civilian medical and health education throughout the Dominion."[142]

This strong endorsement of a re-organization and re-definition of health for military and civilian purposes might easily be read as a way for the psychiatric intelligentsia to legitimize a greater role for themselves in the health field. This would have been to their professional benefit not only in terms of social status, but also economic profitability. That is not to say, however, that what was in their interest was not also in the interest of society more generally. They repeatedly emphasized the broader social concern for "the personal psychological development of the soldier during his period of transition." They go so far as to say that this adjustment process

> be regarded as having long-term importance, rather than as a simple and immediate change from serving soldier to dis-charged veteran; and to be viewed in realistic relationship to Army policy, the Civil Power and Canadian Society generally.[143]

But what interests of Canadian society were they thinking of, precisely, in outlining this relatively abstract and very broad mandate? They perhaps come closer to specifying what they considered that interest to be in the penultimate section (j) of their list of *Demobilization Policy: Basic Principles*: "That in all matters of priorities of demobilization there shall be constant concern for the preservation of a sound social structure in the Canadian Community as a whole."[144]

The socially conservative bias of the doctors appointed to the Civilian Advisory Committee, many of whom like Hincks, Chisolm, and Griffin had shown sympathy for eugenicist ideology prior to the war, comes through quite clearly in these principles. For his part, Chisolm, stated even more directly what he thought the import of the deliberations of the Civilian Advisory Committee in a letter to the Adjutant General, Brigadier M. Noel, dated September 6, 1944: "It is believed that if these measures are carried out aggressively much of the difficulty of the demobilization period of the First World War will be avoided."[145] This is a reference, of course, to the Winnipeg General Strike and the spread of industrial unrest across Canada in the period following the First World War.

It is also interesting to note the impact of those events on the formation of leftist political parties in Canada including the Co-Operative Commonwealth Federation and the Communist Party of Canada in the 1920s and 30s. A similar concern that the spread of the "red menace" might continue its march after the end of hostilities with Germany and Japan may not have been too far under the surface of governmental concern regarding the adjustment of soldiers after World War II. In fact, if this was not already apparent from the events surrounding the Gouzenko Affair in 1945, further evidence of such concern at the policy-making level is given in a memo Captain Seeley of the DPS wrote in the early months just after the German surrender as part of his work for the Civilian Advisory Committee.

Seeley had been asked to do an analysis of Allied planning for the post-war adjustment of the German population. Seeley claimed that this memo went beyond Chisolm, who by this time was Deputy Minister of Health, and was brought to the attention of the Prime Minister and even the American government. There is a record in Seeley's personal archives of a copy that had been read by Chisolm who approved it with the comment scribbled in ink, "Good. No Suggestions."[146] The memo makes the following observation about cold war fears as the war against Germany was reaching its denouement:

> The Russians are already cleverly and methodically at work. Whatever we may think of their views, we cannot accuse them of backwardness or ineptness in putting them over in the areas under their influence.[147]

This memo to Chisolm about the "No-Fraternization Rule" for Canadian Occupation Forces in Germany, was submitted by Seeley as a possible "opening gun," he said, for some unspecified post-war mental health campaign. Seeley writes in the introduction to the Memo, "It has been thought of as something that Clare Hincks might say as an opening gun in some such publication as *Saturday Night*."[148] What new battle was to be fought? It is interesting to recall that that in early 1946, not long after Seeley's memo, Hincks published his infamous post-war article in *Maclean's*, "Sterilizing the Unfit." But what might advocacy for restraint in the punishment of the German population under occupation have to do with advocacy for sterilization of the mentally ill back at home? Unless, of course, they might both serve a common purpose in pacifying the restive post-war populations of Europe and North America. This did seem to be the major concern of the Civilian Advisory Committee.

From Seeley's personal perspective, the question of the discipline of the allied occupation forces in post-war Germany was one that struck at the core of his concern with punishment. Seeley suggested that the freeing up of interpersonal relations between the troops and the locals should be encouraged. If they were allowed to masturbate, as Chisolm had advocated in other places, and if they were allowed to have sex with the locals, they would be happier and more efficient guardians. Here psychoanalysis was being put to use as a social control technique in a way that might anticipate efforts after the war like the Forest Hill Village project. Seeley put it this way in the memo: "[T]he attempt to enforce what is intrinsically unenforceable—with consequent widespread disobedience of orders—is a threat to the maintenance of normal military discipline."[149] At this point, it would seem, the nascent psychoanalytic orientation in Seeley's thinking was compatible with the social control aims of his eugenicist superiors.

There are indeed some other surprising passages in the memo where Seeley's concern for the interpersonal happiness of the troops is counter posed by an obligatory tone of military brutality: "We do not propose to kill more than a few Germans and our peace policy must therefore include some way of dealing with the remainder. What we mean by "dealing with" defines the occupation—and the peace."[150] Seeley proposes the term education as the key goal of the occupation. He writes that the definition of the "educative" goal of the occupation should be understood as to "reform the German character." With his typical penchant for being provocative, Seeley uses Hitler as an example of how to pursue an educative social program, though the boundary between education and propaganda may be blurred:

> We must not let the spectacle character of Hitler's methods delude us into thinking that that was all there was. There was that. But, more important, was the crying need to find a solution to a pressing problem, and the

devoted work at a grass roots level of thousands upon thousands of burning missionaries of the new gospel.[151]

Seeley sees his purpose in missionary terms. But such methods of mass propaganda must be turned to the cause of liberalism and democracy, according to Seeley: "An organized campaign to win over the German people to those attitudes, sentiments, and institutions or habitual ways of acting to which we wish them to become attached."[152] Naturally, Seeley wanted the existing Canadian troops in Germany to lead this effort, though he lamented the fact that there wasn't time to organize a special force for this task, "Or do we propose to recruit and train a special army for the purpose? We do not, and in any case we haven't time."[153] We might detect a Platonist *cum* Freudian tendency in Seeley's plan to organize a special force of psychological experts to "reform the German character."

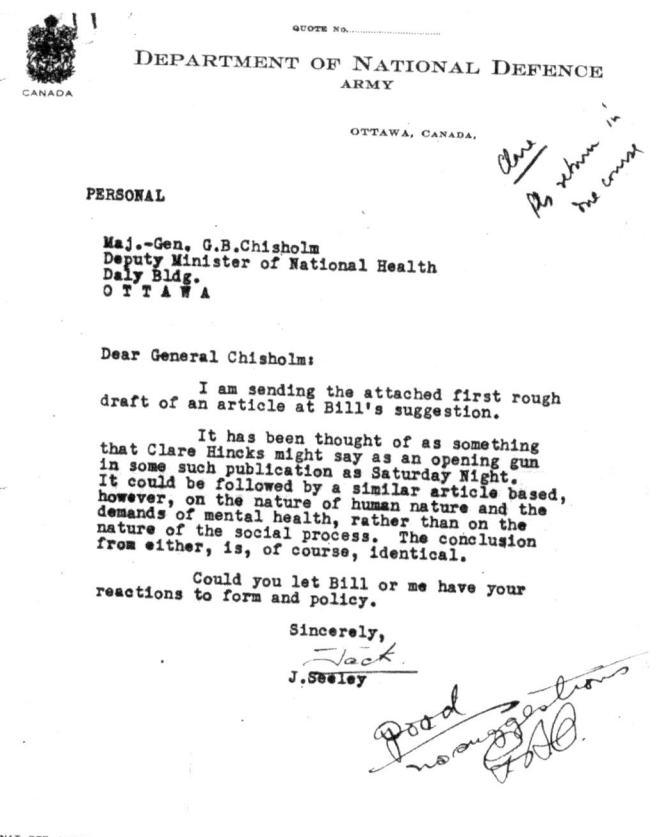

Memo from Seeley to Chisolm, ca. 1945. Seeley Papers, Los Angeles, California.

This philosophical talent was first identified and seized upon by the leaders of the Civilian Advisory Committee, who had asked Seeley to pronounce upon the psychology of occupation. In normal times, as nations trudge through the day-to-day administrative requirements of managing complex economies, there is probably not much tolerance for such grand visionary schemes of the sort Seeley produced during his time in Ottawa. However, the novelty of the immediate post World War II era seen in the total surrender of the enemy; the revelation of mass genocide; the specter of successful communist revolutionary regimes in Russia and China; and the overwhelming reality of the destruction caused by the war; all of this combined to create an era in which visionary promises of renewal were the order of the day. This post-war utopianism would reach its apex in a Canadian educational context with Seeley's Forest Hill Village Project.

Prior to tackling the next task assigned to him by the Civilian Advisory Committee, which was to be entitled a "Functional Chart—Post-Hostilities Period," Seeley made a trip to Europe to do background research. According to Department of Defense records, "he spent some two and one half months overseas, embarking for Britain on 24 November 1944 and returning to Canada on 14 February 1945."[154] It was on this occasion that Seeley visited his mother and brother Frank in London for the first time since he had left for Canada over 15 years before. Perhaps he should have been proud, and felt somewhat vindicated, to appear before them as Captain Seeley on an important mission for the Canadian forces, but that is not what happened as Seeley recounts in a letter to Frank:

> The climax came when I came home the first time. Mamma seemed so small, so unhappy, so robbed of certainty, direct domination and all of her ancient vices that my heart melted—I thought: I now understand this poor, unfortunate, misguided woman; she was a tragic victim of circumstances. At that time elements of the intended revenge lost their value; the desire to demonstrate how wrong she had been; that I had developed a character of my own better than the one she had sought to impose, that I had demonstrated intellectual capacity that made her original estimates patently absurd. But this forgiveness was hate masquerading as love, and as soon as the target of hate seemed to disappear motivation for learning and for an over-moralized way of life disappeared. It became difficult to feel that anything was worth doing, and left me naked to my hate and fear, and that is where I am.[155]

When he returned to Ottawa, Seeley threw himself back into his work with an ambition perhaps re-kindled by this experience with his mamma, yet empty at its core: "Captain Seeley summarized his observations of developments overseas which he had been privileged to witness during December and January. His report centered on the principles of rehabilitation adopted by CMHQ and the development of repatriation training in hospitals in the UK and at the No. 1 Canadian Repatriation Depot."[156] He then presented a very complex flow chart to the Committee:

> In so doing he stressed (and the Committee approved) the necessity for considering such activities as a unified program directed in the interests of the soldier as a person and as a citizen. The Committee welcomed Captain Seeley's presentation and suggested that, since it formed a basis for active participation of all Directorates concerned, unity of the outline might well be symbolized by an appropriate title: <u>Functional Chart—Post Hostilities Period,</u> Relations of DAG (C) and DGMS Directorates in Personal Readjustment Programs.[157]

What the flow chart outlines, essentially, are the different training courses toward which troops with divergent destinations after the war might be directed. For example, troops destined to stay in Germany as part of an Occupation force would be directed toward courses on "Nazism, Democracy." Troops destined to return home to work would be directed toward vocational and psychological counseling. It is interesting to note the way in which the underlying free enterprise values of liberal society worked their way into such post-war planning documents. While the Civilian Advisory Committee claimed to be concerned above all with the soldier's "emotional needs and outlook" it was also quick to point out that, in the end, he was on his own:

> That vocational guidance should not be regarded by the Army as a system whereby every man is guaranteed or placed in a particular job; but rather as a procedure or course of training whereby he is led to think constructively and positively about his own rehabilitation within the framework of the best possible advisory service that the Army can provide.[158]

Next, given the success of Seeley's memo on the "No-Fraternization Rule," and his "Functional Chart—Post-Hostilities Period," he also became the Advisory Committee's special assistant for the issue of adjustment for veterans to their post-war educational programs. The President of U of T at the time, Sydney Smith, had written to Bill Line asking that he "describe a thorough going mental hygiene service for the veterans." Smith said the "university is committed to organize such an undertaking." Smith added as an afterthought in ink on the letter to Line, "but not a guinea-pig laboratory for veterans." His concern was to prevent segregation within the University Community of the veterans, or perhaps even some form of unionization, and to promote their integration back into the civilian community and readjustment to civilian norms of non-aggression, and productivity, "We could head off, I think, the organization of a veteran society or association within the University which, to my mind, would in itself tend to segregate the discharged personnel from civilian students."[159]

Line asked Seeley to write-up a memo in response to Smith's proposal, describing what such a "psychological service should look like." His rather philosophical plan for a psychological service conjured Deweyean motifs of the University as a social microcosm in which the students themselves are involved in the therapeutic process:

> Most of the program should be carried by graduate students in any appropriate science, e.g., psychiatry, psychology, and sociology. . . . For fruitful teaching of the social sciences (whether in public or high school or college) consists in leading the student to acquire tools that enable him first to understand his situation as a member of his society, and later to act intelligently in the light of that insight.[160]

Seeley proposes that this specialized corps of professors and graduate students in the area of the social sciences might play the role of psychoanalyst for the university community. They would treat the veterans as simply one amongst a number of identifiable groups who might benefit from observation and counseling: "The conclusion is that the task of the service is to facilitate the process of liberal education by using the techniques and insights of psychology."[161] This vision of how the social sciences might assume a focal role in graduate studies curricula was a premonition of what Seeley would propose for the "new" post-war university at York.

Perhaps inspired by his own vision of the University, Seeley felt himself drawn back there once the war was over. He was offered a job as Chief of Staff for Paul Martin, the Minister of Health (and the father of a future Prime Minister). But Seeley wrote to Martin that he wanted to keep his feet in both the worlds of scholarship and "the world of practical issues and everyday affairs." If he were to accept Martin's offer, Seeley wrote, he would see his role as that of one whom

> in order to perform adequately must be careful not to lose track of the whole by immersing oneself in successive parts. This implies the necessity for at least a small staff to do necessary bits and pieces of research under the direction of some one person who is free enough to see the implications of these bits and pieces—for the larger designs and long term ends.[162]

Seeley concluded, however, that "the task had been conceived at a much lower level" than this. He decided to return to the University of Chicago to study for a PhD in Sociology. This decision was to prove fateful for his future relations with Ontario's medical elite; that is Chisolm, Hincks, Line, and Griffin, who had promoted him to a position of such influence during the war. Though they would later turn to Seeley again as an intellectual weapon; his experience in Chicago changed him. During his time at the U of C Seeley gravitated toward other Jewish intellectuals steeped in a Freudian world view. This psychoanalytic turn would eventually set Seeley at odds with his waspish, eugenicist colleagues in Canada.

# Pop Sociology

Seeley was officially discharged from the Canadian Army on September 6, 1945.[163] Proudly bearing his "Canadian Volunteer Service Medal with Clasp" and his "War Medal 1939–1945"; Seeley, his wife Margaret, and their first son Michael crossed the border from Sarnia, Ontario to Port Huron, Michigan *en route* for Chicago on September 22.[164] According to a letter of reference later written on Seeley's behalf by eminent American Sociologist David Riesman, who also got his start at the U of C, it took a little while for the Seeleys to find a place to live once they arrived in Chicago, "He lived in our house for a time when he was a graduate student and instructor at the University of Chicago; we were colleagues there in a joint undergraduate course in culture and personality."[165]

For his part, Riesman had come to Sociology by a circuitous route that began with his "unorthodox psychoanalysis" with Erich Fromm in the early 1940s, which was conducted on "alternative weekends for two hour sessions."[166] Eschewing the "surgical" objectivity of the analyst, Fromm befriended his protégé and they became life-long correspondents. As proof of the life-transforming impact of Riesman's relationship with Fromm, one need only notice that when their relationship began Riesman was working as a lawyer, but by the end of the decade, without even a degree in sociology, he was teaching the subject in Chicago.

Unlike his upper class protégés Riesman and Seeley, Fromm was of middle class Jewish-German parentage. His father was a wine trader and his family was full of orthodox Jews who dedicated themselves to the study of the Talmud. Fromm completed his PhD in Sociology at the University of Heidelberg before undergoing his psychoanalytic training with Hans Sachs, who was very close to Freud himself. He then joined the Frankfurt School of Critical Theory as the resident psychoanalytic expert. Given the religious climate in which he was raised, Fromm felt disdain for titles and other things that "you have" as opposed to things that "you are." He raised this prejudice to the level of sociological theory in his concept of the "marketing character" which he saw as a sociological symptom of American capitalism. The typical American, according to Fromm, is mainly concerned with how "salable" he is rather than how happy or free. For individuals who might be typecast as such marketing types, "prestige, status, success, the fact that he is known to others as being a certain person, are a substitute for the genuine feeling of identity."[167] This idea has certainly resonated in post-war American popular culture in works like Arthur Miller's 1949 play *Death of a Salesman* whose hero was so concerned with being "well liked."

Allan Bloom, another U of C intellectual of the time, suggests that Riesman basically re-packaged and popularized Fromm's idea as that of the "other-directed" type in *The Lonely Crowd*. Bloom uses Woody Allen's character *Zelig* to define this type more precisely: "Zelig is a man who literally becomes whoever or whatever is expected of him—a Republican when with the rich; a gangster when with Mafiosi; black, when with blacks. He is nothing in himself, just a collection of roles prescribed by others."[168] In Allen's film, Bruno Bettleheim, who would also have a close and formative relationship with Seeley during his Chicago days, confirms this diagnosis in a cameo appearance where he says of Zelig, "I myself feel that one would describe him as the ultimate conformist."

In his own terms, Riesman defines the other-directed character in the *Lonely Crowd* as, "at once an analysis of the American and of contemporary man."[169] What Riesman sees as linked to the commonly discussed international features of modernity including "capitalism, industrialism and urbanization," is that, "relations with the outer world and with one-self are mediated by the flow of mass communication."[170] The social corollary to this intensified exposure to various media of communication, Riesman argues, is a requirement of "more socialized behavior both for success and for marital and personal adaptation."[171] Insofar as Riesman here reconceptualizes this character-type in social-scientific terms, Bloom argues; he acted as a major conduit for the transplantation of a European, mainly German, identity crisis onto American soil after the war. In particular, Bloom points the blame at Nietzsche and his discovery of the "death of God" for all this moral relativism:

> When I came to the University of Chicago in the mid-forties, just after the war, there were two writers who dominated and generated real enthusiasm—

Freud and Weber. Although it is even now insufficiently appreciated, Freud and Weber were both thinkers who were profoundly influenced by Nietzsche. Everyone knew that they were German thinkers, and that the professors teaching them were a mix of German refugees from Hitler and of Americans who had either studied in Germany prior to Hitler or who had learned from these émigrés.[172]

The "émigrés" referred to, of course, included Fromm and Bettleheim. The fact that Riesman mimicked the integration of sociological and psychoanalytical principles that was characteristic of Fromm's work was openly acknowledged in the preface to the second edition of *The Lonely Crowd*:

> We ourselves were in the tradition of the neo-Freudians, particularly Erich Fromm, with whom I had studied. Fromm's *Escape from Freedom* and *Man for Himself* were decisively influential models in the application of a socially oriented psychoanalytic characterology to problems of historical change.[173]

His book, a triumph, was a gift he proffered his father figure. He makes explicit acknowledgment of Fromm's collaboration during the writing of *The Lonely Crowd* in this passage:

> Among friends who read the manuscript or portions of it, I want to especially thank Lewis Dexter, Herman Finer, Erich Fromm, Everett Hughes, Nathan Leites, Evelyn T. Riesman, John R. Seeley, Milton Singer, M. Brewster Smith, and Martha Wolfenstein.[174]

It is noteworthy that he also includes Seeley on his list of important collaborators. We can begin to see, at this point, just how close Riesman and Seeley were. Of course, the fact that Riesman would later write the introduction to Seeley's book, *Crestwood Heights*, is also an important marker of their intellectual partnership; as is the fact that Seeley openly acknowledged the importance of *The Lonely Crowd* as a template for his book: "Now, I meant this to have about the same relation to reality as does, say *The Lonely Crowd* and not as, say, *1984* or *Brave New World*."[175] In a similar vein, Seeley wrote to Marsh Jeanneret, head of the University of Toronto Press, "I think parts of *Crestwood Heights* will be semi-popular and will receive the same kind of widespread distribution and comment as did *The Lonely Crowd*."[176]

It is not surprising that they would gravitate toward each other given their shared experience as Jews who both converted to other religions. Seeley became an Episcopalian, and Riesman converted to his wife's religion, Unitarianism.[177] They were also similar as intellectuals who shared an interest in the integration of psychoanalytic and sociological theory. For both men, the personal experience of psychoanalysis was formative. Finally, they both made a name for themselves in academia without the conventional qualifications.

It is tempting to attribute to them a shared aristocratic sense of entitlement. In a recently published history of Sociology at U of C entitled, *A Second Chicago School? The Development of Postwar American Sociology*, Riesman is referred to as the "scion of an old Philadelphia Jewish family and proud of its heritage of learning and professionalism."[178] Seeley was also raised in a wealthy Jewish family in England with high social aspirations. It is almost as if they clung to the Elizabethan pretense that a man of leisure must not learn a trade, but should indulge his eclectic interests without concern for money.

But what may be even more suggestive of the importance of the Riesman-Seeley relationship, is the amazing correspondence between the description of the "other-directed" type and Seeley's own character. It is almost as if Seeley constructed his personality based on his reading of Riesman's book, or the other way around. Is it possible that the uncertainties of Seeley's childhood, which left him so malleable or "other-directed"; were only an extreme example of the common experience of a generation which was analyzed so effectively by thinkers like Nietzsche, Freud, Fromm, and Riesman? But before a passage from a letter Seeley wrote to Fischer is presented as evidence of his "other-directedness," we must briefly introduce his second major relationship while a PhD student at the U of C, with the psychoanalyst Bruno Bettleheim, a survivor of Dachau.

American sociologist, professor, and author David Riesman sits and reads a book, early 1950s. Photo by Pictorial Parade, Courtesy of Getty Images.

    Seeley spent a lot of time with Bruno Bettleheim during his undergraduate years at the U of C, 1940–1942, and again during his doctoral program, 1945–1947. Seeley and his wife Margaret were invited to dinner at the Bettleheim's apartment in Chicago on a monthly basis. However a falling out started to take shape over the issue of Seeley's doctoral thesis. Bettleheim wanted Seeley to take a research grant under his supervision for a book entitled, *The Professional Soldier: A Social and Political Portrait*, but by this time Seeley had already begun to feel that Bettleheim was too "dogmatic and dictatorial."[179] He refused to take the research fellowship and instead got involved in participant observation with gangs in the slums of Chicago. A fellow graduate student by the name of Morris Janowitz got the grant to do the work with Bettleheim which led to the publication of the book. Further collaboration between Janowitz and Bettleheim culminated in the 1964 publication of *Social Change and Prejudice*. Starting from his association with Bettleheim, Janowitz established a reputable scholarly career as a sociologist with an expertise on military culture. Seeley on the other hand, got mired down in his work with gangs, and failed to produce anything of substance toward his doctorate.

Seeley said that in his work with the gangs of Chicago he engaged in "a constant Socratic questioning that led to habits of examining their lives and thought-ways and taken for granted apothegms of morality."[180] He said that he only pretended to join the gang, and that he participated in the life of the street as an observer. For example, in his interviews with me he suggested that he went along with the gang on "prostitution crawls" but only on the promise from gang members that "you don't have to fuck nobody."[181] Of course Seeley was married with little children at home at the time. In any event, as he himself admitted, he never wrote anything about his experiences with Chicago gang life in the forties. In his letters to Fischer, however, he did speculate about how he was able to move from gang member, to scholar, without missing a beat. It is here that Seeley articulates the "other-directed" character formation he had developed by this time in his life:

> After toying with the idea of rebellion via a criminal or exploitive career, for which I probably lacked strength—I soon discovered that it was really very easy to "please" people by being helpful, and that I had a talent for it. I tried therefore to develop as many facets very nearly as I knew people, and, as long as I could keep them in separate circles feel little danger except the latent one that they might come together to "compare notes." Hence, in part, the awful threat of Frank's coming here, as against the low-grade danger of my going there as long as he didn't meet my Canadian friends.[182]

Seeley makes reference here to the event of his Jewish brother Frank's visit to Toronto in the 1950s, about which we have already heard in the context of our discussion of Seeley's experience of "de-Judaization" during his childhood. Seeley is explaining that when he visited Frank and his mamma in London while on military duty in 1944, as we have already also reviewed, he did not have to fear exposure as a Jew to his English-Canadian friends. But with Frank's arrival in Toronto, the danger of such exposure was greater. The letter continues:

> The pleasing people pattern was paramount until I met Murray Ross and, partly in order to please him, but also beckoned by the "independent admiration way," I began to prepare for College.[183]

This part refers to the administration of the IQ test by Ross, whom he obviously began to befriend, though it perhaps should be noted that from the beginning the relationship between Ross and Seeley was characterized by a good deal of obsequiousness on the latter's part. Though there were glimmers of hope in Seeley's mind, based on the confirmation of his incredibly high IQ, that perhaps he could be successful based on his own merits, it would seem that his insecurities warred with his hopes:

> The University showed, though I could not for years accept it, that I could operate independently and secure respect without affection, if necessary. However, the emotional effect and the motivation were mixed: It still felt as though I could get along by "pleasing" two different kinds of people: those who liked me to be critical and independent seeming and those who liked me to be sympathetic and helpful. So even in the "independent-critical" role I was still being "pleasing" to and dependent on a new kind of person.[184]

Seeley seems to recognize in this part of the letter to Fischer that, despite his talents, even his intellectual efforts were designed more to please his new friends like Riesman and Bettleheim, whom he imagined wanted him to be a "critical" thinker like they were, than to be an authentic expression of his own interests. What is most curious about Seeley's desire to please, however, is that he would spread it around so freely, to such disparate and conflicting groups. As he writes in the next passage he wanted to fit in with scholars and criminals; those who pursue truth and those who mock it:

> I could usually—not without some sense of danger, however—have it both ways. Even operating with my delinquents Back-of-the-Yards, I could laugh sympathetically with them at the antics of the middle class people, while on campus, I could be "interesting" by describing slum life to comfortable people. The Back-of-the-Yard kids could not hear what I said about them and neither could the good folk.[185]

It is tempting to see the logic of resentment behind such contradictions in Seeley's seemingly random attempt to "fit in" and please others. Perhaps with the denigrating voice of his mama ringing in his ears, Seeley anticipated rejection at every turn. Anticipating that the political world would reject him, Seeley fled to academia, where the vicious cycle recurred. Thus it might be inferred that in order for Seeley to safely rebel against the pretensions and high expectations of his intellectual colleagues, he joined a criminal gang; and *vice versa*, out of his disgust at the behavior of those "back-of-the-yards," he recoiled into middle class respectability in his home life and career. "Not willing to be a part of any club that would have him as a member," as Groucho Marx put it, Seeley invited rejection but possibly harbored resentment when it occurred. Evidence of such unconscious resentments is provided by the pattern of conflict between Seeley and his academic colleagues which first surfaces in his relationship with Bettleheim.

In his review of Bettleheim's book *Love is not Enough*, Seeley identified the "terrifying implications," of the educational theories advanced. Bettleheim suggested that love is a necessary but not sufficient condition of normal development. For example, the autistic child becomes ill according to Bettleheim, even though his mother loves him and wants the best for him, because she cannot fully hide the unconscious wish on her part for the death of her child. Seeley writes, "God, in this case the child, is not mocked." Or, Seeley writes, "to cuddle the child because we wish to make him happy, strong and free, and because we know that this is the way to do it, is, in the absence of genuine and free-flowing love between us, merely to invite in him the feeling that he is being used and manipulated." These terrifying realities about the child's vulnerabilities, and our responsibilities as parents for feelings we may not even be aware of, lead to feelings of helplessness Seeley argued. Seeley concludes his review of *Love is Not Enough* by implicitly objecting to this sense of despair:

> To those who can bear the shock, and let it nerve them the more for the search for a grain of hope in the bushel of despair, it is highly commended for the clarity and importance of its message.[186]

For both Bettleheim and Seeley the only hope for a strategy with which to address the problem of parenting is psychoanalysis. As Seeley wrote in the review, "short of universal psychoanalysis—what can parents, then, do?" At this point in his thinking, Seeley had not yet begun to consider the possibility that public schools could provide the forum for such an experiment. However, he had taken note of Bettleheim's experiment in special education at his laboratory school at the U of C:

> The book suggests that in a controlled setting (such as the Orthogenic School), with a staff of incredibly high quality, with sufficiently large groups and alternate parent figures (as compared with the minute middle-class family) and with the genius and character of Bettleheim—with all these, a great deal (no one knows quite how much) can be done for these badly-disturbed children.[187]

The theme of a guardian class who might guide the troubled, which Seeley had fantasized about in his military memoranda, is repeated in this assessment the Orthogentic School. It would return again when Seeley takes charge of his own educational experiment in Toronto a few years later, as we shall see. Though in this sense Seeley was heavily indebted to Bettleheim, the rift between them that we have detected in the critique of *Love is Not Enough*, had become a chasm by the time, in 1953, Seeley was invited by Bettleheim to comment on his work entitled *Symbolic Wounds: Puberty Rites and the Envious Male*. In the spirit of Freud, to whose memory the book is dedicated, Bettleheim turns his attention in this book away from contemporary parenting issues to the anthropological implications of his clinical observations at the Orthogenic School.

As had been the case with Riesman's *The Lonely Crowd*, Bettleheim acknowledged "Jack Seeley" amongst the list of those who made "many helpful suggestions" in the process of writing the book (how remarkable that Seeley was able to make it onto the list of credits in the works of two such prominent American public intellectuals of the 1950s?).[188] It might be dismissed as projection on Seeley's part when he objected to Bettelheim's "constant speculation about origins to which I have a long-standing aversion in terms of possibility and utility."[189] But Seeley's main objection to Bettleheim's theory of initiation rituals was its presumption in favor of their positive social role because of long practice. Seeley balked when came to this characteristic feature of Conservative social theory, from Burke to Bloom, that the wisdom carried in traditional institutions should be respected even if its reasons are not readily understood during changing times. Bettleheim put it this way:

> Throughout this book I have been guided by the belief that important enterprises of human beings, and certainly those that have continued for centuries to give satisfaction, must serve positive rather than negative ends.[190]

Bettleheim ends the book by saying that the traditional view of initiation rituals and circumcision in psychoanalytic and anthropological theory, "as imposed primarily by the elders on the young, against the will of the young," overlooks their health-promoting functions. Amongst the positive functions of initiation rituals, Bettleheim said, include the opportunity for youth to deal with sexual role confusion. He observes that the blood-letting involved in circumcision of the phallus enables boys to imitate menstruation, or in the case of sub incision, to go so far as to refashion the phallus so that it can take on the look of a vulva without losing its masculine function.

For his part, Seeley objects to this inherent conservatism in Bettleheim's theoretical perspective in the following terms: "[A]t some point you say that you take it for granted that any long-standing institution must have constructive rather than destructive value, otherwise it would not have survived."[191] This, Seeley said in a letter to Bettleheim about the book, is a "seriously dangerous doctrine," that might lead to such conclusions as that

> corporal punishment, capital punishment, torture, and the Catholic Church alike were more in the service of life than death. My feeling is that fascism failed to survive as a growing institution chiefly because of a rare historical accident in terms of a convergence of forces. If it had survived on your argument you would incline researches to look in it for the sense in which it served life rather than death, and while I think this should also be done, I think it would be a regrettable first bias with which to come to the investigation.[192]

This is an interesting exchange between two men who had in their own way suffered under fascist discrimination. Already, Seeley identified the issue which came between Bettleheim and himself; namely, pedagogical authoritarianism and its corollary, corporal punishment. Seeley recalled to me a decisive conversation with Bettleheim. During a plane ride, Bettleheim challenged Seeley to agree with him that it was sometimes necessary to administer *eins links, eins rechts,* "one on the right and then one on the left," for the benefit of students. Seeley said that he could not agree. Years later, Seeley broke off relations entirely when he became more aware of the "psychological violence" Bettleheim inflicted upon his students.[193]

We turn now to the question of Seeley's failure to complete his PhD program. Admittedly, doctorates are interminable programs by their very nature, and perhaps Seeley saw the opportunity to get away without having one in the example of Riesman. But as we shall see, many people unknowingly conferred a doctorate upon him when this clearly was not the case, which raises the question whether Seeley sometimes dressed in borrowed academic robes? This question was dealt with in the correspondence that was exchanged between Seeley and the Head of the Sociology Department at U of C, Everett Hughes. It was Hughes, in fact, who raised the question in a casual letter to Seeley in October of 1958, when Seeley was basking in the academic limelight with the recent publication of *Crestwood Heights* in 1956:

> Earl Johnston just asked me why you aren't a doctor. Of course it is just a matter of time until you will be an honorary one. But I couldn't answer his question. Let me ask you why you aren't a doctor?[194]

Seeing an opportunity in Hughes question, Seeley sent a lengthy reply offering all sorts of excuses for the incomplete thesis, all of which boiled down to placing the blame on others' shoulders. First, Seeley admits in the letter to Hughes that he left Chicago to join the CMHA with both the comprehensive exams and thesis incomplete:

> Only the thesis and final exams stood in the way when I left Chicago to join the Canadian Mental Health Association. With them I had a sensible bargain; after a year's work I was to have six months off to do the dissertation for which I had data. In the first six months there I planned for them, and also worked evenings on my data—long enough to find out that a) the results would be ambiguous, and b) that the questions I was asking were childish, not because I had framed them ill, but because most of the key terms in the mental health field would not bear a second examination.[195]

He goes on to claim that he was forced initially by his personal success at the CMHA to give up the PhD project for a time, and then altogether when he succumbed to mental illness himself under the pressure of writing *Crestwood Heights*. He points the finger for his troubles at colleagues Tom Mallinson and Alex Sims, key members of the Forest Hill Village Project research team, who he says did not do their part in writing up the book:

> The crux came when it was time to write the two books: one on the Human Relations Classes, one on the Village itself. The psychologist responsible for the former couldn't write, though I had done nearly everything else for him, and he got his PhD out of my experiment. Alex Sim couldn't manage the "Anthropology" and, under threat of collapse of that enterprise I had to take over—to write the greater part and supervise, rewrite and edit all of what became *Crestwood Heights*. Under these external pressures (plus whatever was "inside") I began to develop acute anxieties, and went into analysis.

This was beyond our income, and in order to recoup financially I had to accept, I felt, the three-year job in Indianapolis. On my return, I resumed the analysis.[196]

What also emerges from Seeley's account is that he suffered from the common tendency in our culture to over-extend oneself. This may have been a reflection of the other-directedness of Seeley's character which even Riesman himself, the inventor of the concept, had observed:

> There have been times when I have felt that Jack Seeley was almost too sensitive and responsive a human being to cut himself off from some of the demands on his time that students and colleagues make because of this quality, and that there fore his research enterprises would suffer.[197]

His anxiety about the isolation of research and writing may have been traceable to his estrangement from his family of origin. In a remarkable passage from the correspondence with Hughes, Seeley seems to also recognize a link between his childhood feelings of inadequacy and adult pretense in regard to his academic qualifications:

> Yes, I would like to be made, even so late, an honest husband to that wench, research. It has been a hard thing to bear and reconcile the immense (if not excessive) respect I have received in high places and low, among the theoretically oriented and the practically, with the gnawing, nagging feeling that I had not been 'legitimated'. I told myself it didn't matter, but it does: twice over, perhaps, because I was actually an illegitimate child in a very Victorian large family, and was never allowed to forget it. It may be for this very reason that I have put off confronting the 'rite of passage' for so long.[198]

This reference to his "Victorian" family is an example of how Seeley avoided the question of his Jewish heritage. But perhaps the more immediate question raised here is whether in fact Seeley really wanted to turn his attention to completing his studies toward his PhD. Seeley lists all his publications in the letters to Hughes, perhaps in the hope that by themselves these collected works, and especially *Crestwood Heights*, might be accepted on their own terms as enough to warrant being granted the degree. However, he acknowledges they may not be enough:

> How to turn from these enterprises—and the new ones I am embarked on here—to attend properly to a formal dissertation, I do not know. I have a feeling of a task uncompleted, and of having, 'let you down', since

you sponsored me so generously both at Chicago and since. I hope to have a volume of papers on alcoholism published by U of T Press—but it's no dissertation. I do not think I have been 'unproductive'; I have simply not been free—mostly externally, somewhat internally, to produce the document required to prove the 'research competence', I believe I have, and have in different fashion, shown. Do you have—as you so often have had—good counsel for me?[199]

In fact, Hughes does follow through very graciously on behalf of Seeley with his colleagues in the Department of Sociology at the U of C. He got so far as to be able to offer Seeley the chance to organize his works into a coherent whole that he might claim as his own work, and submit this for consideration by the Department as a PhD thesis. The problem, Hughes pointed out, was that *Crestwood Heights* was a co-authored work with Alex Sim and Elizabeth Loosley, which could not be considered original. Seeley responded to Hughes that he simply did not have the time to pull together the various strands of his work as required:

> I don't think the problem is primarily capacity, or self-discipline, or productivity as such. What I can do, under present circumstances is turn out a large amount of publishable material provided no one piece takes more than three working days or two consecutive week-ends.[200]

Seeley never did follow through on Hughes offer. Having discovered the extent of the work involved, he left the matter to some vague future prospect of arranging his life so that he would have more time to write:

> To do something that requires at least a long hard look and an adequate continuous period of preparation and execution—requires either an alteration in my circumstances or in the way I organize my life (or fail to). I am inclined to see about the former, first. With this in mind, I am dickering both at Toronto and Harvard for something that might give me more of a blank check in disposing of my own time than I now have—or have ever had, except for the all–too–brief years at Chicago.[201]

Having the time to research and write any kind of extended academic study never materialized in Seeley's career despite his consistent plea that this was his desire. Much as had been the case when he was a graduate student at Chicago, when the opportunity for serious research was at hand, he consistently turned to the more action-oriented work of a polemicist or administrator. Whether it was an illegal street-gang or a faculty movement conspiring to overthrow a university President, Seeley found himself time and again immersed in the struggle for power rather than in quiet research and reflection. It would seem that there was a tension within Seeley between his quest for justice, or perhaps vengeance, and his intellectual commitments. In a letter to Hughes written much later, in 1970, by which time the PhD issue had long been left unresolved. Seeley himself searches for the meaning of his own actions:

> [W]hat I would like to understand, if you can help me, is what I do or don't do that makes it bad for me and others to administer. (Not that I think that that is my best work; I think my best is research and writing, especially theorizing).

Sadly, the failure of Seeley to follow through on Everett Hughes' invitation to complete his doctorate at U of C, combined with the embarrassment to Hughes, led to the breakdown of their relationship. In response to a letter from Seeley requesting a reference letter in 1970, Hughes responded:

> My answer is going to be one with qualifications. I have known and greatly admired you, your talents and your work since you turned up in Chicago in 1940. Your work in Indianapolis and Toronto are both outstanding, and I know how imaginative and insightful you are. Against this, I have to weigh my judgment of how you played the role of Department Chairman, and as handler of human and organizational matters.
>
> I think it comes to this: that I will gladly recommend you as a teacher and an intellectual of great intelligence and human feeling. But I will do so only if it is clearly understood that the position for which I am recommending you has no administrative duties, major or minor.[202]

Seeley never forgave Hughes for this qualification which may very well have served Seeley's own best interests. He claimed in a letter written much later, in 1982, at the age of seventy, that, despite his own efforts to help Hughes, "... to ensure the extension of your teaching contracts and to secure for you a just salary," Hughes had betrayed him by refusing to give him a reference for an administrative position:

> How sad that your last letter to me should say, in effect, that you would be willing to recommend me for a teaching job but not for anything that

> involved university administration. Next year, I shall be seventy. I do not want to go to my grave with so blank an understanding or so deep a wound after so long a friendship.[203]

There is no record of a reply from Hughes, but a PhD was finally conferred on Seeley in 1975 by the International College of Los Angeles, an unorthodox institution where he had served as a tutor and associate dean of the Faculty and Guild of Tutors. This was much too late to be of any significant scholarly benefit to Seeley whose major works, *Crestwood Heights* and *The Americanization of the Unconscious*, were already behind him. The question may be raised whether the flaws in those works, such as the lack of academic "density" noted by Riesman, might be attributed to this failure of conscientiousness in his academic training.

# Mental Health for Canada

According to his *curriculum vitae*, Seeley served as a Field Research Director at Ohio State University in 1946 on a mental health project in Ohio entitled "Mental Health in a Rural and Semi-Rural Area of Ohio." This was the year prior to beginning a job with the CNCMH in Toronto as Executive Officer and Director of Sociological Research in 1947. In interviews with me, Seeley referred to the Ohio Study as a precursor to the Forest Hill Village Project, though it was "just a survey," he pointed out.

The Ohio Study also served as the outline of an incomplete doctoral thesis that Seeley submitted at the University of Chicago entitled, "Social Structure and Personality in a Small United States City," found amongst the archived papers of Professor Ernest Burgess. It is interesting to point out that despite his failure to complete the PhD, Seeley was considered by Burgess, who was then acting Chair of the Sociology Department, for a tenured appointment in Social Psychology at the University of Chicago.

The Ohio Study was written at a time that a distinction was still being made in America between "whites" and "negroes." Such social classification on the basis of race, however, was in the midst of a transition toward a system based on "normality." Of course, this transition to the language of "normalization" should not necessarily be taken as progress. We sense something disturbingly conformist in the definition adopted by the Ohio Study of "normality" as: "the person who lives easily and comfortably with other normal people and whose behavior does not differ greatly from those of others in ways of which they disapprove, and who is personally happy and socially useful."

"Happiness" is a high standard, so no wonder Seeley's report stresses the high incidence of personality disorder amongst the population, all of whom he claims would benefit from, "mental hygiene counseling services provided by psychiatrists and other professional counsellors." To determine these numbers, Seeley used stats from the military investigation of potential recruits during World War II, and data from schools. These results showed that "superior personal and social adjustment and superior intelligence tend to go together." Also, they showed that "early detection and institutionalization of the feebleminded and the psychotic (or those about to become psychotic) would undoubtedly reduce crime rates substantially." The study also emphasizes the economic losses in terms of working hours and "efficiency" that are caused by mental illness. The study concluded by listing the kinds of psychiatric services that should be organized to treat and prevent the spread of mental health issues; namely, guidance clinics in schools, special education services, and training programs for mental hygiene principles to be applied in classrooms. In these recommendations, the Ohio Study anticipates educational measures which Seeley would advocate as the focus of a mental health campaign to be led by the CNCMH in Canada.

Indeed, it was not long after his return to Toronto that Seeley produced a visionary planning document entitled "Mental Health for Canada," which outlined a national strategy for the promotion of Mental Health in schools. He presented this document in his new role as Executive Officer for the CNCMH to the Committee's Board of Directors on October 17, 1947 in Ottawa:

> The school is chosen because of its accessibility for such a program, because of the compatibility of the goals of the educator and mental hygienist, because of the central and influential place of the school in any community, and because of the need to *concentrate*, but not exclusively on the child.[204]

He sat alongside Hincks and Griffin at this meeting to present his plan for the "psychological sanitization of the schools." The minutes of the meeting record, "Dr. Seeley's" presentation of "Mental Health for Canada" as having been, "a focus of excitement and interest by the Committee." The fact that mental health was defined by Seeley in the document, not so much in terms of the personal mental suffering of individuals, but in terms of wider, and somewhat questionable social implications, is evident in the document's focus on the economic and social costs of mental illness as a justification for a massive intervention in Canada's education system. The list of the costs of mental illness according to Seeley went beyond the usual emphasis on hospital beds and crime to "homosexuality," "pervasive industrial unrest," and most surprisingly, "cults, the sooth-sayers, and mind-readers."[205] The latter may have been perceived as a threat to the claims to scientific legitimacy of the psychological professions. As to the former, we might detect signs of the well-documented anti-communist hysteria that spread through North America in the early post-war era, and the fear of social or sexual deviance, that served as symbolic outlets for these post-war anxieties.

Seeley used military terminology to introduce "Mental Health for Canada" as a plan for the "promotion" of mental health:

> In the field of mental hygiene, as in any other medical field, three major tasks may be distinguished. The first task is therapy—the cure or alleviation of existing disease. This is attempted defense. The second task is prevention—taking steps to stem the increase of disease. This is a containing movement. The third task is the promotion of positive mental health. This is the attack. The plan proposed is one for the promotion of mental health.[206]

The use of military terminology in Seeley's schema may have reflected the historical context of Cold War. Indeed, Seeley believed that the purpose of his recruitment to the CNCMH in 1947 was to help his former military comrades—Hincks, Chisolm, Line and Griffin; create a "civilian similie" for what they had achieved during the war.[207] What was proposed was a national plan to educate a cadre of elite teachers over a period of ten years who would span out across Canada and act as "Liaison Officers" in the "battle for mental health." It is also interesting to note in this context that according to the plan there were to be 10,000 male teachers, or "one teacher in every five now teaching," chosen to be trained to act as a vanguard of mental health liaison officers in schools across Canada:

> These teachers are intended as leaven to the whole teaching profession. These men will be selected from teachers already outstandingly successful, particularly in their relation with children in the classroom.[208]

The role of this elite, masculine vanguard would be to model mental health values and pedagogical methods in the schools. As Seeley put it, "The aim is to turn out practical social engineers." This corps of social engineers in the schools were also to serve as outreach officers for "Child Guidance Clinics" that were to be set up in every school according to the Plan. The principal task of these guidance clinics was to be the "positive promotion of mental health." In the military terminology adopted by the CNCMH for the description of the plan, the guidance clinics were to act as "redoubts from which the Liaison Officer and the Teacher carry on their battle for mental health," as seen in the following diagram found amongst the Forest Hill Village Project files.[209]

Flow Chart "Mental Health in Canada," 1947. Seeley Papers, Los Angeles, California.

Where the politics behind Seeley's plan come to the surface most clearly, however, is in the reaction to it from members of the Board. Strikingly, it was the remarks of Ewan Cameron from McGill University that were the most pointed. According to the minutes of the meeting:

He further commented on the present trend whereby people who were increasingly edgy, nervous and hostile organized themselves into Fascist groups. Dr. Hincks' plan really represented a plan against the disruption of our social structure.[210]

It might be interesting to speculate about who Cameron had in mind as a fascist threat to social stability in Canada? Was Cameron really suggesting that a neo-Nazi party might re-emerge in North America even after the crushing defeat of Germany in 1945? Or, was Cameron identifying the emerging communist bloc as fascist?

It is worth pointing out here that this is the Dr. Cameron who was most famous for his secretive application of CIA funds in mind control experiments on his patients. These "de-patterning" experiments on patients involved isolation, sensory deprivation, massive electroshock therapy and the use of immobilizing drugs, "all in order to facilitate their receptivity to driving statements."[211] The "driving statements" were repetitive restatements of psychologically provocative ideas in the hope of breaking down the patient's resistance to them. It was a scene of psychiatric experimentation reminiscent of Orwell's description in *1984* of the rat torture suffered by Winston in room 101.

In any event, the plan Seeley presented to the Board of the CNCMH in October 1947 was given enthusiastic approval by the members who complimented Hincks, Griffin and Seeley on the "grandiosity," and, "statesman-like," nature of the plan. Only one member of the Board, a Dr. Menckin, was astute enough to warn that the CNCMH should be wary of, "promising more than we can deliver."[212] However, given the spirit of invincibility that characterized the early post-war period, Seeley went forward from the meeting with a broad mandate of approval from the National Committee.

According to Seeley, the reason Forest Hill Village emerged as the site for a pilot project to test out the CNCMH's grand scheme, was a fortuitous meeting of the minds. He wrote in a memo dated April 1948 under the title, "The Forest Hill Village Project of the National Committee for Mental Hygiene, 1948–1949":

> What was needed was a fairly compact community of adequate economic level to support such a program, and of sufficient enlightenment and understanding to appreciate its implications. What was needed in the school system was an unusually progressive body, flexible and bold, devoted to

its children and able and willing to cope with, perhaps the most difficult problem in education. All these criteria characterized Forest Hill, and it was the unanimous first choice of the Committee and its advisors. At precisely that point, some of the Forest Hill staff and Board approached the National Committee and we discovered that we had both been thinking about one another.[213]

On the one hand, there was a certain amount of truth in Seeley's claim that there were progressive forces in Forest Hill open to the application of modern science in schools. The fatherly Don Graham, Director of Education for the Forest Hill Village Schools, was a case in point. Graham was the son of a United Church Minister who was not used to wealth, unlike the majority of members of the community he came to serve in the "velvet ghetto" of Forest Hill. Yet, perhaps driven by the typical desire to succeed of the outsider, and by a deeply imbibed commitment to the Methodist belief in the improvability of mankind, Graham was not content to be just another history teacher. He carefully cultivated relationships with Toronto establishment figures like Bill Line and Jack Griffin with whom he had become associated during the Regal Road Project. According to Margery King, a secretary working for the CNCMH at the time, it was in fact Graham's networking with the leaders of the CNCMH that led to the Forest Hill Village Schools Board "selecting itself" as the site to test out Seeley's project:

> Donald Graham, Director of Education at Forest Hill Village, more than anyone else opened the gates of the community and the doors of the school. At a good deal of professional risk, he took the first steps. Then in recurring crises, he mediated between the forces that were in conflict exhibiting rare diplomacy in maintaining both the community and school involvement in the project.[214]

According to the *Evening Telegram*, however, it was in fact Vernon Trott, Director of the Guidance Department at the school who had sought out Seeley. Perhaps Trott was seeking ways to justify his new position:

> Two years ago last spring the National Committee for Mental Hygiene (now called the Canadian Mental Health Association) was studying the possibilities of caring for mental health in schools. So were some psychologists and psychiatrists at the University of Toronto. In Forest Hill it was a live subject. Largely because of the suggestions of Vernon Trott, Director of Guidance,

Forest Hill asked the Mental Hygiene Group for assistance. So Forest Hill was chosen as the testing ground for an ambitious new mental health plan.[215]

In addition to the enlightened leadership of the schools in Forest Hill by Don Graham and Vernon Trott, the "modern" reputation sought by the schools of Forest Hill was another force that drew its school system toward educational innovations. The Forest Hill Village Project was begun in the same year that high school students moved into an "ultra-modern" building. The new collegiate building was "officially opened in an impressive ceremony by Premier Leslie M. Frost," on September 24, 1949.[216] For the Tories, the new Forest Hill Collegiate was the signature achievement in a massive post-war school-building program designed to co-opt the social planning agenda of the Canadian Commonwealth Federation (CCF). Eerily presaging Foucault's observations about the "panoptic" nature of surveillance in modern prisons and schools, the Journal *Civic Administration* commented on how "well-lit" the new school was: "Its 24 classrooms are painted in light, pleasing colors, while large windows and modern lighting fixtures afford the maximum in natural and artificial illumination."[217]

While there were therefore powerful forces in Forest Hill that welcomed scientifically advanced educational experiments, there is also documentary evidence to suggest that there were also conservative forces in Forest Hill that were skeptical about the plan. That Seeley's portrayal of the agreement between the CNCMH and the Forest Hill Village School Board was somewhat idealized, becomes apparent upon a reading of the rather subdued motion of endorsement for the CNCMH project as it passed the Forest Hill Schools Board Meeting of March 15, 1948. According to the minutes of that meeting:

> The Director of Education and the Principals of the Schools attended the meeting and also Dr. Clare Hincks, Director of the CNCMH and his associates Drs. Griffin, Line, and Seeley. Dr. Hincks asked for permission to use the schools as a laboratory for extending the work of the National Committee. Dr. Hincks' associates also addressed the Board explaining the work which they had in mind for the schools if permitted to use them as a laboratory for the Project.
>
> That Dr. Hincks and his associates be advised that the Board would co-operate with the Committee for the use of the Village Schools as a laboratory with the understanding that the Board would not assume any financial responsibility,

but that the Director of Education would work out an agreement with the CNCMH with respect to using the present teaching staff so that the equivalent of *one* teacher's time may be available to the Committee.

*Carried*[218]

It is interesting to note that at this very same meeting, Vernon Trott was appointed as Head of the new Guidance Department to be established at Forest Hill Collegiate.

The planning documents and meeting minutes from late 1948 for the Forest Hill Village Project suggest that Seeley and his colleagues were well aware that there may have been sensitivity amongst people in the Village to their being treated like laboratory rats. Perhaps, the growing Jewish population of Forest Hill was not completely blind to the dangers of modernism. On the one hand, they hoped that the benefits of a scientific educational system could help lift them out of social and economic marginality, and on the other, in the immediate aftermath of the Holocaust, perhaps they had heard that the clinic held terrors of its own.

The documents would suggest that their suspicions were justified. Surprisingly invasive new elements were introduced into the research project at the late stages in the planning process. These included a focus on research into anti-Semitism in Forest Hill, and the surveillance of the performance of teachers and students that were not obviously related to the original aim of mental health promotion in the schools. These disturbing aspects of the Forest Hill Village Project emerged in tandem with two developments during the school year of 1948 and 1949 in the organization of the Project; the shift from a national plan to a local pilot project; and the shift from the CNCMH to the U of T Department of Psychiatry as the organizational base of the project.

For his part, Seeley's reminiscences about his move from the CNCMH to the Department of Psychiatry in order to take the helm as Director of the Forest Hill Village Project had two different levels. On one level, it had to do with securing government funding. Seeley wrote in an autobiographical letter to Everett Hughes to this effect:

> I went from the C.M.H.A (1948) to the Department of Psychiatry at Toronto by agreement with both, simply because the Dominion Government would only support our joint research-and-action scheme under University auspices.[219]

It is at this point in the story that federal bureaucrats assigned to a new Mental Health Division, at work behind the scenes on funding issues, make their presence known. It was under Chisolm's direction that this Mental Health Division was established and, as historian Harvey Simmons observed, "with the establishment of a federal Department of National Health and Welfare in 1944, and the appointment of a chief of the mental health division, the federal government began to play an active role in mental health policy."[220] Federal funding was forthcoming from this Division for the CNCMH's "Mental Health for Canada" campaign, despite the strong reservations of the staff.

The intra-governmental debate about Seeley's project began with an exchange of memoranda between Dr. Charles Stodghill, Chief of the new Mental Health Division, and Dr. G.D.W. Cameron, Deputy Minister of Health during the winter of 1948. Stogdill reminded his superior in a March 30 memo of an earlier discussion they held about Seeley's blueprint in January of 1948. They had both agreed to support the proposed plan with the following caveat: "At that time I believe you felt as I did that the aim of the undertaking could not be quarreled with but that more information was necessary."[221] Stogdill did, however, raise concerns about potential implementation problems with Seeley's plan:

> I feel that the aim of this project, *viz.* to concentrate our efforts on the child, is good. However, I have no information on the attitude of the educational world beyond what is contained in a paragraph on p. 16 of the attached brief on the subject. Further, I do not know what has been obtained in the way of cooperation from the Deputy Ministers of Health. In view of these serious deficiencies I do not see that I can make a recommendation with regard to this project, beyond the general one that more information be supplied. If the Dominion Government contributes, it should have a voice in the planning and administration of the project.[222]

In response, the Deputy Minister was even more "puzzled" about implementation issues than Stogdill seemed to be, and called for further comment from Stogdill on Seeley's plan:

> I am puzzled about the one year people who are going to busy themselves with school teachers and children. What do you think about this aspect of the proposal? I don't see how the National Committee of Mental Hygiene can hope to gather their subscriptions in the amounts proposed. It seems to

me that a tremendous amount of public education would be required to do that. They have been sold on T. B. largely because a very definite and easily understood course of action has been explained to them. I don't think this is the case with the mental health program.[223]

At least one other official in the Mental Health Division, by the name of Gordon H. Josie, agreed with Cameron's skepticism in regard to Seeley's blueprint. On April 19 he wrote up a more extensive critique of "Mental Health for Canada" in a memorandum submitted to Dr. Stogdill. Josie was critical of Seeley's claim that the up-front costs of government investment in mental health programs would be offset by the long-term reductions in expenditures that were projected to ensue. He wrote:

> This type of reduction of expenditure or saving represented by the anticipated success of remedial or preventive programs, which we have also considered in connection with the drug addiction problem, seems to me to be somewhat misleading, since the national bill for mental ill health and the economic loss to drug addiction are both paper figures and do not represent actual expenditures from which deductions may be anticipated.[224]

Furthermore, in regard to financial issues, Josie thought that the sums of money that Seeley was asking for were too ambitious:

> The total of 12 million dollars per anuum seems a large expenditure as an additional item in view of the fact that this is approximately equal to the general public health expenditures in Canada. It is not clear to me at least why the public should be called on to contribute one-third of this large sum.[225]

On the other hand, the most penetrating critique Josie offers was not in regard to financial issues, but rather to the vague institutional architecture proposed in the plan:

> The upshot of the plan seems to be an expansion of the development of mental clinics and educational and preventive measures concentrated around the school. These are both sound and generally accepted objectives but do not represent a new or unique program. The new element in the plan seems to be the recognition of the importance of the school as an accessible focal point, so to speak, and the proposal to develop a new type of specialist—the liaison or guidance officer. Regarding the special training of school teachers

in mental hygiene principles and practice, it would seem that if the teachers are not already receiving sufficient of this type of training, effort might best be addressed at emphasizing these factors in present normal schools. The proposed training course for the liaison officers which is intended to be "very much down to earth" would seem to have the danger of producing individuals with only a superficial knowledge of the basic sciences and skills.[226]

Josie's memorandum raises the question as to why mental health programs for teachers should be organized by the CNCMH or the U of T Department of Psychiatry rather than by the Normal Schools, as Teacher's Colleges were then known. In the absence of such integration into the professional education of teachers, whatever learning such a program achieved would be bound to be superficial, as Josie rightly points out. Moreover, the knowledge and experience gained in mental health techniques for teachers would have no lasting institutional base from which to be built upon and transmitted.

Yet, despite these very reasonable concerns about a lack of commitment, excessive costs, and misguided institutional arrangements, the plan was not rejected. Rather a way was sought to minimize the risks to the federal government from participation in the scheme. It would appear that Cameron, Stodghill and Josie strove to support Hincks' proposal even against their better judgment. There is a note in the handwriting of Josie in the Mental Health Division records from April 1948 in which he records what appears to be a discussion with Stodghill that hints at a desire to appease Hincks for some reason:

> Everyone says fine—but somebody else must make final move. What would be attitude of the provinces if only 2 centers—Toronto and Montreal—were started for first five years?[227]

So the solution was to narrow down the scheme. Eventually, as it turned out, this little note jotted on a federal bureaucrats pad turned out to be decisive, for this was what in fact happened. The maneuvering of the federal Mental Health Division to ensure that Seeley's project, "Mental Health for Canada," was reduced to a manageable size and subjected to proper management is visible in the correspondence between Stodghill and Hincks over the summer of 1948 which revealed that a few more subtly communicated changes to the plan were required in exchange for federal cooperation.

First, the federal government wanted the project supervised by the U of T Department of Psychiatry. In a letter from Stodghill to Hincks of June 26, 1948, this is spelled out:

> I had a letter from Jack Griffin a few days ago about expanding the activities of the Mental Hygiene Consultation Services. I think the best way for him to go about getting government support for this is through the University Department concerned with the training of the types of personnel involved. It seems too that the same procedure would apply to your Forest Hill Village pilot plan.[228]

The recommended shift to University auspices, which we have already seen Seeley himself acknowledge as a "condition of the grant money," might very well have been designed as a way to address the federal mental health division's concern about the effectiveness of a training program for teachers that did not have an academic base. The point was quickly taken by Hincks, who responded in a letter to Stodghill just days later, on June 30, 1948:

> In this office we will immediately explore ways and means of developing a linkage between the University of Toronto and two of our projects—the Mental Hygiene Consultation Service and the Forest Hill undertaking.[229]

A further condition of the grant money was a *quid pro quo* in terms of respect for a certain amount of federal surveillance of the program. As Paul Martin, the federal Minister of Health, was quick to point out, the mental health grant was to be the largest of the government grants in the health field to be awarded in 1948. In fact, the federal government promised to commit more money to various mental health initiatives across the country than the four million that had initially been requested in Seeley's proposal, "Mental Health for Canada." Paul Martin wrote to Dr. Meakins, the official President of the CNCMH on March 1, 1949:

> The Mental Health Grant is, as you know, the largest of the grants in specific health fields, increasing over the years from $4,000,000 to $7,000,000.[230]

With such a large sum invested, the federal government wanted to keep an eye on how the money was spent, and yet it faced the difficulty of having to demand surveillance powers in what, constitutionally speaking, was a matter of provincial concern. The way Martin sought to straddle this line, as is typical in politics, was to say one thing but do another. In an earlier letter to Dr. Meakins of July 13th, 1948, the Minister of Health,

Paul Martin, starts out by declaring his intention to respect provincial jurisdiction:

> The mental health grant, like the other grants announced by the Prime Minister on May 14th, 1948 is a grant to the provinces. There is no intention on the part of the Federal government to dictate to the provinces as to the use of the grant.[231]

However, in the space of a mere two paragraphs in the same letter, in which he has spelled out the purpose of the grant for, "the expansion and improvement of preventive and treatment services," Martin shifts to a much more interventionist tone:

> You will appreciate that it will be necessary for me to be informed as to the effective use being made of these large sums of money, as I am answerable to Parliament. This will necessitate a certain amount of supervision of the expenditure of funds. You will be glad to know that it is planned to strengthen the Mental Health Division of this Department for this purpose.[232]

In a rather cryptic comment, Martin even goes so far as to allude to an overall policy direction for the historically-unprecedented federal foray in Mental Health and Education in 1948: "I agree that misinformation and erroneous attitudes must be dispelled and more healthful attitudes inculcated in the rural parts as well as in the urban portions of our population."[233]

On the one hand, it seems that Martin is recommending here that the goal of the mental health initiative was to address the stigma problem with regard to mental health issues. On the other hand, the use of the phrase "inculcate in the population" carries with it connotations of forcefulness that may betray underlying social control intentions. Moreover, we may suspect that in the early post-war era governmental concern in regard to "misinformation and erroneous attitudes" extended beyond mental health issues. We may do well to recall that C. K. Clarke and other early leaders in the Canadian mental health field considered socialism to be a symptom of mental illness.

Given this complex panorama of interests involved in governmental decision-making, it comes as no surprise that federal funding was rapidly forthcoming once the CNCMH won the co-operation of the Forest Hills Schools Board of Education for the Project. This was confirmed in research that Alex Sim, one of the other authors of *Crestwood Heights*, retrospectively conducted into the history of the Forest Hill Village Project:

We find a record of a committee meeting of July 1948 entitled, "The President's Ad-Hoc Committee to Consider University Training Programs under Provincial Mental Health Grants." Already the interested departments were assembled—psychology, social work, medicine, nursing and psychiatry—along with Professor William Line representing the Forest Hill Village Project. The Forest Hill Project was mentioned in the ad-hoc committee's report as an activity of the Department of Psychiatry, but there was no specific budgetary proposal. However, provision was made for the appointment of a sociologist to the Department of Psychiatry, a position which was later filled by John R. Seeley, who moved from the CNCMH to the University.[234]

There was, however, another level of political maneuvering in play behind Seeley's move from the CNCMH to the U of T Department of Psychiatry. In part, this move also resulted from Seeley's success in cultivating his personal connection as a fellow Englishmen with the new Chair of the Department of Psychiatry, Aldwyn Stokes. Seeley remembered having become concerned at the time that Hincks was so unreliable because of his semi-annual depressions that even keeping a watchful eye on him would not have been enough to enable him to see through such a gigantic undertaking as the Forest Hill Village Project. Seeley may have used his keen social antennae to determine that Stokes would be a more reliable and influential ally in the pursuit of his project. For his part, Stokes was likely eager to befriend a fellow Englishmen in the strange frontier world of Upper Canada, but he also had reasons of his own to bring Seeley into the Department of Psychiatry.

As Seeley himself said, once Stokes arrived in Toronto he would regularly attend brainstorming sessions over dinner with the other leaders of the CNCMH. Stokes was therefore intimately involved in the early planning and organization of the Project. The Forest Hill Village Project was obviously intended by Stokes as a way of distinguishing himself from his predecessors Farrar and Clarke through a more eclectic commitment to the integration of social science and psychiatry, and the expansion of the purview of psychiatry beyond the asylum and into the community. Despite such liberal intentions on Stokes's part there still lurked in his approach the old eugenicist agenda of the U of T Department of Psychiatry.

Farrar had lobbied hard to ensure that his successor at the Toronto Psychiatric Hospital shared his views. According to Dowbiggin, it was

Farrar's effectiveness as a lobbyist, demonstrated in the appointment of Aldwyn Stokes as his successor, which was mainly responsible for eugenics retaining a stronger foothold in Canada than it had in the United States.[235] Stokes came from the Maudsley Psychiatric Hospital in London, England. During the formative years of Stokes's career at the Maudsley in the 1930s and 40s, he would have had to conform to the eugenicist views that were held at the highest reaches of that institution. According to Pauline Mazmdar in her book, *Eugenics, Human Genetics and Human Failings: The Eugenics Society, its Sources and its Critics in Britain*, the Maudsley had a longstanding institutional relationship with Kraeplin's clinic in Germany, where Farrar had been trained.[236]

After World War I, the Maudsley had emerged as a bastion of medical experimentation and treatment in regard to the psychiatric casualties of war. Stokes rose through the ranks of the Hospital to the role of Medical Superintendent working alongside Aubrey Lewis as Clinical Director and Professor of Psychiatry. Under the leadership of Stokes and Lewis, the institution inclined toward traditional medical approaches to deal with psychiatric problems in contrast to its principal competitor, the Tavistock Clinic. Sigmund Freud and Carl Jung were associated with the Tavistock and it produced such leaders of avant-garde British psychoanalysis as John Bowlby and Wilfred Bion.

The leading academic lights at the Maudsley like Lewis and his personal friend and colleague C. P. Blacker, on the other hand, were active members of the British Eugenics Society. In fact, Blacker was the General Secretary of the English Eugenics Society from 1931–1952 and Lewis was a Vice-President of the Society alongside a group of other illustrious Englishmen like Winston Churchill and John Maynard Keynes.[237] These men were respectful but skeptical about psychoanalysis as a treatment modality, an attitude which Stokes would maintain throughout his career.[238] Douglas Frayn, a distinguished psychoanalyst in Toronto, remembers that in the 1960s, upon his first encounter with Stokes at the Clarke Institute of Psychiatry, the latter had quipped something to the effect, "So you are to be the resident psychoanalyst in the Department of Psychiatry eh? Well, I suppose it is good to have one psychoanalyst in the Department, but only one."[239]

Despite Stokes's claim to open-mindedness regarding psychoanalysis, one knowledgeable observer, Toronto Psychoanalyst Peter Thompson has written that: "I have always been uncertain as to the degree that

Aldwyn Stokes encouraged or discouraged the development of psychoanalysis in Toronto. Stokes always held his cards very close to his vest. I think he was ambivalent on the whole."[240] Thompson based this opinion on a letter written by Stokes to Dr. Boulanger, Director of the Canadian Psychoanalytic Society in 1958, in which Stokes took the position that any psychoanalytic practice should be under the supervision of the U of T Department of Psychiatry. Quite a bit earlier than this, in the midst of the Forest Hill Village Project's operations, Stokes had made his position on this issue already quite clear in correspondence with Dr. Ewan Cameron, the notorious CIA-sponsored Head of Psychiatry at McGill University. He wrote to Cameron warning that: "the opportunity in Canada of avoiding extra University training centers of sectarian movements seems to be threatened," by the forming of a Canadian Society of Psychoanalysis in Montreal.[241]

The biological tendency in Toronto and London psychiatry, inclined Stokes and his mentor at the Maudsley, Aubrey Lewis, toward the containment of psychoanalysis and the promotion of eugenics and other bio-chemical methods. However, as a Jew, Aubrey Lewis, was torn between his attraction to, "prevention through voluntary sterilization of families with an established history of major mental illness;" and his objection to eugenics being, "hi-jacked by the Nazi Party to pursue overt racial discrimination."[242]

On the question of eugenics, the Nazi issue pitted Lewis's class identifications as an aspiring member of the British aristocracy against his ethnic identity as a Jew. However, such conflicts would not have bothered either his friend C. P. Blacker or his colleague Aldwyn Stokes. Indeed, the elitism that was natural to Blacker as a graduate of "Eton, Oxford and Guard's" may have been what attracted Lewis to befriend him and to support his work on eugenics at the Maudsley. As for Stokes, eugenics may have appealed to him because, like Lewis, he was of lower class origins and thus an aspirant after a more respectable status in English society.

Lewis's father was a poor Jewish watchmaker in Australia, and Stokes father was a clerk in a Welsh law office. The careers of both Lewis and Stokes had ridden the waves of philanthropic scholarships from Oxford and the Rockefeller Fund to great heights on the basis of their work-ethic, intelligence, and undoubtedly their conformity to expectations of class allegiance that came along with the money.

It is therefore not surprising to see that Stokes engaged in speculation on eugenic methods even after the experience of the war. In an article he presented to an Ontario Nursing Association Meeting on September 10, 1948 in Orillia entitled "Eugenic Aspects of Social Psychiatry," Stokes shows that he was not in principal opposed to sterilization:

> Sterilization on a compulsory basis has probably been most thoroughgoing in respect to the social problem groups. Genetic reasons here give way to social urgency which demands the use of practical measures and which cannot wait on further development of the academic theories of heredity. A sterilization measure of this sort approaches to a punitive procedure: it may or may not be justified according to an unbiased appraisement of results.[243]

Nevertheless, in order to demonstrate his liberal tolerance of alternative approaches to psychiatry, Stokes moved swiftly to bring Seeley into the Department of Psychiatry by January of 1949. This was attested to in the announcement by Stokes, with some pride of accomplishment, of a bold interdisciplinary undertaking at a presentation he gave on the, "Biosocial Aspects of Psychiatry" to the Academy of Medicine Meeting on January 7, 1949:

> The movement in psychiatry which is giving due emphasis to groups, to social structure and function, and to cultural pressures is, therefore, to be fostered. In that movement, as I see it, is to be found a corrective to the theoretical psychopathological structures reared on the findings of individual techniques. In line with this general outlook a full time social scientist has been appointed to the Department of Psychiatry. This appointment is I think unique and from the establishment of a liaison with another discipline great psychiatric benefit should accrue. In any event, I commend Mr. Seeley to you and ask for your attention to a short discourse, preparatory to the case presentations, on "Some possible contributions from social sciences to clinical insight in Psychiatry."[244]

Prof. John Seeley, 1950s. Photo by Jeff Goode, *Toronto Star*, Getty Images.

As Seeley recounts in another of his lengthy letters to Everett Hughes, with this appointment by Stokes, he had not only maneuvered himself into the U of T Department of Psychiatry, he also suddenly found himself operating as a novel psychiatric practitioner of sorts: "I thus found myself training psychiatrists, teaching teachers, instructing sociologists in the making and running an "empire" bigger than some departments."[245] This was acknowledged by Stokes in the following terms:

> Mr. Seeley's appointment represents one of the few full time appointments anywhere of a sociologist in the Health field. His organization of the Forest Hill Village Project has been exemplary. This is a pilot research into the Mental Health problems of a community approached through the school setting. Mr. Seeley has been active in the training program of doctors and teachers.[246]

# The Transmission of Anti-Semitism

Despite the apparently interdisciplinary and progressive nature of Stokes's promotion of Seeley into the ranks of psychiatry (without anything more than a two-year BA from U of C, it might be added), the extent to which the regressive values latent in the history of eugenics also informed his policy becomes evident when we begin next to examine the early stages of the implementation of the Forest Hill Village Project. His presence alongside Hincks, Griffin, Line and Seeley at a meeting of the Scientific Advisory Committee of the CNCMH of June 21, 1948, should be noted as we begin to confront some startling twists in the plan. For suddenly, at this meeting, it becomes clear that the meaning of mental health promotion in the schools to the leadership of the CNCMH was not simply that of guaranteeing the well-being of students and teachers, but rather, also to segregate those identified as mentally ill. In regard to the education of teachers, the Scientific Advisory Committee of the CNCMH "carried" the following motion:

> The Committee is also of the opinion that any effective program in the selection of candidates for teaching, or in the weeding out of mentally unhealthy candidates for teacher's certificates, is directly dependent on the extent to which the staff of the teacher training institution, and the Superintendent of Schools hold a mental hygiene point of view.[247]

Similarly, in regard to students in the High Schools, the ambition of the CNCMH was to weed out those students not suited for education, according to the Scientific Advisory Committee of the CNCMH; not because of "mental defectiveness" as was the case before the war, but because of "mental ill-health." The purpose of the training of teachers in mental hygiene would be so that they could come to understand themselves and their reactions and improve their adjustments as well as to guide toward other occupations those students whose personality patterns and mental ill-health make them un-suitable for the work of the classroom.[248]

What is the reader to make of the designation "mental ill-health" that would render certain prospective teachers or students unfit for the classroom? Given the historical background of the leadership of the CNCMH in the Directorate of Personnel Selection in the Canadian Forces during World War II, it would seem that a comparison with the soldier who is deemed unfit for combat might be illuminating. Would this mean that those without the proper levels of aggression and obedience to authority were too mentally ill to go to school?

If this segregationist approach to the problem of mental health in schools is not surprising enough, it is even more startling that "Dr. Seeley," as he was referred to in the minutes from this meeting, and who was now actively in charge of the day to day organization of the Forest Hill Village Project, also introduced the fact that another of the principal aims of the research component of the Forest Hill Village Project was to be: "A Study of the Pattern and the Transmission of Anti-Semitism."[249]

The historical context of ethnic tensions between Jews and Gentiles in Toronto, and possibly also the new arrival of Holocaust survivors, makes this sudden appearance of the "History of the Jews in Toronto," and the "Causes and Effects of Anti-Semitism" as a major focus of the Forest Hill Village Project somewhat curious. It would appear that the concern of the Forest Hill Village Project Planners was to acquire knowledge that might help to prevent the dangers of a re-emergence of the social unrest that had characterized relations between the two communities prior to the war. The Jewish community of Toronto happened to be at the time encroaching on the traditionally Anglo-Saxon enclave of Forest Hill, and the Jewish children at Forest Hill Collegiate were rapidly coming to outnumber the Gentile kids. But if the intent of the research was thus rather benign, then why was Seeley so guarded about any public statements in regard to this research aspect of the Forest Hill Village Project? In fact, Seeley explicitly requested in a Memorandum to Aldwyn Stokes dated June 30, 1949 that the part of the research program that involved anti-Semitism be kept confidential and not released to the public out of concern for the reaction of the people of Forest Hill:

Further to our conversation I am sending copies of two reports on the Forest Hill Village Project. The first is marked <u>CONFIDENTIAL</u> and is for the information only of the President of the University of Toronto and such other persons not themselves the subject of the research as he deems fit. The second is smaller and suitable for general publication. I know that you agree that it is vital to the welfare of the whole project that nothing should be published which emphasizes research or experiment. This would only re-evoke the already latent definition of themselves as "guinea pigs" which Forest Hill Village people have. This would militate seriously against research possibilities, if it did not actually destroy them.[250]

The first, "confidential" part of the report, makes mention of research interests in regard to the "history of the Jews" and "anti-Semitism" in two or three different places alongside the outline of a project to collect very personal data on the population of Forest Hill including the development of a "personality inventory," a "teachers rating scale," and the collection of data in regard to "family structure, sex, ethnicity and personality characteristics." In the second part of the report, which Seeley suggested was suitable for publication, no mention whatever was made about anti-Semitism, or about the collection of social data more generally.

One might expect that because of the recent memory of the Holocaust there would have been a particular level of caution on the part of the doctors, and alarm on the part of the Jewish community, in regard to any signs of mass experimentation or any other form of governmental surveillance. Yet, this was precisely what the Forest Hill Village Project, and its ambitious social engineers, proposed to do. Of course, Seeley and the founders of the project would claim that any interest on their part in anti-Semitism was only for the sake of improving the mental health and social stability of Jewish–Gentile relations in Forest Hill. The Jewish community in Forest Hill at the time was surely not naïve in this regard, but perhaps being so eager to repress for a time the memory of recent events, to avoid the limelight, and to take advantage of their growing wealth by advancing their social status and educational opportunities; they went along with what from their perspective was a minor recurrence of the same old tribalism to which they had been subjected from time immemorial. As one Jewish man was recorded as having said in regard to concerns in the Jewish community about the Forest Hill Village Project: "[L]et sleeping dogs lie—things have been like this for 3000 years and we can't change them. . . ."[251]

It is hard not to speculate at this point about Seeley's personal feelings regarding the emerging focus on anti-Semitism given his concerns about his Jewish identity. As we have seen, in letters to Fischer he worried that people might suspect him of being Jewish if his brother Frank were to visit Toronto, or that the "discovery of his origins" would ruin his career.[252] This feeling of danger was intensified by the fact that, whether out of a desire to flee or from ambition, Seeley had just left behind a somewhat immersed Jewish intellectual experience at U of C where he had become associated with famous Jewish scholars like Bettleheim and Riesman. He had returned instead into the fold of the WASP establishment in Toronto led by men like Hincks, Stokes, Line and Griffin who were inclined to be suspicious of the intimidating Jewish presence in the field of psychiatry, especially in relation to the spreading popularity of psychoanalysis about which they were at best ambivalent.

On the one hand, Seeley was therefore quite eager to blend in with the Gentile establishment out of his anxiety not to jeopardize his new status. Unlike other Jews living in Toronto in the 1950s, perhaps Seeley felt free because of the "Wolff Child" story to stand outside the community and offer criticism. Perhaps being one of them, but not really one of them, he was uniquely qualified to act in the role of cultural spy on behalf of the Gentile establishment. From this standpoint, perhaps Seeley relished the opportunity to prove his allegiance through his work in the Jewish community of Forest Hill.

On the other hand, Seeley might have harbored considerable anxiety at the unhappy coincidence that the community of Forest Hill was fifty percent Jewish. Not only did this increase the risk that his identity issues would be exposed to the public, but also that he might be forced into an uncomfortable confrontation with himself. Whatever was really happening, it certainly stretches the bounds of credulity to believe that it was a mere coincidence that brought Forest Hill Village and John R. Friedeberg Seeley together in the late 1940s.

# The Cold White Light of Detachment

To picture the Forest Hill Village Project in action one tends to conjure an image of Mengelian doctors patrolling the halls of the school, and terrified students being sent down for examination under clinical conditions, which Seeley referred to as the, "cold white light of detachment."[253] One might imagine Seeley as an Orwellian figure sitting in bemused judgment while students struggle through such torturous psychological inquisitions. Seeley himself projected his self-doubts onto the professional psychological worker when he wrote about the danger that psychological expertise could be used for ill:

> It was hoped that a "professionally specialized person" might be able to conduct such classes in the schools, and if properly trained, he would safeguard the process against the perversion to sadistic uses of which it is clearly capable.[254]

There is evidence that Seeley was involved with the treatment of high school students. An example is a "Confidential Memo," regarding the case of a "dark-haired boy of gentle, but not soft contour," who wanted to run away from home. Seeley described the way the session began in the following excerpt, "He was told, on ordinary grounds of honesty but as a chosen part of the definition that the writer was not a psychiatrist (or, indeed, a doctor) but that he 'understood' some of these things." Seeley wrote that the boy complained of a critical nagging father. Seeley recommended that the boy be allowed to "flee" by going to boarding school at Ridley College. Though permissive, Seeley certainly could not be accused of the kind of abuse of power that he feared in others.[255]

Of course, Forest Hill Village was not Auschwitz, but there is some evidence that at least some of the Project staff showed authoritarian tendencies.

For example, one field note observes an encounter between an "expert" and a student in less than flattering terms:

> I believe he is quite opinionated—sure that he's correct. He feels he's quite a psychologist and a lover of children, although I don't notice any particular rapport between him and his pupils. He always seems pretty authoritarian to me. I was in his office today when one of his pupils came in crying—sent there by D.N. I thought I'd practice reflecting the boy's feelings to him. He responded by pouring out his strong dislike of a classmate who was always bullying him and others. When D. N. came in the boy did not make much of a case for himself, partly perhaps because his original strong emotions had subsided. D. N. didn't give him much chance to state his side or to draw him out—accused him of being the trouble maker and of swearing and sent him home. I refrained from comment. This was an interview on the role of the specialist. The whole interview reinforces the opinion that D. N. believes in advanced educational views, believes he is a good psychologist—and can possibly carry out many of his ideas, except in actual face to face dealings with the children.[256]

This doctor, D.N., sounds like he could have become another Mengele under the same conditions as prevailed in Nazi Germany, but in the wealthy suburbs of Toronto would do no more harm than the everyday snarly and detached clinician. We should explain at this point that Seeley developed a code by which the real identities of the persons involved in the Forest Hill Village Project, as referred to in the project notes, would be known only to staff members.

Actually, of the former students at the school still around to talk about it, very few can recall much about the Forest Hill Village Project. One said that he had vague memories of Seeley, "sitting in his room at the front office writing his book." Another said:

> I don't remember Dr. Seeley much at all—I have a vague mental picture of what he looked like, which may or may not be accurate. I was in elementary school (South Prep) and the study may have continued into my junior years. I do recall the impression that he was at times subjective and judgmental, and asked us, through his questionnaires, to be the same, whether he realized it or not. Questions like, "who do you like the most and who do you like the least in your class, and why"? I had never thought in those terms before, and I believe it was damaging to the way we looked at our classmates.[257]

Forest Hill Junior High School, 1948. Baldwin Collection, Toronto Reference Library.

Perhaps these notes and vague memories do suggest that some feelings of intrusiveness were invoked in the students by their experience of the Forest Hill Village Project, but they still do not get at what really went on in the schools. There was one component of the Forest Hill Village Project, where "white clad doctors" did actually enter the schools, which might give us some clues. This was called the Child Guidance Clinic set up at the new high school building. The Clinic was put under the leadership of pioneering female U of T Psychiatrist, Dr. Lila Frances Coates (Maltby). Seeley described the Child Guidance Clinic in detail in an article he co-authored with Griffin in 1952, while the project was still underway:

> The Service aspect meant the provision of a formal mental health or child guidance clinic comprising the traditional team of psychiatrist, clinical psychologist, psychiatric social worker, and secretary. This has been made available on a full time basis for work in the schools through the Department of Psychiatry of the University of Toronto. In a school system in which there

are only 2,000 children one might well ask whether a full time clinic of this nature is justifiable. It must be remembered, however, that this is an experiment to see what would happen if an attempt were made to provide relatively generous mental health services according to our present state of knowledge. It is interesting that this clinic has hitherto had no difficulty in keeping fully occupied providing therapy for those children who are showing the early signs of breakdown—in most cases well before the breakdown has become too serious.[258]

Yet, the impact on students may not have been as beneficial, as Seeley's account would suggest. The Minutes from a "Meeting of the Liaison Officers" on February 17, 1949, suggest that from the outset of the project there was a problem of the availability of the medical doctors and psychologists to the teaching staff and students. Either they were not able to always juggle their various professional obligations, or they fell into the inevitable tendency to spend most of their time working with teachers and Guidance Counsellors, not students:

Clinic
The group appreciates the difficulties and practical problems that have been met with in the setting up of the Clinic. However, they hope that it will be possible for them to get considerable clinical experience in Forest Hill Village, and if possible, in other clinics before the end of the year.

Counselling
It is the opinion of the group that the efforts in this area have been for the most part successful, and that the Forest Hill Village people are impressed with its value. There is, however, an opinion that if some method might be worked out whereby the counseling teams would have contact with students themselves, the value of the programme [sic] might be enhanced.[259]

The complaint that the professional U of T medical personnel and professors assigned to the Forest Hill Village Project were often too busy to be available as needed was one that endured throughout the Project. In an academic follow-up study out of Queen's University on the efficacy of the Forest Hill Village Project entitled, "Mental Health in Education: An Evaluation of a Special Mental Health Training Program for Selected Teachers," one teacher explained the problem:

It was felt disappointing, for example, that so often a course of talks and discussions would be announced to be taken by a certain lecturer as a regular, say weekly feature. This lecturer would then often be called away at that time on some other job or duty, and the whole course, so eagerly looked forward to, was felt thwarting and disappointing to the class. One year, too, felt that its course was being made up as it went along, and however good this may have been as an experiment, it must have failed of some of its purpose when no explanation was forthcoming about vagueness, changes of plan, or rather unplanned spells.[260]

The last mention in the Seeley Papers to the Clinic Records mentions their being left in the basement of the Toronto Psychiatry Hospital at 2 Surrey Place on the campus of the University of Toronto: "I am planning to put most of the 'dead' material (e.g., Maltby files, Sim Records, etc.) into cartons and store them in the TPH basement."[261] The "Maltby files" would be the Child Guidance Clinic files, because Dr. Lila Frances (Coates) Maltby was in charge of the Clinic. In *Crestwood Heights* there is listed in the acknowledgements of "Contributory Studies," a "Report on Work of the Clinical Team, Crestwood Heights Schools Child Guidance Services," by L.F. Maltby. This report might presumably have been included amongst her other files, but these files cannot be traced in any Canadian archive. Indeed, according to a book that chronicles the history of the Toronto Psychiatric Hospital:

> The archives of TPH have largely disappeared. Although the records of individual patients have been preserved, the administrative correspondence on which the history of such a hospital would normally be based has vanished.[262]

This conclusion would seem to be borne out by the author's own experience. When I visited 2 Surrey Place, originally the Toronto Psychiatric Hospital, I was told by the librarians working there as part of the new "Surrey Place Centre for Education and Research on Developmental Disabilities," that there was nothing left in the basement of that building but an empty crawl space.

The Toronto Psychiatric Hospital opened in 1925 at 2 Surrey Place. Its focus expanded to encompass all branches of psychiatry following the arrival of Dr. Aldwyn Stokes in 1947 as its director and head of psychiatry. Courtesy of CAMH Archives.

There is, however, one file found amongst the Seeley Papers in Los Angeles that did escape loss (or destruction). It is a quite suggestive "staff memo" written by Norm Bell, who was a junior researcher with the Forest Hill Village Project Staff, and who was a Master's Degree student in the U of T Department of Political Economy at the time. Bell's memo was entitled "A Note on Emotionally Disturbing Triads." Bell speculates that the perceived weaknesses of the Clinic, which had not been entirely resolved as the Project neared its end in 1952, was due to its mode of operation. Bell cites an article by Alfred Stanton and Morris Schwartz entitled, "Institutional Participation in Mental Illness" which "relates outbursts of patients on a psychiatric ward to certain interpersonal processes amongst staff members," as a possible model on the basis of which to analyze problems faced in the Child Guidance Clinic at Forest Hill Collegiate. These processes, according to the article, are usually triangular situations which Bell describes in the following way:

The process briefly is one of differences of opinion about the patient between two people who differ in status and involvement, with the difference coming into the open or being recognized. This is the quiet stage. It is followed by open disagreement, at which point the patient outburst occurs. In the resulting conflict the division is solidified and appeal is made to a larger group. The one unsuccessful in appeal, who becomes a minority, tends to flee from the situation, often by resigning, but this can be averted by authority forcing the two combatants to thrash out their difference of opinion.[264]

Bell goes on to suggest that if similar, "such processes are identifiable, they would seem to lend much to our explanations of the dynamics of clinic, school, and family behavior which are often rather weak."[265] If we now follow Bell's application of the ideas in Stanton's article to the situation at the Child Guidance Clinic, we do get an insight into how it operated, and what went wrong:

The parents are deeply involved emotionally and interested in the patient on personal grounds. The clinic disagrees with the way the parents operate— and it always does insofar as it considers parents as involved in the child's emotional problem. So far the process resembles the quiet period. At the point where the clinic tries to make the parent be committed to involvement in the clinic, the difference in opinion is brought into the open (the therapeutic process relative to the parent). In many cases the clinic's operation breaks down here. The parent refuses to become involved and withdraws, or more often, hesitates and wavers to the extent that the clinic withdraws. Very often it seems that rather than working out the differences, combat is closed.[266]

Bell continues in his memo to emphasize that he sees the evidence of the Clinic as showing that it did frequently fail in its mission, and he wondered if it was because of such triangulations as he has described: "Is the notably poor success of the clinic due to the fact it unwittingly gets caught in triangles which it doesn't understand and can't handle?"[267] He offers a particular example from the "Maltby Files" to demonstrate that his analysis may have merit:

A recent case that of Jonnie Gould, looks as though it might lend weight to the theory. There the mother is separated from the father and is having difficulty reaching a divorce agreement. Mrs Gould has recurrent crises and the son has frequent upsets.[268]

Alex Sim, also commented on the missing "Maltby Report," in another errant file from the Forest Hill Village Project found amongst his papers. He argued that the report placed too much emphasis on the mental health problems associated with the traditional patriarchal model of parenting. He saw this as rooted in the Freudian emphasis on underlying oedipal conflicts in parent-child relations. He was apparently reaching for something more along the lines of a sociological analysis of the effects of the new "other-directed" personality formation, in the following comment:

> As to the content of psychopathology, I am convinced, despite the material in the clinic files, that the traditional content of the neuroses, with stern father induced superegos in conflict with relatively unknown, surgent, sex-and-aggression-oriented ids, is a largely disappearing phenomenon pointing to a survival of passing attitudes and practices; the new phenomenon is a much less sharp, much more a generalized malaise, much closer to under-organization and in-definition than to over-organization of sharply defined incompatibles.[269]

This review of the evidence in regard to the activities of the Child Guidance Clinic suggests that real anxiety was induced by the Forest Hill Village Project; patriarchal fathers rushed to the school to put a stop to some impractical psychiatric intervention in their child's upbringing; emotionally abandoned mothers used the Clinic for their own needs as much as their child's; teachers complained, as usual, that they were being infantilized by the so-called professionals; doctors, rushed off their feet, resented the new expectation that they were not only cure bodies but also minds; and children felt confused by these strange new adult games.

# Free Discussion

Luckily, one revealing primary document has survived from the days of the Forest Hill Village Project about how it played out in the classroom, as distinct from the Clinic. This was a record of the minutes of a "meeting held on February 14th, 1949 at 4 pm, 111 St. George Street, in order to discuss the Human Relations Teaching at Forest Hill Village School."[270] Seeley explained the ways in which the "Human Relations Classes" were intended as an experiment in mass psychoanalysis as follows:

> It will be recognized from what has been said that the Project as a whole may be viewed as a species of attempted social therapy. Just as the therapist has a "patient who comes to him for help" so we had a community that came to us for help. Like the therapist, we started with "what was on the patient's mind" –; and, again like him, we followed up these comments in relatively free association. Again, like the therapist, we assumed that if the process of communication continued long enough, the pattern or structure for which we and they were looking together would emerge with greater clarity. Perhaps the technique used was manifest in greatest clarity in the "Human Relations Classes" conducted with the children. Here, generally, nothing more was said than "we talk about a lot of things in school every day, but perhaps these are not all the things that you are interested in talking about. If you like, we will set aside an hour every week, for the rest of the school year to talk about all the things that you like. What we talk about and how we talk about it, will be up to you."[271]

Thus, the Human Relations Classes took the form of "free discussion," much along the lines of the psychoanalytical technique of free association. The students were free for one period a week at school to talk about whatever topic they wanted. Moreover, the teacher's role was simply to assume a non-judgmental air that would allow as open a discussion as possible. The theory was that such talk therapy would prove itself to be therapeutic and, indirectly, also benefit the overall academic performance of the students in the experimental classes. It would seem that this psychoanalytical design of the project would have reflected Seeley's preoccupations to a greater extent than anyone else involved. As we have seen, neither Stokes, nor Hincks and Griffin were very enthusiastic about psychoanalysis, seeing it as a form of "mysticism."

But Seeley describes the roots of the human relations class methodology as traversing the psychoanalytic theory of Bettleheim and the sociological theory of Riesman. Seeley returns to Riesman's theme of "other-directedness" in connection to the human relations classes in an early lecture which he presented as an "Interim Report" on the progress of the Forest Hill Village Project. He speaks of the issue of autonomy, as does Riesman, in a society so bent on enforcing behavioral conformity:

> We have been concerned about the peculiar distressing situation of the middle class child in particular, who, in our society, seems to be at the focus of all the manipulative, other-directed facilities of the society, and which poses for that child, a peculiarly difficult problem of obtaining any kind of autonomy, any kind of ability to think and feel himself, or for himself. Out of these concerns, we of the Uppertown experiment, set out to devise, if we could, a social activity, in which on an egalitarian basis, and not on the usual "teacher up here and children down there" basis, in an atmosphere that was warm and value judgment free, the children could carry on for themselves, routinely, an investigation that would help them understand themselves.[272]

Though Seeley traces the importance of the Human Relations method to his intellectual mentors, others pointed to the humbler origins of the practice in the work of a mental hygienist from Delaware, a retired American Colonel Edmund Bullis. Thomas Mallinson, a statistician working simultaneously on his PhD and on the Forest Hill Village Project Staff, drew attention to this fact:

> These sessions came to be called "Human Relations Classes" although this is obviously unjust to Col. Edmund Bullis' earlier use of and prior claim to the term.[273]

But Mallinson did hasten to point out in his completed Doctoral Dissertation, which won significant praise from Stokes who served on the Examination Committee, that Bullis's method was much more directive than that which emerged from the Forest Hill Village Project. It was much more analogous to the process used by Griffin and Blatz during the Regal Road School Project. According to Bullis, the Human Relations Class should begin with the reading of a story or a play that involves an emotionally charged situation where mental health issues are at stake. The teacher would then direct the discussion toward an exploration of the issues raised, and whether the students in the class had ever experienced such issues themselves in their own lives as family members, or in their peer group at school. By contrast, the more psychoanalytic methodology of Seeley's "Free Discussion Classes," as he preferred to call them, was highly in-directive. Mallinson explained as follows:

> The term 'Human Relations Classes' which we used to describe these sessions has been employed to cover many types of class activities, with priority probably going to Col. Edmund Bullis. However, we cannot underline too strongly the felt difference between the dialogic experience we were prepared to 'offer' and the obvious guidance employed by Bullis and others; while we strove to provide the opportunity for 'human relating' in the belief that whatever values and learning there might be would accrue from the experience itself, others have sought to utilize the occasion for introducing specific 'rules' (social and moral) on 'how to relate'.[274]

It makes sense given the prominence of Bullis in the American mental hygiene movement and his acquaintance with Canadian leaders in the field like Hincks and Griffin, that there was a cross-fertilization of language and theory between the American and Canadian wings of the mental hygiene movement. One might even speculate that Griffin and Line's ideas about human relations classes as implemented by them during the Regal Road Schools Project of the 1930s might have found their way into Bullis' work, first published during the 1940s, and then boomeranged back to Canada when Seeley took up the idea again during the Forest Hill Village Project of the 1950s.

It is also interesting to note that just as was the case with Line, Griffin and Seeley, Bullis was a military man who was inspired by his wartime experience to devise preventive mental health techniques. As has already been identified, the question is whether the military origins of these techniques suggested a concern for ensuring social conformity. At first sight, it would seem that "free discussion" would be antithetical to military virtues like discipline and obedience. From the perspective of Foucault, however, the Human Relations Class could easily fall along the continuum from the medieval confession to the modern psychoanalytic session as investigative procedures designed for purposes of thought control. As he wrote in *Discipline and Punish*, in such social engineering projects we must "hear the distant roar of battle."[275]

Seeley had returned from Chicago with a very positive view of psychoanalysis. From his perspective, the problem was simply one of how to teach laymen to apply it in a school setting; a formidable task that was ahead of its time. For the teachers, on the other hand, questions about the integrity of psychoanalysis were secondary those of classroom management. To return to the minutes of the meeting between Seeley, Line and Griffin with the teachers who were being trained to implement the Human Relations Class method, we are immediately impressed by the teacher's discomfort with the lack of a traditional academic structure in these lessons. A Mr. Mahon, according to the minutes, "said he felt more comfortable now but did not seem to think this was the way he should feel since he was more comfortable only because his lessons now were more structured and he had been told he should not structure them."[276] Line responded to this and other such complaints in a subtle, dialectical way:

> Dr. Line felt that although the students now felt more at home with the teacher of the class, very little progress had been made, partly because there was confusion about the direction. He thought the classes would have to be given a good deal more form, which might mean the complete effacement of the teacher or might mean having an objective in mind. Giving more form to the classes did not mean structuring them as structure is usually thought of something that will happen teacher-centered. He said there's dynamite in what can be drawn from a class.[277]

The greater form Line wanted to give to the classes, even over the objections of the teachers, was not to set learning goals but the opposite, as he put it, to achieve "complete effacement of the teacher" or, as he said later in this same meeting, "to let the problem emerge through the students and the adult should not be in a position of having the right answers."

Griffin, on the other hand, made gestures to appease the teacher's anxieties about the lack of structure in the human relations classes. Griffin acknowledged that the "children were anxious because they don't know where they are going or why." He suggested that the classes begin with an expected level of structure as comparable with other classes, and then gradually let this structure fade into the background:

Dr. Griffin thought that Grade 11 should be given more information at the start because they were most accustomed to intellectualism. They had been exposed to discussions and felt that our classes suffered from comparison with other discussions. They had conveyed this attitude to their regular teachers. Dr. Griffin felt that it is best to introduce what you want to say and then move away from it. He thought that plunging in right at the start and exposing the students to a process that is so different from what they are accustomed to, had made them uncomfortable and had made it much more difficult for the liaison officers in the long run.[278]

Line disagreed with even this level of structure suggesting that "growth takes place" when students discover for themselves what their concerns are. In such an open-ended process they also realize that "no single answer to a problem is satisfactory and that there is more to this than they had thought; that living is more interesting and more complicated than they had thought."[279]

Trying another angle on the structure issue, Seeley suggested that while judgments on matters of opinion or value should be reserved in the spirit of Line's more adventurous perspective, perhaps the teachers could intervene on matters of fact to correct student errors. But Line, "insisted that the teachers should not go in as an authority." As the meeting came to an end, the teachers were obviously not satisfied that their issue had been addressed: "Mr. Mathews said there were two opposing ideas here—are they going to supply answers or not"? "Dr." Seeley brought the meeting to a close by using his authority as "Director" of the project to overrule the objections of Line:

> Dr. Seeley then said he thought the result of the meeting was the decision not to supply answers and not to smuggle answers in. He said he would like to see premature answers avoided but if facts seem necessary to make an important point these facts should be supplied.[280]

It is interesting that Seeley seems to undercut Line in his summary of the results of the meeting. Though it might seem a minor instance, an escalating accumulation of such slights, was likely to have had a negative effect. We should remember here that as Seeley's immediate superior at the Personnel Directorate of the Canadian Armed Forces, and the person who had promoted him to the highest levels of that organization, Seeley certainly owed some loyalty to Line. In this context, the appearance that Seeley was undermining his former boss in the meeting might have seemed ungrateful. In letters exchanged with Mallinson, Seeley further exhibited this tendency to be critical of Line:

> I didn't think for a moment that Bill would be of any help to us in giving us advice. This is completely outside his realm technically and as far as responsibility goes.[281]

And yet, Line was supportive of the psychoanalytic direction Seeley was taking the Human Relations Classes. Indeed, it is interesting that Line would have such a willingness to consider the group psychotherapy model for the Human Relations Classroom given his background as a protégé of Blatz. In regard to therapeutic technique Blatz said: "Non-directive: Non-effective." Griffin, on the other hand, showed himself to be much less willing to let go of structure. Even Seeley was not willing to go as far as Line. But the flipside of Seeley's problem with authority was his need to be in power himself. The fact that throughout his life he maintained cordial relations with Line and his family despite at times seeming overly competitive, however, shows that he was able to keep his combative side in check.[282] That he seemed aware of this tragic flaw in his character was expressed in the very last line of "Getting Along with Others," a lecture he gave on the Human Relations Class:

> How can you create a kind of situation in which some enterprise which you care about as an enterprise will determine of itself the kinds of relations which are desirable, whether they consist of getting along with one another or fighting one another and fighting has its values too.[283]

# Anti-Semitic Segregation

The events of the Forest Hill Village Project reveal that ethnic tensions were a major concern of the adult community behind closed doors. We know of these concerns because of parental participation in a series of adult study groups, alternatively referred to as "Adult Seminars." These seminars were organized by Seeley through the Home and School Association. According to an entry on January 24, 1950 in the "Minute Book of the Forest Hill Village Home and School Association, 1949–1953," the Adult Seminars appeared to be well attended:

> Dr. Seeley's Seminar Group has speakers on Education. There are in all a total of 11 study groups. The study groups are functioning with good attendance, February 14th will be Father's Night.[284]

Of course, as we can see in the special attention given in the minute book to the participation of the fathers, it was primarily the mothers who attended. Given that the Home and School Association itself was so popular in the community, it is not surprising that Seeley had been able to attract a large number of Village women to participate in these seminars. In fact, the Home and School Association reached the "pinnacle of power in the community" during the time of the Forest Hill Village Project.[285] In another minute book entry for March 25, the large membership numbers were proudly brought to the attention of the meeting and duly noted:

> Membership: Mrs. Graham announced that there were 2046 members of the Forest Hill Home and School Associations—an increase of 346 over the last year's registration. There are 11 honorary members and 101 Staff members bringing the total to 2163.[286]

The purpose of the Adult Seminars, like the Human Relations Classes, was twofold; first, to experiment with "social therapy," and second to gather evidence for the sociological analysis of suburbia which took final shape as the book, *Crestwood Heights*. It would seem that Seeley modeled his approach, not only on that of Riesman, but on that of Freud himself who had used the material excavated "archaeologically" in the analysis of his patients to address larger issues of the human condition. That Seeley was consciously pursuing a similar plan during the Forest Hill Village Project is exhibited in the following staff memo:

> I think it should be clearly recognizable that we are making two studies. (a) a study of selected effects of Human Relations Classes; and, (b) a study of Forest Hill Village as a community with special reference to the formation of personality, and with primary concentration on the school (and the home) as agents therein. It should seem expedient to discuss problems related to study (a) in a series of memoranda separate from this, but in dismissing this study for separate consideration, we must not neglect to recognize that the content of H. R. Classes discussion provides material of the highest relevance for study.[287]

As to the content of the discussions that were held in the Adult Seminars, according to the minutes, the superficial focus on child-raising issues varied. Most of the topics taken up by various groups related to psychological questions like, "Child Adjustment Problems, Family Relations, Adjusting to the Opposite Sex, Achieving Emancipation, Looking at Ourselves, Discipline, and Adolescence." Jewish and Gentile relations in Forest Hill was nowhere on the list of topics according to the "Minute Book," and yet they simmered beneath the surface.

In the chapter of *Crestwood Heights* entitled, "Parent Education," an excerpt from a document that originated out of the Project suggests that the issue of Jewish-Gentile relations was addressed, however obliquely:

> Both Jewish and Gentile women joined the seminars; but at no time were there more than thirty women in these groups during any one year. Topics discussed included personality and culture theory; educational philosophy and the school, Jewish-Gentile values; a study of the family; reports by mothers on the day-to-day happenings in the home; reading of, and comments on, some of the research in progress. At least two women enrolled in university courses in sociology as a direct result of their seminar participation.[288]

The emphasis in *Crestwood Heights* on the place of Jewish-Gentile issues in the Adult Seminars was on how they served as a "central integrating point between the two ethnic groups in Crestwood Heights."[289] Moreover, to the extent that *Crestwood Heights* did address Jewish-Gentile conflict, the perspective adopted was to emphasize that the Jewish community voluntarily submitted to their own marginalization. For example, the book points out: "No Jewish woman has at the time of writing been President of the central Home and School organization." Yet the book explains this as a "joint effect of Gentile and Jewish wishes," which was, "carefully maintained, largely through the clique structure of the Home and School Association, which operates by telephone behind the official scenes."[290]

The book goes on to emphasize that the Jewish community was willing to make such sacrifices because they "prize their half-acceptance by the Gentiles." The authors of *Crestwood Heights* were willing to go so far as to suggest that, "For the sake of acceptance by Gentiles, the Jews are prepared to support the status quo on the Board of Education, in the Home and School Association, and in the school system," even though, "time may very well bring about a situation in the schools where all the students will be Jewish, although the school staff and administration would remain Gentile."[291] The text failed to explain that the reason for the growing majority of Jews in the public schools of Forest Hill was not only that there was such a large influx of the Jewish population after the war, but also that many of the wealthier Gentile families of Forest Hill sent their children to local Anglican private schools like Upper Canada College and Bishop Strachan (the equivalent of British public schools like Henfield, which Seeley attended).

Not only, therefore, was the topic of Jewish-Gentile relations avoided on the surface in the Adult Seminars, its more difficult aspects never found their way into *Crestwood Heights*. The book emphasized the stereotype of religious conformity in American suburbs that predominated in the "pop sociology" of the time. But as influential American sociologist Will Herberg pointed out in *Protestant, Catholic and Jew*, published contemporaneously with *Crestwood Heights* in 1955, this conformity did not take the form of an abandonment of religion. Quite the contrary, membership in the acceptable religious denominations rose dramatically during the period. Herberg may have rightfully lamented the loss of authentic religious experience. The churches and synagogues were full because of their propaganda value during the Cold War. They served as proof of the benefits of consumer choice and religious freedom in a capitalist society. In a Veblenesque display of "conspicuous consumption," the new suburbanite

Jew or Christian sought to show-off their religious affiliation in the same way as their "trophy wife," their membership at the local sports club, and their new car or TV. As Seeley put it, religious institutions in Forest Hill, did not "preach a fundamental cleavage between the way of the world and the way of the spirit."[292] Religion had "utility" as a sign of one's adherence to the transcendent value attached to participation in the "American Way of Life," according to Herberg.[293]

In adopting this point of view Seeley may have glossed over significant differentiating factors in the Canadian situation, as Riesman pointed out, which he himself embodied as a British Home Child and "non-Jewish Jew." These stem from the history of more fraught relations between Jew and Gentile north of the border, especially in Ontario, perhaps traceable to the provinces colonial heritage. Unlike in the United States, India, and other former territories of the British Empire, resistance by the small population in Canada was easily crushed in the nineteenth century. In fact, sovereignty in Canada still rests, at least symbolically, with the British crown and the Union Jack still flies in Ontario. Thus, the class consciousness which is characteristic of British society has had a long time to entrench itself in Canadian culture. Along with it, we might suspect, lies a deeply rooted anti-Semitism that found expression in the 1290 Act of Expulsion, Shakespeare's "Shylock," and in twentieth-century eugenics.

Historian G. R. Searle observed in *Eugenics and Politics in Britain* that, "the Jews entering Britain from Eastern Europe in the post-1880 period aroused the class hostility of many eugenicists."[294] We may not be surprised, therefore, to find a pervasive anti-Semitism also lurking at many levels in the Canadian response to increasing Jewish immigration during the early twentieth century. At the highest levels of government the effort to block Jews from entering Canada, most famously exemplified in their deportation aboard the *St. Louis* in 1939, is well documented in Troper and Abella's book, *None Is Too Many*. But even in social terms, the involvement of the medical elite in eugenics, which was largely centered in Toronto, betrayed their belief in the "superiority of the white race."[295]

We have seen that the Anglo-Saxons to whom Seeley reported as an agent of the CMHA, were all implicated with eugenics; and as Angus McLaren noted in *Our Own Master Race*, "many eugenicists were in fact Anti-Semites."[296] In interviews, Beatrice Fischer and Reva Gerstein remembered feelings of distrust toward men like Aldwyn Stokes and William Blatz on the grounds of anti-Semitism. Seeley also feared that his relationship with Fischer might have been unfavorable with Stokes, presumably not just because of arid academic debates. "It was all part of the politics of psychoanalysis at the time," Seeley said to me when we discussed these issues.[297]

Still, there was more to Jewish-Gentile tensions in Toronto than the maneuvering of politicians and interpersonal atmospherics. In fact, the worst outbreak of Anti-Semitic violence in Canadian history took place on Toronto streets in 1933, the "Christie Pits Riots." While the spark that triggered the violence was the unfurling of swastikas at a baseball game between local Jewish and Gentile teams, the increasing population of Jews in Toronto during the Depression era who were beginning to break-out of their downtown Ghetto, "the Ward," laid the incendiary social groundwork.

The northward migration of the growing Jewish population in Toronto to more desirable neighborhoods like Forest Hill met with "Restrictive Covenants" against Jewish home ownership that "barred Jews from certain streets." In another episode reported by Jack Lipinski in *Imposing Their Will: An Organizational History of Jewish Toronto*, the Forest Hill Village Council "prevented the Brunswick Avenue Talmud Torah from using a storefront" and forced the school to "move outside the village boundaries." Nevertheless, according to Lipinsky, the Jewish population of Forest Hill Village increased from 1,293 Jews in 1931 to 6,073 by 1941, and, "by 1951, over one-third of the city's Jews had settled there."[298] According to the Canadian Jewish Congress, Toronto had become the third largest Jewish community in the British Commonwealth by 1954: "The estimate of Jewish population of metropolitan Toronto as of June 1954 is 74,500, an increase of 7,727 over the 1951 census."[299]

In the context of the suburbanite need for status symbols, it must have been very frustrating for the Jews of Forest Hill to continue to be subtly banned from joining prestigious local clubs and schools even after they had surmounted obstacles to home ownership. While it is true, for example, that the desirable Badminton and Racquet Club (B & R) has never acknowledged its ban on Jewish members for which it received a commonly used nick-name, the "B and a'R'yan Club," it has publicly refused to divulge the number of Jewish members.[300] Similarly, the contrast between the large numbers of Jewish children in Forest Hill in the Fifties and the very small number who attended its most prestigious school, Upper Canada College, must have served as painful evidence of the rumored anti-Semitism and informal quotas which existed in so many elite schools in Canada during that era.[301]

The reality of a greater level of tension between Jews and Gentiles against this historical backdrop than was acknowledged in *Crestwood Heights*, is revealed in many unpublished Forest Hill Village Project notes taken by the team of field researchers under Seeley's supervision. One participant in the Adult Seminars suggested in a letter to Seeley that simmering Jewish-Gentile tensions were actually their central focus:

> It seemed to me that you came into the community when the anxious trial and error attempts of a number of people to stem the separation desires of the majority in both groups was approaching its peak, and, at least from what I knew of your activities, these were the people with whom you had many contacts. Although I believe this group had various motives and understandings, I think they agreed that, to them, contact was a better policy than separation. I believed and explained in my attempt to describe the Seminar group, that contact was the underlying motive. It was expressed to me by some in the seminar that discussion of the warp and woof of life would lead to group disintegration, and by others, that not to discuss such affairs would lead to disintegration. All seemed to desire the same end but differed regarding the means. It appeared to me that specific child rearing topics were only discussed when tensions became too difficult.[302]

The perception of Mary Doan that the participants in the Forest Hill Village Project Seminars were preoccupied with Jewish-Gentile issues to a far greater degree than child-rearing, is borne out in the field notes taken by Alex Sim, Elizabeth Loosley and other members of the Project research team. In the first place, the notes confirm that there was discussion and disagreement in the Adult Seminars over how to handle ethnic tensions within each group. For example, one Jewish female participant in a Seminar with Alex Sim made the following comment:

> Re—breaking our Group into Jewish and Gentile factions. I think it is a very ill-advised thing to do. I don't agree with Dot Henderson that it might be indicative of defeat. It could only be experimental, nothing else. Visualize an all Gentile Group. Mrs. S. knows Mrs. K. very well, hence Mrs. S. cloaks her opinions in heavy veiling. She wants to keep on being friendly—she wishes to invite no strained feelings. But the discussion proceeds and rather petty points are picked up and attacked. No one gets hurt. It becomes an artificial sort of discussion. I may be wrong, but I rather experienced this sort of thing myself—and thenceforward vowed to silence. I evidently sounded

Anti-Semitic—and shocked a member of the group—or felt I did. A Jew mustn't knock a Jew. We, the persecuted are too vulnerable—have suffered too much and are too damned sensitive. Hence an all Jewish Group—or an all Gentile group is a negative undertaking in my humble opinion.[303]

The notes also confirm as might be expected, that the talk around the Village gave vent to a generalized anxiety about the influx of Jews in the post-war period. The fact is that the Jewish population in Forest Hill between 1941 and 1951 increased from 11 percent to 40 percent of the total population. By the 1960s the majority of people living in Forest Hill were Jewish.[304] Strangely, however, in his letter of response to Mary Doan, Seeley claims to have been oblivious to the fact that addressing issues in Jewish-Gentile relations was a dominant area of concern:

> Some of the material in your letter is not only extraordinarily helpful but is news of the first importance. The fact that it is news, after a five or six year exposure to the community, is of course itself significant. What you say about developing an interest area as a conscious attempt to prevent the separation of Jews and Gentiles in the Village is extremely important. The fact that up to this point no one had told us this or anything like it or even hinted at it throws fresh light either on village life or our interpenetration with it or both.[305]

A cursory review of the themes in Jewish-Gentile relations that recurred time and again in the notes of the Project Staff reveals that either Seeley had not paid enough attention to what his staff had done, or that, Seeley was being disingenuous in his response to Mrs. Doan. The resentment toward Jewish migration into the suburbs seemed to focus around suspicions that Jews had not come by their money honestly. In other words, the notes give us variations on the ancient Gentile myth of the Jew as "Shylock," a ruthless and greedy money lender. In Alex Sim's notes, one female participant in the Adults Seminars came up with the following list of Gentile complaints:

1. All Jews are rich
2. Jewish children are luxuriously dressed
3. All Jews have television
4. All Jews have mink coats.[306]

And she writes, "This one's on me—I've heard it oft repeated: There isn't a Gentile who sincerely likes a Jew." In a subtler, but perhaps also more menacing way because of the source, the same suspicions seemed to be latent in the following comment made to Alex Sim, November 7,1949, by Forest Hill Police Chief Frazer, "The Jews will pay two or three thousand dollars more than anyone else to get into the Village." Another woman, who attended Sim's Adult Seminar, wrote to him that, "I've heard it said that people, particularly Jews, made a good deal of money during the war, and moved to Forest Hill." She expanded on the theme of mistrust of Jewish success in business in a little anecdotal story she passed along to Sim:

> In conversation with a gentleman I told him my Dad was a blouse manufacturer. He then very seriously asked me how my Dad could possibly compete with THOSE PEOPLE. "What people," I asked, innocently—"You know, those Jews." "Well," I said, "I have no desire to embarrass you, but the reason my father gets along so well is because he is one of those people." The chap was quite flustered and said,
>
> "But you don't look Jewish."
> "What is looking Jewish?"
> "Well, you speak so quietly."
> "Many Jews do."
> "Well, you dress so neatly."
> "Many Jews do. I think you must have had an unfortunate experience with some Jewish firm. Did you?"
> "Yes, yes, etc. . . . & etc. . . ."
> He apologized himself right into Windsor stadium in Montreal—ending up with the classic—"some of my best friends are Jews."[307]

The resentment toward upwardly mobile Jews is revealed in the Project notes to also emanate from the working class Jews of Toronto who were left behind. According to Sim's notes, it was common amongst them to speak, "disparagingly about Mortgage Hill." Some also referred with similar derision to the new Reform Synagogue, Holy Blossom Temple, built in Forest Hill in 1938, as the "Church on the Hill."[308]

Exterior View of Holy Blossom Temple, Bathurst St., Toronto (ca.1956). Ontario Jewish Archives, Blankenstein Family Heritage Center, Item 932.

Also, in a somewhat humorous vein, Sim summons up the following vignette:

> Somewhere in the files there is an anecdote about a Jewish family whose less wealthy relatives continued to visit them—in trucks and broken down jalopies—and the ensuing remarks made by other residents on the street.[309]

At another level of omission, *Crestwood Heights* was seemingly oblivious to the impact on ethnic tensions in Forest Hill of the Holocaust. Seeley admitted that this was a "rather singular omission."[310] This omission is particularly surprising given that, as we have already seen, one of the original aims of the research component of the Forest Hill Village Project was: "A study of the pattern and the transmission of anti-Semitism."[311] It would certainly have been logical at this time for public policy makers to be concerned, not only about the causes of such virulent outbreaks of anti-Semitism, but also about the consequences of the trauma in Europe for the large numbers of Holocaust survivors who came to Toronto as emigrants. It is important to point out that, in fact, most of the 30,000 to 35,000 survivors and their descendants who came to Canada between 1945 and 1956, settled in Toronto. Moreover, this group of survivors came to constitute up to 15–20% of the local Jewish population in the Greater Metropolitan Toronto area which by 1961 had reached a total of about 89,000 Jewish inhabitants.[312] These survivors, or "Greenies," as part of a very tight-knit community with many levels of social relations through family, synagogue and workplace gatherings; must have had an impact on the consciousness of the whole community including those living in Forest Hill.

The most compelling argument that has been put forward to explain the general silence about the Holocaust in Canada during the immediate period after the war is given by Franklin Bialystok in *Delayed Impact*, where he observes that the Jewish community, for many complicated reasons, sought to avoid the issue:

> Interest in the Holocaust was late in coming. For the first twenty years after the war, Canadians knew little about the event. This amnesia was not restricted to the gentile world, it was also pervasive within the Canadian Jewish community, as it was in other Jewish communities outside continental Europe. Certainly, many Canadian Jews had lost family members and now lived with the reality that a civilization had been destroyed, but the community, as represented by its leaders, did little to instill knowledge of the catastrophe, and there was no grassroots desire for this situation to change.[313]

According to Bialystok, for the survivors, the memories were often too fresh and painful to be spoken of. They sought to protect their children from the pain, and shame, of what had happened to them. For the community, the Holocaust was seen at first as a "blot on Jewish history." Like so many victims, they blamed themselves for not successfully resisting this attack, or for collaborating in their own self-destruction. Thus, Jewish schools omitted teaching about the Holocaust; Jewish newspapers "ignored the topic"; and the leaders of the Canadian Jewish Congress, "had little to say about the impact of the Holocaust on Canadian Jews."[314] According to Bialystok, the Jewish community as a whole was, like the "greenies," more concerned during the fifties with fitting in than with dealing with the ghosts of the past.[315]

Yet, the reality is that despite the best efforts of their parents to spare them, these children of survivors came to know very deeply what had happened. As one of them said to me in the context of telling a story about how his mother, who was a survivor of Auschwitz, had left the house for weeks after encountering a mouse, "we did not have to talk about it, we lived it."[316] The authors of *Crestwood Heights* nevertheless seemed oblivious to this deeper reality of Holocaust memory that underlay the post-war silence of the Jewish community. Was this because they were fooled by this silence into believing that it did not matter?

The one place in the Forest Hill Village Project notes where we do see subtle references to the Holocaust was in regard to the storm that took place in 1950 about a proposal to segregate classes of Jewish and Gentile students in the High School. Ostensibly, the decision of the Forest Hill School Board to assign students to their high school classes based on ethnicity was for the sake of "better balance," in the words of then Superintendent of Schools for Forest Hill, Don Graham.[317] The *Toronto Daily Star* reported sympathetically on Graham's "scheme under which classes have been re-grouped and four all-Jewish classes formed in the predominantly Jewish student body, in order to increase the ratio of non-Jewish students in the other classes."[318] Rather than refer to the "scheme" as "anti-Semitic segregation," as had been done in the rival tabloid *Flash*, the *Star* used a more scientific sounding label, referring to it as an "Educational Experiment." Indeed, the *Star* reported that H. Rogers, the Chairman of the Forest Hill Village Board of Education, said that "complaints of segregation are ridiculous." In order to further accentuate this aura of scientific neutrality around the "scheme," the *Star* sought to portray it as a strictly administrative maneuver:

> [T]here was no pressure from outside groups advocating the change, and school officials themselves worked it out, then got the go-ahead from the Board of Education. Since then Mr. Graham has been waging a vigorous campaign of informing parents of the reasons for the set-up, and the way it works. The plan is in effect only in the classes from Grade 8 to 12. In each of these grades, one class has purposely been made up of all Jewish students, increasing the ratio of non-Jewish students in the other classes.[319]

*Toronto Daily Star* coverage of School "Regrouping," October 14, 1950.

The extent of newspaper coverage of the classroom segregation issue suggests, however, that efforts to downplay it failed to fully suppress reaction in the Jewish community. The *Flash* wrote about the, "reports and rumors of Anti-Semitic segregation which have been permeating Toronto lately." The *Toronto Daily Star* reported a "crowded" meeting at Holy Blossom Temple to discuss the issue of the "Forest Hill CI experiment":

> Rabbi A. L. Feinberg chairman of the Canadian Jewish Congress and a leader in Forest Hill Jewry, last night assured a crowded open forum at Holy Blossom Temple that the people of good will in the village who are studying the new scheme of regrouping students in the collegiate would not scuttle the principles of freedom and non-discrimination for which Jewish people have fought for hundreds of years. The meeting, which included a large number of Forest Hill residents, indicated the probable attitude of Forest Hill Jews to the plan: a wait-and-see, don't get alarmed attitude.[320]

Was this really the "probable" attitude of the Jewish community in Forest Hill, or was it the attitude the papers and the institutional leaders from the School Board to the Jewish Congress wanted to inculcate? In any event, the fact that this meeting took place, is a clear sign there was considerable concern in the Jewish community about Anti-Semitic segregation.

The most striking feature of the controversy that emerges from the Forest Hill Village Project field notes, was that it was blamed on the unrealistic sensitivities of Holocaust survivors. The extremity of the situation in the schools in Forest Hill may have been cause for survivors to look-up from their daily work, at least briefly, in a reaction that anticipated the "delayed" explosion of their anger in the 1960s in response to the Eichmann Trial and the Allen Gardens Riots.

One, un-named researcher from the Forest Hill Village Project staff, who attended the meeting at Holy Blossom Temple, took quite revealing notes about what happened. He or she entitled the file, "How to Murder a Community" Sermon by Rabbi Feinberg, Filed under "Churches" (the segregation of the classrooms issue).[321] The note-taker did not refer to the re-grouping scheme as an educational experiment but, calling a-spade-a-spade, referred to it as "segregation." The possibility that the events of the Holocaust had an important impact on the reaction in the Jewish community seems implicit in the title chosen by Rabbi Feinberg for his sermon. The title is ironic because Feinberg intended to compare those who were questioning the School Board's classroom segregation policy to the Biblical figure of Cain who murders his brother. Feinberg suggested that an over-reaction to a policy that was well intentioned would only serve to increase frictions between the Jewish and Gentile members of the Forest Hill Community. In this way, the protestors might become, like Cain, the "murderers of their community." It is hard not to read a particular commentary on the Holocaust into this presentation of the segregation issue; the message being that in Europe the suffering of the Jewish people had been caused by their own political meddling. Instead, he suggested that the school leaders be given the benefit of the doubt, and priority be placed on maintaining good relations with Gentiles.

But Rabbi Feinberg was an American-born Jew who had no personal experience of what happened in Europe. Like many other Jews who had grown up in relative safety in North America, and who were anxious to take advantage of the opportunities for economic progress that the post-war era offered, his tendency was to assume that the "greenies" had done something to deserve their terrible fate, as had the Biblical figure of Cain. Unlike their European ancestors, the already Americanized Jews were not interested in continuing the pattern of dispersion that tormented the children of Cain.

However, this attitude came into direct conflict with the experience of the Holocaust survivors arriving in great numbers in Toronto. Indeed, there is historical evidence that some of these survivors, at least, were active in the Holy Blossom Temple at the time of these events. According to Adara Goldberg's *Holocaust Survivors in Canada*, "Some briefly attended services at the Reform Holy Blossom Temple, one of Toronto's older synagogues."[322] The possibility that it was these Holocaust survivors who agitated against the school's segregation policy during the meeting at Holy Blossom, is suggested in the following note taken by the member of the Forest Hill Village Project Staff who attended:

> A questioner asked Feinberg to elaborate on his sermon statement that "children were better community leaders." Feinberg replied that he did not say "better community leaders." He then expanded the theme of those adults who had suffered in Europe and as a consequence were more ready to see threats to their security than would the children. "We must be less emotional and less ready to jump to hasty conclusions." The questioner then said he had been at a dinner with a Forest Hill Village family and the girl had said the kids were quite happy about the classroom arrangements, whereupon the mother had rebuked her for saying this. Feinberg observed, "You mean the parent was more worried about the child's experiences than the child who was having the experience?" Question from behind me—What is so terrible about all this? Why is there all this agitation? The kids aren't agitating—the parents are.[323]

Feinberg's concern was that the survivors who had been through the Holocaust might be exercising undue influence in the Jewish Community in Forest Hill. Under their influence, the parents' natural desire to protect their children was fobbed off by Feinberg as "emotional" and "hasty," in contrast to the naïve innocence of the children, whose reaction better served his agenda. The *Toronto Daily Star*'s report on the Holy Blossom Temple meeting also noted the connections that were being made in the meeting to the Holocaust:

> Questioned later in the forum the rabbi explained that, "adults are too often conditioned by experience and preconceptions and prejudices. Adults are in the same relation to children as Jews who had gone through the pogroms of the Nazis and the Fascists were to those who had lived all their lives in Canada."[324]

Feinberg's claim here was that the sensitivities of the survivors were a form of prejudice in contrast to his more enlightened progressivism on matters of racial relations. He was claiming that his conditioning was superior in these matters because he had not been persecuted like the Holocaust survivors. However, from the perspective of twenty-first-century Jews who have themselves experienced the emergence of neo-fascist movements and the continuing struggles of Israel, it may have been Rabbi Feinberg's conditioning that was the more illusory.

As to the children themselves, unlike what Feinberg and others at the meeting assumed about their being unaffected by the racial prejudices of the adults, it would appear that they too were distressed in their own ways about Jewish-Gentile issues. According to *Crestwood Heights*, the issue of segregation affected the high school fraternities and sororities that were so popular across North America in the fifties. The fact is the students themselves practiced segregation between Jews and Gentiles through their selection practices for these teenage clubs. When, at a "joint meeting of parents and collegiate students to discuss the problem of fraternities and sororities," the parents objected to the practice of such blatant discrimination, the students were quick to point out the hypocrisy of the adults. The students brought forward examples of similar adult forms of exclusion practiced in organizations from the United Nations to the Forest Hill School System itself. In the only reference to the classroom segregation issue that found its way into *Crestwood Heights*, one student is reported to have challenged the Collegiate Principal on this point:

> Student (Female): You say that the school has always been democratic and not shown discrimination. How about the segregation of the Jewish and Gentile classes that took place two years ago? She was groaned down. Several teachers spoke at once, saying that the move had been taken all in good faith, that it was an error, and had been corrected: that the school was not infallible; that they tried to correct all such errors immediately, etc.[325]

According to Seeley, the importance of the issue of Jewish-Gentile segregation also emerged amongst the adolescent population in the Human Relations Classes. Seeley said, in regard to dating, that:

> If in a Jewish family a girl fell in love with a gentile, suddenly an unknown grandma would appear for dinner, then grandma would discourage the Jewish girl and she would be sent off to a Jewish school or out of town. Exile to prevent inter-mixing. Torrents of emotion. Deceived, banished by their own parents. After 2–3 weeks damning their parents they began to wonder,

"when I get to be a parent, will I do any better." They started to invent ways that parents might not deceive their children.[326]

This issue was also reported in Tom Mallinson's PhD thesis about the Human Relations Classes:

> They were able to share in an honest discussion of their feelings around the vital area to (to them) of Jewish-Gentile dating, marriage and courtship; what the problem was; and why it was so complicated; and what they could do about it. The terminal point at the end of the year was; no agreement amongst them as to what should be done about the problem, but some clarification as to where they stood, and in a final burst of insight, some notion of what kind of character is required if you are going to build a new world in which you are willing to over-step traditional bounds, be they right or wrong.[327]

In another revealing passage in Mallinson's thesis concerning the Forest Hill Collegiate student discussions, a very young group of students made their way toward the important issue of Jewish–Gentile relations through a discussion about African-Americans:

> Initial sessions of this class discussed at length the question of slavery in the early Americas. Gradually, the discussion moved toward the question of the treatment of the negro today, but when this was related to a recent example of discrimination in a nearby small town, the discussion immediately veered back to conditions many years ago. Again the discussion turned to more recent times and immediate surroundings, but when a local club was cited as discriminating against negros, and a boy asked if they had any other kinds of discrimination there, the class again veered away from the question. It was not until two or three sessions later that the class was able to verbalize, and look at, their feelings about discrimination against Jews—a problem that was of quite some concern to the community in which they lived, hence to them.[328]

It is clear from a look at the various levels at which anti-Semitism plagued the Village of Forest Hill in the fifties, that it was a heated issue. Contrary to Seeley's emphasis in *Crestwood Heights* on a convergence of interest around the instrumentality of religion, it would seem that there was active segregation. With regard to the incident of Anti-Semitic segregation in the schools, we can see how *Crestwood Heights* participated in the silencing of the community in regard to the events of the Holocaust. Such repression served the interests of the hierarchy in maintaining social order. These forces included the media whose spin on the issue was to dismiss the concerns as "idle talk" in the words of *Flash*; the Board of Education whose chairman called concerns about segregation, "ridiculous"; and, the Canadian Jewish Congress and its spokesperson Rabbi Feinberg who suggested that the Jewish survivors were "prejudiced" by their traumatic experiences in Europe. Feinberg's approach was to attempt to mollify the community with public reassurances to the effect that "what Mr. Graham has done to better overall relations between Jewish and Christian children will ultimately be of great benefit to all of Canada," while at the same time working behind the scenes to quietly ensure that the practice of regrouping classrooms was put to an end. According to Martin Sable, Feinberg's approach was effective:

> Congress objected, but very carefully, couching its objections in terms of a breach of democratic principles. Indeed, Congress backed off quickly when the Forest Hill Board of Education agreed to consider an alternative course of action for the following year. As far as Congress was concerned, it had brokered a satisfactory resolution for the Jewish community, and had forestalled extensive public discussion. Nothing more was necessary. *Time Magazine* commented at the time that "the situation would have provoked uproar in the United States, but with typical Canadian restraint, Jewish organizations decided against a public outcry because the Board of Education had acted in good faith."[329]

No doubt, as leader of the Forest Hill Village Project, Seeley also played his part in the effort to keep a lid on ethnic conflict in Forest Hill. Despite his commitment to free discussion in the Human Relations Classes, he was perhaps ready to make an exception when it came to Jewish issues because of his own identity confusion and the politics of Jewish-Gentile relations in Toronto at the time. On the one hand, *Crestwood Heights* for its time may have deserved the applause granted it in the "Introduction" to the book by David Riesman for at least opening up consideration of Jewish-Gentile relations. On the other hand, Seeley may have exaggerated the extent of the cooperative spirit between the two solitudes of Forest Hill.

# Film Noir

The growing Jewish population in Toronto was not alone in its desire to move into the expanding new suburbs in the early post-war period. In Ontario, the rate of population expansion in the suburbs exceeded that in the city cores by over 100% between 1951 and 1961.[330] This was driven by many economic factors including the need for housing for veterans, a booming population and economy, dramatic increases in car ownership, the invention of low-cost tract housing, and an increased supply of oil, gas, and hydroelectric power amongst others. The move to the suburbs also satisfied certain social needs that had intensified in the aftermath of War and Holocaust. These took the form of various utopian dreams of return to small town democracy, nature, and leisure.

Amongst these dreams was a desire to hold onto a "natural" division of labor between the sexes which the "spatial segregation of the suburban frontier" reinforced.[331] The distance of the suburbs from the factories and office towers ensured that women remained close to home, and dedicated their energy to creating an idyllic pastoral realm for their children to grow up in, and their husbands to return to at the end of the day. Ideally, such an effort to clarify roles would serve to reduce conflict and preserve marital harmony. Historian Doug Owram's explanation of such post-war social conservatism was that the physical and emotional disruptions caused by the war oriented Canadians toward home, family, and stability to a degree unparalleled in other historical periods.[332] Perhaps, the reality of rapidly increasing female participation in the labor force and politics during the twentieth century, and the threat it posed to patriarchy, may have provided an added incentive. The question was whether people found what they were looking for in the suburbs.

Just as was reflected in film noir, an art form characteristic of the period, Seeley and other pop sociologists were skeptical. Of course, in art the perception of hopelessness in the flight to the suburbs was carried to an extreme. Events always take place in the night-time. Like Plato's prisoners, the audience was forced visually to follow the shadows on the walls. As in psychoanalysis, the narrative runs backward as characters haunted by their past remember what brought them to such a state of desperation. Not only was sexual infidelity, rather than monogamy, the norm in film noir, there was also a leftist political consciousness operating at a subtle level. Film noir often focus on corruption in the daily business world of the banks, insurance companies and media. In *Double Indemnity*, the femme fatale's plot to induce a lover to murder her rich but abusive oil executive husband seems justified. In *The Naked City* a contrast is sharply drawn between the exhaustion of the working class who must work the night shift and the idle rich closing out another night on the town.

Seeley promised, on the dust jacket to *Crestwood Heights*, a similar kind of expose. The book attempted to sell itself as a kind of sociological noir that offered a "penetrating study," a "revelation," or an "illumination" of the "dilemmas in which modern Western middle-class people find themselves" in any North American "Big City." Some critics think that Seeley did achieve such a penetrating critique of suburbia. For example, Veronica Strong-Boag wrote in *Home Dreams*:

> The indictments of social critics were elaborated most fully in *Crestwood Heights*, a case study of Toronto's Forest Hill, an 'inner suburb' built before the Second World War. Dissecting the family lives of an upper middle class sample of Wasp and Jewish Torontonians, the authors revealed what many critics of mass society feared. Men concentrated on making money, ignoring families emotional and spiritual needs. Dissatisfied women wielded power in a community in which they were the dominant adults for the daylight hours. Mothers were preoccupied with their offspring, to the detriment of themselves and their offspring. Both sexes were overly materialistic. The contribution of men and women to the wider society was intrinsically limited. Despite the lack of comparability of this older suburb to what was happening on the periphery of Canadian cities, *Crestwood Heights* rapidly became the measure by which modern suburbia was judged.[333]

Other critics, however, argued that in the very process of establishing the "measure" for evaluation of suburban culture, *Crestwood Heights* normalized its values. Wini Breines, for example, argued that:

> The work under consideration takes for granted and studies the "great American celebration" of white middle-class America, as does much of the work written during the fifties. One is hard pressed to find awareness that the social and ideological conflicts of the 1960s were germinating and would soon burst forth. . . . Its locations are the new suburbs and expanding corporations and it is written by men, again, as was most social science of the period.[334]

Mary Louise Adams, in her book *The Trouble with Normal*, also argued that *Crestwood Heights* invented the norm of the ideal family in the name of which a retreat to the suburbs could be justified. Despite Seeley's intent in *Crestwood Heights* to indict the moral vacuity he observed in suburbia, according to Adams the paramount effect of the book at the time was to reinforce banal stereotypes of smug middle class self-satisfaction:

> For the most part the image of the family that was used to represent the ideal was drawn from urban, white, Anglo-Saxon, middle-class and upper-middle-class communities.[335]

American scholar, Stephanie Coontz, in her influential book, *The Way We Never Were*, also invited readers to consult *Crestwood Heights* for a traditional, "defense of the suburbs" perspective.[336]

Those who did not feel Seeley went far enough in his critique of Suburbia were joined by Riesman who, as we have already seen, felt that Seeley could have dug deeper in his exploration not only of Jewish-Gentile issues, but also interpersonal and emotional experience in Forest Hill. It may be significant in this context to review material that was collected by Seeley and the Forest Hill Village Project team which would have made such an in-depth study possible. This may point us in the direction of those forces which blocked Seeley's attention to it, including his own emotional inhibitions. We begin with the following passage, found amidst the notes taken by the Forest Hill Village Project research team, in which a housewife vividly describes the subtle way that the compartmentalization of suburban life led to alienation:

> Informant # 15 was brought up as a young girl in an old farmhouse on the outskirts of the city. The kitchen was rather small and in it we did our nightly work. In front of it was the dining room where all the meals were served. In

the evenings, after the dishes were washed in the kitchen, the cleared table would have a red cloth placed over it and I sat there to do my homework with my mother nearby sewing or mending. My father had a desk in the same room where he did his accounts. There was a fireplace in this room which was invariably burning as a partial source of heat, and we used to eat apples in the winter evenings. Now in our house here in *Crestwood Heights* we try to have our meals together in the dining room, but these are hurried and that is all we do in that room. After supper my husband and I may sit in the living room to read but the children do their homework in their own rooms. In the afternoon, the children may use the living room for playing records and doing dance exercises and so on, but when they do that my husband is at work and I am usually out.[337]

What this woman revealed, it would seem, is that the retreat from public into domestic life during the fifties did not stop at the front door. It was possible, especially in the Forest Hill Mansion, for family members to continue their retreat within the home itself. Husbands became isolated from their wives, children from their parents, and brothers from their sisters as they each beat a retreat into their separate rooms and their separate socially assigned functions. Yet this social impoverishment was justified as a sign of material progress:

> The teachers took a number of students in a bus somewhere and some of them leaned out of the windows and said "there's the place where grandma lives." Still lives. And they were shacks. The children used to live there themselves. Some people in FHV don't use their living rooms. Most of them eat in the kitchen or sunroom. Their living room furniture is covered with sheets.[338]

It was as if the separation into economic classes reverberated in a fractal series of disjunctions at other social levels. Even rooms in the domestic home reflected social divisions by being designated as either the "family room" where family members actually lived, or as the "living room," where no one actually went because it was only to be used for "company." The word "company" may here be seen as a portmanteau that is suggestive of the emphasis on salability in the other-directed social relations of the time.

Forest Hill, Looking S.W. from Old Forest Hill Road, 1953. Photo by James Victor Salmon, Baldwin Collection. Courtesy of the Toronto Reference Library.

It was because of socially enforced gender segregation that most of the Forest Hill Village Project interviews were with women. The mothers of Forest Hill participated in the research project as part of their volunteer work for the Forest Hill Village Collegiate Home and School Association, which kept them busy while their husbands had gone off to work downtown. Of course, it wasn't just that the husbands went off to work every day that left the village women with a desperate sense of loneliness and isolation; it was that often, they never really came home. The following passage tells the story of a fifties housewife better than any post-modern film, because it is not fiction:

> Mrs M. Lep; (about 44 or 45). It's just terrible being a widow. I feel so lonesome and lost. I spent my whole life being crazy clean, cultivated no friends, developed no hobbies; just made sure my home was spotless and germ free; fed my children the correct vitamins, etc. What a fool I was, all I knew was my home, my four walls. I had a maid, but I watched her closely. Yes! My house was clean—so what? Then my husband died and I have no one and nothing. One daughter is married and has her own life while the other is busy with the young crowd. I am not needed. I am invited to an

occasional party, and I sometimes attend, but I'm the only one without a husband. I sit close to the wives, lest they suspect me of being interested in their husbands. It is really awful to have to live without a man. I realize now that I wasted my life worrying about the dust free corners.[339]

In this woman's experience the suburban home, which was supposed to be a safe haven, had turned into a jail. But who guarded the jail? While her husband lived, Mrs. Lep had been obsessed about the cleanliness of her "store front windows," to quote a line from *Crestwood Heights*, but then, once he died, she realized that it hadn't really mattered. This would suggest that in some sense the men played the role of watch-dog, or was it in fact the other housewives, jealous lest any of their number be set free? A big part of it may have been the pervasive role of the "company" in social surveillance. This was suggested in the following interview excerpt from the *Toronto Star*, May 24, 1955, entitled "Unselfish Wife Can Contribute Greatly to Success of Executive":

> The quality of the wife is so important for executive success in today's business world that some firms even hire private investigating firms to report on the wife's fitness, Edwin C. Phillips, Vice-President of Trane Co. of Canada Ltd, said Saturday. Mr. Phillips said, "The number of executives being held back by their wives is terrific." He said many firms now have direct interviews with the wives, others make subtle inquiries; some even have checks by private investigators. Business today is not looking so much as previously for the wife who can prepare a good meal for the boss, or is good-looking, or will have 15 children who she can guarantee will eat only the company's products," he said. "They're looking now for the girl who's going to be ambitious for her husband; who is anxious for her husband to be something, for her children to be something, in fact, to push him." Mr. Phillips said: "It doesn't take a seasoned executive long to spot the man who's got a neurotic wife.[340]

What the "company" wanted, therefore, was little "Lady Macbeths," who would drive their husbands' and children's achievement complexes. In the process of doing so, however, they fell prey to an obsession with cleanliness and mental hygiene; "Out, out damned spot," reverberated through the hallways of the suburban castle.

Yes, it was a time when outward calm masked intense inner pressures that must have driven them all, men and women alike, to seek out extramural sources of sexual release like Mrs. Lep's interest in the other husbands. In fact, this was a central theme of Riesman's study, *The Lonely Crowd*, in which he identified a pattern of intensified sexual activity in the post-war era as a manifestation of other–directedness. However, he saw it as a kind of "anxious competitiveness" where each new sexual partner was like a new brand that one must have before anyone else.[341] According to Riesman, sex had become the most sought after object of consumption. But, contrary to this rather sporting approach to sex amongst the other-directed types, we find signs of a more desperate and even perverse form of sexual activity amongst the people of Forest Hill in the 1950s.

For example, there is evidence in the Forest Hill Village Project field notes of porn being sold door to door in this fashionable suburb, and that there were indeed "Mrs. Robinson" style encounters between lonely wives and oedipal teenagers:

> This is a fairly detailed and complicated story about her (Informant # 70) relations with an 18 year old boy, # 201, who is a class mate of her eldest son. She first met him when he was peddling from door to door a book written by his father called "Toronto Doctor," which from the innuendo in her voice appeared to be a scurrilous and pornographic work. She then described a peculiar relationship with this boy in which he stated that he had a crush on her and that he hated his mother. He hates her because she is over affectionate and her love is incestuous. He and # 70's boy had run out of gas one night and early the next morning # 201 brought over the gallon of gas to put in the car. She said, "You didn't have to do that." He said, "I only did it for you. I have a crush on you." She said he is suffering from acne and girls often would not go out with him. His comment on this was, "I don't blame them." Yet when a girl goes by he "simply drools" and makes detailed comments about her figure. When somebody offers to introduce him to her he says, "oh, don't do that, she will know I asked." In reporting this # 70 made the following slip. Instead of saying "she will know I asked her," she said, "I will know he asked her," whatever that means.[342]

While on the one hand the sexually frustrated housewives of Forest Hill may have fantasized about their teen-age son's friends, not all the boys were so naive as to seek their sexual education through relationships with the local moms. The culture of gender segregation in Toronto had left behind a long tradition of men going downtown for work and for play. Indeed, it was the practice of Prime Minister William Lyon Mackenzie-King during his younger days in Toronto to regularly indulge in this sort of "night-walking." The following excerpt sets the reality of the wartime problems of prostitution and venereal disease within the naive discourse of the fifties:

> Mrs. Marcus asked Alan (her son) if they had been given any talks on venereal disease, and how to protect themselves against the possibility.
> Alan: Mom, the boys know all about that. There's hardly any of that around here.
> Mrs Marcus: How about when the lads go to these so called houses, do they call them cat houses?
> Alan: When the boys go, they go together and to a place they know is all right. The boys wouldn't take us to just any place. Yes! They are sometimes called cat houses. The girls are all checked regularly, anyhow.[343]

But the sexual adventures of the fifties were not all about prostitution and porn. The Forest Hill Village Project researchers came across many examples of adultery amongst the "moral and monogamous" couples Seeley claimed were characteristic of Forest Hill Village:

> <u>Unfaithful Wife</u>
> The facts in this case revolve around retaliation, for the husband had been having an affair whilst in Winnipeg. During this time, his wife was in Toronto, having an abortion. The reason for the latter was purely economic. This was her third such operation. She had been suspicious, for whilst they were both in Winnipeg, he had been paying a great deal of attention to the "other woman." The latter was unmarried. When he returned back to live in Toronto, his wife asked him point blank, and he admitted that he had been living with the "other woman" all the while his wife was here, a matter of months. Evidently, apart from normal reactions, the wife had suffered a great deal and was quite ill as the result of the operation. She resented the fact that he was so carelessly having a very enjoyable time. Months after his return, she met someone to whom she was attracted and eventually met him at a hotel. Her action was deliberative. It happened the once, and that was that. She says it did not help at all and she is very sorry that she was so foolish, but at the time it seemed the only thing that would purge her. Whether she told her husband or whether he found out, I don't know, but she did say he knows about it. The wife is now 39 and the husband is 48. They have a two year old child, on whom they both dote. This affair happened about ten or twelve years ago, as far as I was able to judge. They appear to be happy, have

many interests in common. The most devouring interest being politics, and following closely with music and the arts.[344]

The darkness here, it would seem, was in the felt powerlessness of the "unfaithful wife." From our perspective today it might seem that she was too faithful in her response to her husband's insensitivity. Yet the forces behind her guilt and her loyalty in these circumstances were hidden. If we think back to the *Toronto Star* article about what was expected from a Forest Hill Village wife, we might imagine that the economic importance of keeping up appearances was what drove this woman's ultimate acceptance of her husband's behavior. In the following case of adultery, the wife is better able to articulate the psychological price she paid for her willingness to repress her marital disappointment:

<u>Unfaithful Husband</u>
Accidently, I discovered that my husband had been unfaithful to me. It came to light nine years after the incident, which in no way lessened the shock. A chance remark of his—"Imagine Mr. Blank has been married for 15 years and has never been unfaithful." His incredulity amazed me, because I was naïve enough to believe that most husbands were faithful, especially mine. I brooded for days and nights. In casual talks during the years we had both discussed what we might do if faithlessness on either side were discovered. I'd always said, so glibly, that I was sure I would understand and forgive. It seemed to me that it had to be a thing of the moment, a temptation, desire, all of which would not mean that my husband had stopped loving me, or even loved me less. After a few days I decided to challenge him. I knew a great deal was at stake and I also realized it might break our marriage. One evening, with a carefully rehearsed speech, and whilst having a midnight snack, I recited my lines. I told him I had good reason to believe that he had been unfaithful to me. He turned a deep red and to me, looked guilty as sin. He replied, "I have been, but it was many years ago." I expected it, but I shook like a leaf. Regaining my composure, I asked him if it had occurred often. No, just the once. It didn't really matter then, once or often, all I felt was a deep desire to hurt and hurt deeply. I said, "Then that makes us even." Not a word was said while both of us tried to drink our coffee, cups rattling from nervous fingers. What I had said was a lie, and after a few moments I began to feel nervous lest he really believe it, so fumbling along, I tried to clarify the matter by telling him that my lapses were mental and physical—saying that it was almost the same. He said there was no comparison and that it was

very natural to dream about individuals and to picture situations etc. I let him talk on, wanting desperately to be as big as I thought I was. I tried, really tried. Two miserable people retired to their separate beds. Neither slept all night. Early the following morning, having told myself that I could not go on living if it weren't on good terms with my husband, I hopped into his bed and invited the only course that could make us one again. I was proud of my so-called bigness and even felt happy, but it didn't last long. I would start thinking again, and the realization that he had lied to me would nag, then I thought of my or our way of life and how wonderful and complete it had been. I had felt secure, but that had altered. I was unsure and shaky. All this happened years ago. Admittedly, I have never really forgotten. I have tried very hard to resume life as though nothing had happened. In truth, it is my own private cancer. I sometimes picture him, in a hotel room, with a woman, nude, in a variety of positions. I know I shall never forget nor possibly forgive. It's like black spot in my life.[345]

The negative social effects of masculine autocracy in the fifties must have resonated out into the community, for the unhappiness of the women would have taken its toll on the children.

Another central topic of concern to the woman of Forest Hill was menstruation. The Forest Hill women ranged in their discussion of this topic from the effect of the "change of life" on women's interest in sex, to speculation on whether men themselves also go through some form of the same experience. In this context, stories of sexual failure and adventure poured out of the informants. One woman related how, after many years of frustration, just as she had finally reached the point of being able to enjoy sexual relations with her husband, he became impotent:

My husband was a real animal in his younger days. I loathed sex life and he didn't give a damn how I felt. I never enjoyed it, until I was married a long time. I guess I must have been 33 or 34 (having been married 13 or 14 years) before I knew anything about an orgasm. Even then I didn't yearn for intercourse or want it as often as I had to submit. When I was about 38 and my husband was 40, I went to England, alone, and was away for 3 months. Upon my return, my husband met me at the dock, took me home, and could hardly wait until I took my coat off. It was in the afternoon and I told him not to be so silly, but he insisted. I was so ashamed. Nothing happened, however, and then he was ashamed—and I was glad, glad, glad. Since then, and that's a very early age, he has been almost useless. No! He took about a year or was it two, but I can really say since then he has been useless. I often think of my own ignorance of sex, and regret that just when I was beginning to appreciate sexual intercourse, my husband was incapable. I often suspect him of chasing around a lot in his younger days, and, so, it serves him right. I am now fifty-seven, and I don't care anyways.[346]

In a very poignant vignette, another woman spoke of her friend's despair over the loss of her son and the impact of this event on her relations with her husband:

She told me years ago that she was looking forward to the Change of Life hoping it meant the end of sex life. The loss of a brilliant 14 year old son from a brain tumor had a great deal to do with her attitudes and reactions.[347]

It was at points such as these that the descent into mental illness for the women of Forest Hill began. In the following conversation between two Village women named Lillian and Muriel, we see most vividly what form this illness often took. The note-taker first introduces us to Muriel, who was suffering from a terrible depression long before the availability of effective medication that might have helped her:

Muriel is a woman of forty-two, married to a very fine young man—they are financially very secure. They have a ten year old daughter. Her parents were cousins. The mother suffered a mental depression following the birth of the last child. Muriel started feeling very depressed about 18 months ago. She finally went to a psychiatrist. She visited him three times a week. She goes nowhere, sees no one, and doesn't seem to care about anything at all.[348]

The note-taker then recounts a conversation between Lillian and Muriel over the phone about her husband Al:

Tell me Muriel, is Al patient; do you feel he is understanding?
I don't know. You see, it's really in reverse, I think.
You mean he's going through the change?
Yes, it happens to men too.
Yes, I know, do you and Al discuss it, talk about it and wonder about it together?
Listen Lillian, I'm not capable of listening or understanding for more than 2 seconds. I'm just in a fog, a deep freeze. Al talks to me, but I don't follow. I can't concentrate, and then he falls asleep. He's fed up. I have another pain or ache every day, and I nag, nag, nag. He has every right to be fed up.

Muriel, maybe he's trying to help and to understand—he may be going about it in the wrong way, but trying anyways.
Perhaps, but there's a tension in the house.
Do you have much company in the house, the family etc.?
No, no one comes around anymore. I don't feel up to it, and I can't listen to anyone—I just sink down under my fog.
Well I certainly hope you will be feeling better soon.
Thanks Lillian but this has been going on I guess for five or six years, and I'm not really getting better. This fog, I just can't clear it.
Would you and Al like to pop in tonight for a while?
I haven't been out in six months—yes I think I would. I'll speak to Al and call you back.
8 pm Al had a meeting.
Well you come up and Al can pick you up later?
No, he won't be in until very late, and anyways I'm in bed for the night. Thanks.
All right Muriel, but perhaps one evening we will go out for dinner and have fun, just like old times.
I'd like that if I'm able to. Thanks for calling and for listening. Bye![349]

Again and again in these stories, we see how the women of Forest Hill suffered under the restricted conditions of their suburban lives. They were isolated to their homes, forced into almost slavish conditions in relations with their husbands, and all the while seemingly helpless in regard to finding a solution to their problems. This took its toll on their mental health, and probably also returned in its own way to punish their children.

These women turned for help to medical experts like Seeley. Unfortunately, these experts were also men who shared the same sense of power and privilege as their husbands. Moreover, Seeley, who was promising the people of Forest Hill an educational utopia in which such mental health issues might be resolved, was faced with symptoms of his own. Just as Seeley's identity issues may have made it difficult for him to fully explore the ethnic tensions in Forest Hill, so might the emotional trauma he experienced in his relations with his parents have interfered with his sensitivity to certain psychological issues, especially the plight of women in suburbia.

In a letter to Fischer, Seeley described his private life at the time as if he were himself a character in the blackest of the film noir genre: "It is just there," he writes, "on its small scale, our obscure lives, total tragedy with no one and nothing visibly at fault."[350] This leads us to an exploration of Seeley's own mental health issues during the writing-up period of the Forest Hill Village Project, and his attempt to wrestle with his demons through psychoanalysis.

# Unorthodox Psycho-Analysis

Beatrice Fischer and John R. Seeley in her Home, 1990s. Courtesy of Beatrice Fischer.

Beatrice told me in an interview that "Jack loved the word analysand." She was sitting with me by an upstairs window looking out over expansive gardens that recede into a deep ravine. We were reading together Seeley's eulogy to her husband, Martin Fischer. She read out loud the following passage:

> Psychoanalysis is a long and costly process. It is not out of the way now for two thousand or more hours of talk to pass between analyst and analysand (nearly all the analysands talk). And the process is surrounded, first on the analyst's side and then on both, by an unremitting devotion to the discovery

of truth, and again on the side of the analyst, by an invariant showing of faith in (and love for) the analysand.[351]

We both shared a laugh over the verbosity of Seeley's idealized account of psychoanalysis. I said it was "windy," but she went further exclaiming, "windy city." She said that Seeley loved the sound of his own rhetoric. The resonance of the word analysand for Seeley may have been related to its association for him with the memory of his lifelong colleague and friend. It was in his capacity as Fischer's analysand that Seeley felt he had been "returned from the grave."[352]

It is singular, however, that this blending of the roles of colleague, friend and "analysand" materialized in the relationship between Fischer and Seeley. They met as colleagues working at the U of T Department of Psychiatry. In fact, according to Seeley, it was because of his influence that Fischer was hired by the Department of Psychiatry at U of T as its first psychoanalyst, even though officially this had been done by the new Head of the Toronto Psychiatric Hospital, Aldwyn Stokes:

> In hiring professionals to staff the TPH, Dr. Stokes' eclecticism was very evident. For example, he appointed the first psychoanalyst to the University of Toronto, Dr. Martin Fischer. His first professionally trained social worker, Morton Teicher, was lured from the Philadelphia Child Guidance Clinic, and sociologist Jack Seeley was also appointed. As interest was high in social psychiatry in the 1960s (as it had been in psychoanalysis in the 1950s), Dr. Stokes hired people from various disciplines to establish a therapeutic community approach.[353]

On the one hand, there are reasons to accept Seeley's claim considering the star status that he had achieved in the eyes of the senior mandarins at the CNCMH and the Toronto Psychiatric Hospital. Stokes quickly made this brash, brainy young sociologist the centerpiece of his new initiative to broaden the scope of the psychiatric hospital's jurisdiction into the field of social medicine. Perhaps as a *quid pro quo*, Seeley had asked that the Department broaden its horizons by opening up its loopholes in order to hire a Jewish, psychoanalytically oriented psychiatrist like Fischer; for, there were hidden quotas at the University on the number of Jews who could be hired.[354]

While on the one hand, Fischer's experimentation with psychoanalysis may have been, globally speaking, typical of the time; on the other hand, he would likely have been one of the few psychiatrists in Toronto to have such an interest. As we have seen, the leadership at the Toronto Psychiatric Hospital and the Department of Psychiatry from C. K. Clarke to C. B. Farrar was notoriously resistant to psychoanalysis. It was not until Robyn Hunter, who became a founding member and training analyst with the Canadian Institute of Psychoanalysis in 1967, and at the same time accepted an appointment as successor to Aldwyn Stokes at the U of T Department of Psychiatry, that psychoanalysis gained any legitimacy at all in the inner circles of Toronto psychiatric establishment. According to Doug Frayn, who was a student of Robyn Hunter's and accompanied him from Queen's University to the U of T, there was a very hostile environment to psychoanalysis in Toronto at the time:

> The rumors I had heard about there being intellectual hostility towards depth psychology at the U of T seemed to be confirmed, because whenever the subject of psychoanalysis arose, it was spoken of as an unscientific activity, practiced by unenlightened if not amoral therapists. Studies suggested that being on the waiting list without any treatment was superior to having psychoanalytic therapy, and they saw it as essentially a moribund procedure conducted by a ship of fools. The Clarke associates informed me that my psychoanalytic training at the Toronto Institute of Psychoanalysis could not be considered an academic pursuit. I have found little evidence that there has been any change in this negative attitude by the University's medical school, even now after thirty years.[355]

So, in light of this context of hostility toward psychoanalysis in Toronto, there was some truth in the idea that Fischer was amongst the first psychiatrists to have had an interest in integrating psychoanalytic techniques. What may carry more significance for an understanding of the relationship between Fischer and Seeley, however, was the solidarity they must have felt as they pursued their intuitive preference for psychoanalysis. Perhaps, in part, the under-currents of professional disapproval pushed them toward conducting their psychoanalytic project informally and secretively. Undoubtedly, they felt that the resistance to psychoanalysis in English culture was associated to subtle forms of anti-Semitism that lurked in Canadian society at the time.

Moreover, the plausibility of Seeley's story that he intervened on Fischer's behalf is supported by the natural attraction the two men were likely to have had given their personal backgrounds. They were both from

German-speaking-Jewish families. They were both intellectuals with a dedicated interest in psychoanalysis. They were both in Canada as refugees from abusive situations in Europe, though in the case of Seeley his had been a private kind of terror, rather than the more publicly administered Nazi terror that Fischer escaped. Even their differences must have had a magnetic effect. Fischer was from a poor family, while Seeley's family was rich. At six feet tall, with a gracious Viennese accent, the commanding presence of Fischer stood in contrast to the elfin stature of Seeley, who rolled his r's in the fashion of a British aristocrat, and whose faint German accent was barely detectable. Fischer was practical in thought and gesture; Seeley waved his arms, and adorned even the most mundane observations with flowery language. Perhaps most importantly, Seeley was accepted as part of the in-crowd amongst the Toronto medical elite as a British aristocrat, where Fischer struggled to break in from the outside. He wanted to ensure the security of his place in a society he knew was not that different from the one he fled. In other words, these two men were the perfect foils for each other.

Seeley also found a father figure in Fischer. His first memory of Fischer, which he shared with Fischer's daughter Erica, captured this idealized role. She reported that on the car ride back from the cemetery after the burial of Fischer in the winter of 1992, Seeley reminisced about how he had been attending rounds at the Doctors' Hospital near Kensington Market in Toronto, which had been established so that young Jewish doctors could complete internships, when Martin Fischer was called upon to demonstrate psychiatric technique in the treatment of a catatonic child.

Apparently, no one at the hospital had succeeded in getting this child to speak. As Seeley watched in awe, Martin Fischer sat down facing the child and placed his hands on his lap with their palms facing up. The child got up and walked over to Martin Fischer who had undone the buttons on his white coat as a gesture of openness. The boy sat on Fischer's lap and nuzzled inside. From there, the boy could be heard to speak to the Doctor. This memory trace seems more like a dream than historical testimony. The use of the hands gives the story the aura of an eighteenth-century exercise in magnetism in the style of Franz Anton Mesmer. Seeley may have wished he too could hide under the protective cloak of Martin Fischer's strength and courage. The depth of Seeley's transferential feelings for Fischer are revealed in the letter below, written early in their relationship.

*[Handwritten letter:]*

> Mein lieber Martin:
>
> It is only a week — though it seems like a month or more — since you left, and I gather from Beatrice that you arrived safely. I hope the trip is not too hard on you, and that you will soon be back with your mission accomplished and your mother well on the way to recovery.
>
> I have missed you far more even than I would have believed possible. I feel largely in a state of suspended animation —

Letter from Seeley to Fischer, 1952. Fischer Papers, Toronto, Ontario.

Seeley and Fischer's shared interest in psychoanalysis involved them in many joint ventures. Fischer collected Seeley's drafts of sociological articles and Seeley went with Fischer to visit hospitals and group homes for kids like "Warrendale," made famous in Allan King's documentary *Warrendale* which won the International Critics Prize at the Cannes Film Festival in 1967. It may be worth noting that the timing of their sessions in Fischer's appointment books often coincided with visits to Warrendale.[356] Fischer founded Warrendale to explore group psychotherapy modalities as part of his work with teen agers in cooperation with the "Grey Nuns" of Ontario. Indeed, Fischer was a amongst the first pioneers of group psychotherapy in Canada: "Group therapy in Canada was established through the efforts of early group advocates and practitioners, such as Fern Cramer-Azima (Montreal), William Powles (Kingston), and Martin Fischer, Violet Head, and Yvonne Shaker (Toronto)."[357] Seeley was never so bold as to claim that he and Fischer were the North American equivalent of Freud and Jung, but their experimentation with group psychotherapy at Warrendale and Forest Hill Collegiate was highly innovative.

The question remains, however, whether a description of Seeley's confessions to Fischer could realistically be called a "psychoanalysis." On the one hand, the casual and intermittent nature of their "sessions" calls

Seeley's claims in this regard into question. Given the nature of their social relationship which involved personal, collegial and family get-togethers at the office, the park, at home and in restaurants, it would have been very difficult to determine when a session had begun or ended.

There are sporadic therapy "process notes" recording meetings between Fischer and Seeley for the months of September 1952 through January 1953. They do not contain any diagnostic or even interpretive work on Fischer's part, but merely indicate that they are transcriptions of Seeley's "free associations." Many of the otherwise blank pages on which these "process notes" are recorded were undated and could record sessions held at later times. The informality and personal context of the Fischer-Seeley sessions raises the question whether these "process notes" might be more accurately referred to as the record of Seeley's "confessions," than as a medical record. Nevertheless; setting aside the fact that Seeley directed me to the Fischer's and Beatrice consented to my use of the Fischer Files *in toto*; I have not referred to the contents of the "process notes" in order to respect the ethical principle of psychiatrist-patient confidentiality, which may extend beyond death. Whether or not there are legal prohibitions involved is even more dubious, and eventually with the passage of time, and of Seeley's descendants, all such constraints will fall away. A potential loss to history of this censure would only occur if the records do not survive.[358]

In addition to the "process notes" of their early sessions, the correspondence thereafter between them, and the recollections of Beatrice Fischer, would suggest that Fischer and Seeley held irregular meetings in Toronto, and perhaps also during visits to New York, Indianapolis, Los Angeles or other American cities that Seeley lived in over the course of his nomadic lifestyle. Fischer and Seeley also corresponded by mail and over the phone throughout their lives. The following is a letter Seeley wrote to Fischer in 1966 from Los Angeles, which reveals how casual the psychoanalytically oriented exchange between them was:

> Dear Martin,
> Had a unique dream—the first one ever about Frank. He was on my back, digging his knuckles most painfully into my spine. I was running, trying to shake him off, and biting his little finger. He dug harder, I bit harder. I had to decide whether to bite as hard as I could. He hurt more, I decided and bit, and bit as hard as I could—down to the bone.
> I woke up, not dissatisfied.

Will you interpret? Phone me at home, collect,

Love, Jack[359]

Perhaps that is why, as Beatrice Fischer recounted with frustration, Martin Fischer once said to her, "Don't make him pay," as she struggled to manage her husband's accounts.[360] During our interviews in which we discussed the Fischer Papers, Beatrice was surprised to learn that there was any record of payments having been made by Seeley at all. Her recollection was that Seeley would always arrange informal meetings with Martin in order to continue their psychoanalysis, but not have to pay. She had always been very suspicious about these attempts, in her eyes, to avoid making payments because, she said, "he was cheap" and "a fraud."[361]

In the next breath, however, Beatrice would share fond memories of his very friendly relations with her children. A vignette of Seeley with her four kids in a *Vunelleh*, or bathtub, in the backyard flashed across her mind at one point during an interview.

Indeed, if we look at the sardonic tone of the following letter we very well might suspect that payments made to Fischer were, in fact, more for Beatrice's sake than for Martin's:

> Here is Beatrice's pin money for February. Pretty big pin! Now you've put it on that basis I'm going to feel like a heel when the payments quit. Visions of Beatrice and the children in rags—or, the modern day equivalent, unable to afford a good psychiatrist. When are you coming to Indianapolis? We are saving a special bottle for the happy event.[362]

At another time Seeley sent a letter addressed to both Martin and Beatrice with regard to payments:

> Dear Martin and Beatrice, Another little blue slip—but not many more to come (how many by the way?). How are things going? And when are you coming to see us—both of you? We think of you often and fondly. 'Jack'[363]

In addition to this and the other evidence of boundary-crossing between the professional and personal realm in the Fischer-Seeley relationship, the physical context in which the "Seeley" file was kept in Martin Fischer's basement also becomes noteworthy. The file marked "Seeley" was quite independently located in a rather empty filing cabinet, unattached to any patient files, or other professional papers. Its contents were also quite unique. In addition to the notes of their conversations which were often undated, it also included personal letters that Seeley had sent Fischer over the course of many years. In addition, there were letters that Seeley had written to his brother and mother; letters and cards sent by his wife Margaret addressed to either or both of Martin and Beatrice Fischer; drafts of articles, and even a draft for a preliminary chapter in *Crestwood Heights;* intra-departmental memoranda addressed from Seeley to others including Aldwyn Stokes; and finally, there were also copies of poems that Seeley had written, some in German.

In fact, the very personal nature of the Fischer-Seeley relationship is verified by Erica Fischer, Martin's eldest daughter, who said that Seeley was her father's "only real friend."[364] Otherwise, his time was consumed with his work and to a subordinate extent with his family, which included his wife and their five children. When questioned by me as to why her husband would agree to informal meetings with Seeley at airports, coffee shops, and for walks in the park, Beatrice responded simply that Martin enjoyed the intellectual dialogue. Attraction to Seeley as an intellectual sounding-board was not uncommon. Many men including Murray Ross, Clayton Ruby, and Rick Salutin, were also mesmerized by Seeley's intellect. Members of the Fischer family fondly remember Seeley's eulogy: "Martin is my dearest friend," Seeley said, "—and both my son and my father."[365]

In addition to the very personal nature of their relationship, a further problem in regard to the authenticity of Seeley's "psychoanalysis" was that Fischer never actually undertook his own psychoanalysis. This is particularly surprising given that he was a member of the original Toronto Psychoanalytic Study Circle founded in 1956, along with Drs. Parkin, Schiffer and Thomson who were to become founding members of the Toronto Psychoanalytic Institute in 1969. As part of that germinal group Fischer attended regular Wednesday evening meetings, presumably in honor of the meetings Freud had held of the original group in Vienna.

Fischer wrote a letter in 1958 requesting an application form for psychoanalytic training to Johann Aufreiter, who had joined the Montreal Psychoanalytic Institute as an émigré from Vienna.[366] Aufreiter had done his own training analysis with August Aichorn, a principal member of Freud's Wednesday night group meetings. One would think this would have been of great interest to Fischer, but the training analysis was never undertaken. Perhaps with five small children and a busy practise in Toronto, Fischer just did not have the time for regular travel to Montreal.

Erica Fischer suggested that her father had never wanted to undertake his own analysis. She said that that he was not a very introspective type of person! Perhaps having already qualified as a medical psychiatrist, Fischer was reluctant to pursue further training. Fischer was able to teach courses to psychiatric residents at U of T by 1948 in psychodynamics without further psychoanalytic qualifications.

According to Beatrice, however, the reality was that Fischer was formally rejected as an unsuitable candidate by one of the founding training analysts with the Canadian Psychoanalytic Society, Nathan B. Epstein. Beatrice's recollection of this rejection was that her husband had been terribly angered by it. Beatrice remembers that the reasons given by Epstein had been that Fischer was not, "ready for," or, "accessible to," psychoanalysis.[367]

We might rule out anti-Semitism as a motivation for Epstein's rejection of Fischer, since both men were Jewish, but this does leave us with one other possible explanation. Perhaps, in the course of a training analysis already being undertaken between Epstein and Fischer, the boundary violations that the latter had already committed by the late 1950s in his relationship with Seeley were revealed. Indeed, Fischer's "flexibility" as a psychiatrist was far-reaching. For example, Erica said that rather than make a taxi driver pay for sessions, he would offer therapy during rides to and from work. This approach may have raised concerns amongst early leaders of psychoanalysis like Epstein who were likely very protective of the reputation of their controversial new profession.

There is other evidence in the Fischer Papers of an unorthodox quality in Fischer's approach to psychiatry. For example, his appointment records indicate that he used electro-convulsive therapy (E.C.T.) with some patients. He was certainly not alone during this period, and ECT is still widely accepted as an effective treatment, but psychiatric applications in the fifties and sixties, prior to the routine use of anesthesia and the establishment of contemporary standards for informed consent, became a quite controversial focus of concern for the anti-psychiatry movement in the seventies.[368] It is interesting to note that (aside from the fact that Fischer's c's look like g's as proven by the writing of the word "Charges") an appointment with Seeley comes right after the use of E.C.T with another patient. This raises the question as to whether Fischer and Seeley also experimented with E.C.T during their sessions?

Fischer's Appointment Book, Fischer Papers, Toronto, Ontario.

One other sign of Fischer's unorthodoxy is an undated letter in the Fischer Papers, written in the hand of Seeley, in which Fischer complains of injustice at having been forced to resign as the head of the psychiatric service at Mt. Sinai Hospital. According to Erica, Fischer's resignation was prompted by his objections to a decision by hospital administrators to cancel free clinics at a time when there was no public health insurance. Fischer turned to his friend Seeley to bring to bear his great expressive skills in the writing of the resignation letter:

> I would be dishonest if I did not say that I would have wished to carry to completion or at least a stage further the work I have begun and carried along so far. I say "would have wished" because from my conversation with Dr. Kohan, the continued holding of the wish has been made impossible. Without even arguing that it is just, or indicating that it is in some demonstrable way to the best interest of the service or the hospital, he has advised me that my interests would be best served by my resigning. He adds that the M. A. C. has recommended against reappointment in any case, and that the lay board automatically (!) endorses such recommendations. In effect, I have, without a semblance of judicial or judicious process, been asked to resign under the contention that the alternative consequences would be worse.[369]

The fact of the writing of this letter by Seeley on behalf of Fischer is almost as interesting as what its contents reveal. It illustrates the close collegial and friendly relationship between the two men. It also may help to explain their feelings of being isolated and under siege as Jewish intellectuals committed to psychoanalysis in a Gentile dominated system of institutions that had little tolerance for "free association" of any kind.

At another level, however, it is possible that Fischer's unorthodoxies as a psychiatric practitioner had again got him into trouble with the authorities in the field. In Fischer's defense, however, it was not until the 1980s that the Canadian Medical Association had begun to work on an annotated Code of Ethics for Psychiatrists which clarified many of the ambiguities around doctor-patient relationships in terms of consent, experimentation, and exploitation. It is interesting to note in this regard that the <u>1996 CMA Code of Ethics Annotated for Psychiatrists</u>, states that "the nature of the psychiatrist-patient relationship generally precludes the psychiatric treatment of anyone whose personal or family history is familial knowledge."[370] Clearly, then, the relationship between Fischer and Seeley would be viewed as unethical by present-day standards. But is it fair to apply present standards to past situations?

Jacalyn Duffin, in her book entitled *Langstaff: A Nineteenth Century Medical Life*, argued against such anachronism. She published the names and details about the suffering of Langstaff's psychiatric patients, pointing out that these were "one hundred years old." To transpose her argument, we might question whether the imposition of twenty-first-century standards of confidentiality, and of "what diagnoses might have been (or would have been) "sensitive," on a mid-twentieth-century-psychoanalysis, "borders on hubris?"[371]

We have seen that David Riesman's psychoanalysis with Erich Fromm was also irregular in comparison to today's expectations. Like Fischer and Seeley they were as much friends and colleagues, as doctor and patient, over the course of their whole lives. It may have been that in this early stage of its development, with its relationship to medical psychiatry as yet uncertain, psychoanalysis was thought of in the early 1940s and 1950s as something far more private and experimental than a medical treatment. From this perspective it was perhaps the threat of the professionalization of psychoanalysis; especially in Toronto where the medical establishment had a long history of alignment with eugenicist and bio-chemical approaches; that made Fischer unpopular.

Seeley said that Fischer was controversial because of his interest in ways to address the problem of the individualized focus of psychoanalysis. He wanted to reach more people with the technique, and this was why he sought to apply it in the form of group therapy. It was perhaps also why he conducted his psychoanalytic experiment after hours with Seeley. Martin Fischer was so motivated to create opportunities for self-expression for others, Seeley suggested, that he perhaps could have been criticized for not having spent enough time with his family. Comments by members of the family in regard to his frequent absence due to his workload, would seem to bear out Seeley's observation, but do not explain the behavior in terms of its historical antecedents. For such an explanation, we must undertake a digression into Fischer's past as a Holocaust survivor.

# Nazi Terror

Martin A. Fischer was born on the 22 of May 1913 in a small town, then in eastern Poland, now in the Ukraine, that was known as Kamionka-Strumilowa, which historically had a large Jewish population.[372] His parents Mr. Effraim Fischer and his wife Sara left Poland for Vienna in 1920 at the end of the Great War. His parents were not wealthy. According to Fischer's school records at the University of Vienna, his father was a "plumber's assistant."[373] Fischer told his wife Beatrice that he was no ordinary plumber. Rather, he was an "artist in the design of plumbing parts."

Beatrice remembers her husband's mother in similarly glorified terms as a woman who could do no wrong. Sara Fischer was completely devoted to her three sons, Martin being the oldest. Fischer himself referred to his mother as, "Meiner selige Mutter," my sainted mother. He was crushed by the way the tragic events of the Holocaust affected her.

Up until the time of the Anschluss, Fischer had progressed successfully through school to the fifth year of his studies at the Medical School of the University of Vienna. Fischer was an observant Jew, who in his youth was active in the "Students' Aid Committee of the Kultusgemeinde in Vienna as a representative of the Judea Students' Organization."[374] In this capacity, Fischer sought to sell Sigmund Freud tickets to a B'nai Brith dance, but Freud's busy schedule had forced him to decline the offer. Though he had artistic talents, having spent much time, for example, sketching the works of Michelangelo on his frequent visits to Italy, Freud acknowledged his more limited aptitude for music. He may therefore have shied away from the dance, but in any case he was gracious enough to send his regrets in writing to the Fischer boy along with a cheque for the purchase of two tickets *in absentia*. Somehow, Fischer managed to retain this letter throughout his family's travails during the Holocaust and to this day it holds a special place in the Fischer library.

Dr. Douglas Frayn, a former Director of the Toronto Institute of Psychoanalysis, offered a quite different interpretation of Freud's interest in the tickets to the dance: "My guess is that the dance tickets were for Lou Andreas Salome and Anna Freud. Lou often visited the Freud's and was the only follower allowed to attend Freud's Wednesday night group, as well as Adler's Monday group. She loved to dance and party and particularly to bring August Aichorn to Freud's for dinner despite Freud's admonition to her request—'Why do you always ask for the Goy to come?'" Anna Freud had an interest in August Aichorn, Frayn suggested.[375]

There are other signs of an early interest on Fischer's part in psychoanalysis. He studied psychiatry and neurology for two terms as part of his medical program at the University of Vienna between the years 1933 and 1938. Fischer notes the details of this practicum on an information sheet he sent to the Canadian National Committee for Mental Hygiene to be used for a "Biographical Directory of Canadian Psychiatrists." Though the form is not dated, it must have been submitted sometime after Fischer's certification as a psychiatrist in 1947 by the U of T. In the space on the form set for information regarding "Professional experience," Fischer writes: "Internship at the Psychiatric Clinic of the Viennese General Hospital, 1937."[376]

Though Freud himself was elderly and ill with cancer by 1937, certainly psychoanalysis had a great influence on the work of psychiatrists in Vienna at that time. For example, the Chair of the Department of Psychiatry was Dr. Otto Pötzl. He succeeded Freud's erstwhile colleague and competitor Wagner-Jauregg in 1928, and remained in the position until 1945. Pötzl conducted experimental research designed to prove the empirical validity of Freud's theory of the unconscious. In June 1917 he delivered a paper on the theme of experimentally provoked dream images as an illustration of Freudian dream analysis. Six months later he was admitted as a member of the Vienna Psychoanalytic Society and retained this membership until 1933. In a letter to Freud, Pötzl wrote: "I cannot imagine my teaching work without psychoanalysis. My audience and I are your fervent supporters."[377] Surely, Fischer too was infected with this enthusiasm for Freud's intrepid intellectual adventures as a young student of psychiatry in Vienna. If nothing else, the straight path he follows toward a psychiatric career as a refugee in Canada and the importance he attaches to Freudian approaches over the course of his career would suggest that this had been the case. One could interpret his career as a pioneering Canadian psychiatrist as nostalgic.

Beatrice joked that her husband was a born psychoanalyst who emerged from the womb with a beard and a note-pad ready for the first patient!³⁷⁸

However, like his parents before him, who had left Poland in the aftermath of World War I, Fischer was forced to leave Vienna and pursue his studies in psychiatry in Canada as a consequence of the events of World War II. He might very well have found himself continuing his studies at the Hebrew University in Israel but for the deportation of his brother David to Dachau. Erica Fischer recounts that Fischer's "selige Mutter" persuaded Nazi officials to release his brother, pleading for his removal to Israel where the cost of his upkeep would no longer have to be borne by the German government. She managed to convince them that Martin's scholarship was in fact intended for her younger son. As it was, the Nazi intervention in Austria in March of 1938 forced Fischer out of medical school in the midst of writing his final examinations. He wrote on the *Curriculum Vitae* he typed up for Canadian Authorities in 1940 that, "I was preparing myself for the examinations of the last two Rigorosa, when I was forced by the Nazi Authorities to interrupt my study."³⁷⁹ The trauma of his final day in Medical School in Vienna lends insight into Fischer's determination to ameliorate the conditions in schools in Canada, and also serves as a dramatic reminder of the role of eugenicist medicine in the Holocaust.

Immediately upon the Anschluss having taken effect on March 15, committed Nazi activist Eduard Pernkopf was made Dean of the Vienna Medical School. Pernkopf had joined the Nazi Party Storm Troops in Austria as far back as 1933. He presided over the immediate expulsion of all Jewish Professors and students from the medical school in the months just after the Anschluss. According to the University of Vienna Medical School Memorial Book, Fischer is listed in the category of expelled students:

> Martin Fischer was enrolled finally in the spring term at this medical school in the fourth year of his studies. He could continue his studies in the context of the numerus clausus of Jewish students until the end of the spring term 1938.³⁸⁰

What is perhaps most thought-provoking about Pernkopf's purge was the extent to which such measures were concentrated in the medical faculty rather than other faculties at the University of Vienna:

> Of 770 professors and 221 "Dozenten" (assistant professors), 322 (45%) were forced to leave, most of them within weeks after the German takeover. The

percentage of those in the Faculty who had to leave was significantly larger (78%) than in any other faculty of Vienna or indeed of any university in Europe. For most of the 118 persons evicted, the sole reasons for dismissal were Jewish origin or marriage to a Jewish partner.[381]

It would seem that the priority the Nazi Party placed on controlling the Vienna Medical School reflected the emphasis in their program on eugenics, and in particular, on the culling of the Jewish population in Europe. The implementation of such programs would require both the elimination of Jewish physicians and the indoctrination of the remaining, so called Aryan, staff.

According to Beatrice, one day while Fischer was writing an exam, National Socialist Storm Troopers marched into the school. Fischer and other students at the time referred to these Nazis as "verbrechers," criminals. They forced all of the students to get down on the floor and called for the appearance of a certain professor who handed them a list of the Jewish students who were to be expelled from the school. From his perspective on the floor, Fischer recognized the boots of the man that entered the class, and who handed the list to the "verbrechers," as those of his favourite professor.

Beatrice could not remember the name of that professor, but it may very well have been the infamous Nazi Doctor Hans Eppinger who became notorious for his cruel medical experiments on the condemned at the Dachau concentration camp. According to Fischer's *Curriculum Vitae*, "From 4.1.1937 till 12.3.1938 I practiced as cand. med. at the Allgemeines Krankenhaus Vienna, at the first Medical University Clinic [under the supervision of] Professor Dr. Hans Eppinger, Vienna IX. Lazarettegrasse 14."[382] In his last term at the University of Vienna prior to his expulsion he had been registered in Dr. Eppinger's class in "Internal Medicine."[383]

It is hard to imagine that Fischer could have ever liked Dr. Eppinger who experimented at Dachau on Gypsies. Eppinger wanted to know how long people can live on seawater. The Gypsies who died from dehydration as a result of his experiments were witnessed licking the floor after it had been mopped in the last days before their death. Eppinger committed suicide rather than face sentencing during the Nuremburg Tribunal on War Crimes in 1946. Fischer was not alone in his admiration for Eppinger's medical skills; his fame was so widespread that he was called upon to treat Stalin in 1936.

The list was read out and a struggle ensued between the Jewish students and the "verbrechers." Many of the students actually died in that struggle from being thrown down the stairs. Fischer himself was knocked unconscious by the fall, and was left by the "verbrechers," who did not take the time to distinguish between the living and the dead. When he came to, he managed to get to a streetcar that took him to his parents' apartment. The storm troopers had already been there, following through on their list, and Fischer fled to a nearby wood, the Wiener-Wald. The Vienna Woods is a forested area of the lower Austrian Alps that reaches into Vienna. Fischer hid there in a hut known to his friends, until the cold forced him back to his parents' apartment.

When he returned, Fischer continued the process of arranging emigration for himself and his family to the United States. He must have begun this process soon after expulsion from the Medical School in July, or earlier, because on September 7, 1938 he went along with his father to the US Consulate in Vienna to register for a travel visa. He and his parents had already received affidavits for emigration to the US during August because they had relatives in New York. This must have seemed so promising to them at the time, but little did they know the enemies of their continued family life together were not the Nazis alone, but also the actions of governments in England, Canada and the US; all of whom would succumb to the confusion, fear, and resultant bureaucratic rigidity that accompanies a breakdown of the political order.

At the US Consulate that day, Martin and Ephraim Fischer registered as part of the "Polish Quota" because they were not native Austrians, which meant they had to wait their turn within this restricted group to receive their visas. Sadly, they learned that this process could take two years or more, but that was not the worst of it. According to Erica Fischer, Nazi Storm Troopers opened fire on the crowd that day and again he witnessed the death of innocent members of the "Kultusgemeinde." Though Martin and his father managed to get back to their apartment, they arrived only to be subjected to a bizarre scene of the "verbrechers" arriving later that same day to arrest them both on the charge of illegal possession of a gun that had been planted in the apartment. Martin Fischer's recollections were that a lady in an apartment on a lower floor had served as an informant about their presence in the building. Though these memories may contain some distortions that are inevitable in the recounting of oral history, such as the conflation of events that could have occurred on separate occasions, they are invaluable in giving us a feeling for the desperation of Jewish people in Vienna at this time.

According to the family oral tradition, Martin Fischer and his father were detained in the "Kripo–Leitstelle # 9 building on Rossauer Lande 5–7 in Vienna," the Criminal Police Control Station. By this time the local Austrian Kripo, or Criminal Police, had been integrated with the Gestapo under the ultimate command of senior Nazis in Berlin, and were assigned the responsibility for implementation of the reactionary new racial regime. Erica Fischer remembers her father's reluctant recounting of having been dragged from a large gym-like area where they were held at the Kripo–Leistelle, to an office where he was bludgeoned with the butt of a gun on the head for the impertinence of standing on the carpet. Martin fell to the ground bloodied. In a ruse to psychologically torment the already demoralized prisoner, the "verbrechers," demanded of him: "Are you a socialist"? Martin said, "Yes, I am a socialist."[384] The Kripo then dug through his wallet and found what they thought was evidence that he had worked for the "Judentisch," to gather and distribute food for medical students in need at the University of Vienna. Fischer's punishment for the crimes of being a socialist and a Jew was to be sent to work building roads somewhere near Salzburg *en route* to a concentration camp.

However, he was one of the lucky ones. Before too long, he was selected as part of a group of one hundred unmarried young Jewish men destined for concentration camps that were sold to the Central British Fund for Jewish Refugees in Britain. Fischer's migration through British refugee camps can be followed through documents in relation to his requests to British authorities for release to travel to the United States. According to one document entitled, "Application for Release," Fischer arrived in England on May 1, 1939 at Dover and proceeded from there to the Kitchener Refugee Transit Camp, Richborough, near Sandwich, Kent:[385]

> I was admitted to come to England on ground of the possibility to emigrate to the USA after my turn to go there would become due. My landing permit included the following remark: "S14 Leave is hereby granted at Dover on the condition that the holder proceeds forthwith to Richboro Refugee Camp, registers at once with the police and remains at the Camp until he emigrates."[386]

Kitchener Camp, according to Eric Koch's account in *Deemed Suspect* was a "City of Refuge" maintained by the "Council for German Jewry." Launched at the end of 1938 after the horror of Kristallnacht, it accommodated the men who had been thrown in concentration camps such as Sachsenhausen during the Pogrom only to be released if they could prove that they had an English Visa, as well as those who were in acute danger of being arrested unless they left Germany or Austria immediately. The camp designed to house transients who waited for visas to the United States or other countries, was a self-governing enterprise, and hundreds received agricultural and technical training there.[387]

Tribunals for the review of the status of Germans and Austrians in Britain were set up immediately after war was declared on September 3, 1939 but the public was not in a trusting mood toward enemy aliens. When the war broke out Fischer was interrogated for the purpose of assessing whether or not he might pose a risk to British National Security. The tribunal determined in October 1939 that Martin Fischer was not a threat. He was labeled a Category C "Refugee from Nazi Oppression," in contrast to those identified in Categories A and B who were "deemed suspect."[388] Those classified like Fischer in Category C were originally free to travel. Despite this, as the war intensified with the German invasion of France in 1940, the British government became increasingly concerned that enemy aliens might be planted as fifth columnists amongst the refugee population. Thus, "plans were made to intern all male enemy aliens in Category C between the ages of sixteen and seventy, even the ones who had been completely cleared by the Tribunals."[389]

In the meantime Fischer volunteered and served admirably in the British military. He worked for British intelligence in translating German naval messages to great effect, according to Beatrice Fischer's recollections, even preventing an attack on a British ship. According to his, "Application for Release," Martin Fischer served as a Camp Leader in the Kitchener Camp, and as a "Civilian Leader and responsible for 180 men who were working at the Radio Security Section," where these men were conducting work of "national importance."[390]

Nevertheless, by the summer of 1940 Fischer's internment as a potential fifth columnist, even though he was in fact a determined enemy of the Nazi Regime, led to his deportation along with other enemy aliens to Canada. This was in order to relieve the burden on British Troops of supervising them at a time when there was a real fear of a German invasion across the

English Channel. Rather than travelling to the United States as an émigré, Fischer found himself amongst other Category B and C internees on board the Polish Liner, Sobieski, *en route* to Canada. Upon their arrival, Fischer and the other "prisoners," as they were at first understood by their Canadian guards, had another long wet journey ahead of them to what had previously been called Fort Lennox. This old British Fort dated back to the War of 1812, but had been quickly converted into an island prison replete with barbed wire, watchtowers, and sentries. When they got to the Fort, with their belongings soaked and torn, the sight of another prison camp, which may have conjured memories of the German concentration camps, terrified them once more. This prison-camp for suspected fifth columnists was ironically situated on the, "Isle-of-Nuts (Isle-Aux-Noix)," in the middle of the St Lawrence River. Fischer hastened to point this out with a rare flash of humor in a letter to his brothers who had managed to escape Vienna for Israel.

Letter from Fischer to his Brothers, March 31, 1941. Fischer Papers, Toronto, Ontario.

Martin Fischer recollected that, "The desperation was global on that first night, people were crying; they were breaking down."[391] Again Fischer was forced into a leadership role:

> He had been singled out as the camp leader, not only because he spoke English, but because, as apparently the authorities quickly discovered, he had already performed special duties in the Kitchener Camp in England.[392]

It was in his role as leader at Camp I in the early1940s during the dark days of World War II that Fischer confirmed for himself his calling as a therapist. The treatment of the prisoners in the Camp was relatively humane in terms of the availability of food, recreational opportunities and books. It was the psychological distress caused by indefinite internment while a Holocaust was being inflicted on their relatives and friends in Europe that at times verged on being intolerable.

In addition to their powerlessness in relation to what was going on overseas, these men were concerned that Canadian authorities were misunderstanding their situation. In the following letter to Canadian authorities of August 3, 1940, within weeks of their arrival, Fischer communicated the concerns of his fellow inmates about their status:

> We understand from a big sign put on the wall of our House today that we are considered and described as "Prisoners of War" (Kriegsgefangene), a statement against which we must protest. We do not know whether there are two sorts of Internment Camps and different regulations for Prisoners of War and Civilian Internees. In any case, we must maintain that we are Refugees from Nazi Oppression and certainly not prisoners of war in any sense of the word—a fact which is known to the officers in charge of Internment Camp I but possibly not to all authorities concerned. A simple investigation would prove that there is not the slightest reason to consider us, and consequently treat us, as Prisoners of War or possible fifth columnists. Should such an investigation be omitted, we are very afraid we would not only be treated as Prisoners of War as long as the war may last, but would also have to face all legal and political consequences resulting from such a status. We might even be put at the disposal of the German government just the same as a regular German soldier taken prisoner, as it is usual at the end of the war. To this we beg to point out that we are Jews without exception, that we were forced to flee from Germany after most of us had been kept in German concentration camps for months. It is not our intention to return to Germany under any

circumstances. In the name of justice and human rights we beg you to take note of our present protest, to pass it on to the British authorities competent, to recognize our particular position as Refugees from Nazi Oppression, and to have our status rectified accordingly. Thanking you in anticipation, we beg to remain, very respectfully yours, Martin Fischer.[393]

In the letter of 1941 to his brothers in Israel, quoted earlier, Fischer alludes to the fact that he had achieved some progress by that time in gaining recognition by Canadian authorities of the real situation of these poor refugees whose unjust internment at the hands of Nazi, British and Canadian authorities was dragging on into its third or fourth years. "Being regarded as refugees now, we are permitted to receive visitors," Fischer wrote.[394]

The primary stressor during his internment at Camp I on the Isle-aux-Noix, was Fischer's inability to contact and help his parents who remained stranded in Vienna under the "Nazi terror" as he described it in his letters. Indeed, the central focus of the stream of letters and documents that Martin Fischer sent to relatives, friends and government officials from Camp I was the effort to get his parents out of Austria. His anxiety about his parents is revealed in the following letter sent just months after his arrival at Camp I on December 15, 1940. He plead for help in getting a new affidavit for his parents to emigrate to the United States:

> You will undoubtedly realize the terrible situation my parents are in. Their hope for rescue which kept their spirit to endure the ruthless persecution by the Nazis is now gone. Robbed of their property, deprived of their home, separated from their three sons, suffering from starvation and cold they have now to continue to stand the brutal and barbarous Nazi terror. Unfortunately, being interned myself, I cannot do anything to mitigate their fate.[395]

Even toward the end of his internment at Camp I Fischer was still struggling with his powerlessness about his parents' situation. This was reflected in the following excerpt from a letter to his brothers:

> First, I should like to inform you that according to letters of September 3rd and September 9th, which I received the other day, our dearest parents are alright. Father is still working with the Kultusgemeinde. Unfortunately, since there is no American Consulate there anymore, it is impossible for them to get a visa right now, though I succeeded in getting a new affidavit for them. Even the Schneider family who have already got ship tickets are still there, and as mother reports, there is no telling when they will have a chance

to leave, since they have to get a new visa. Still the danger of an imminent deportation is always present for our dearest ones and all others there. I am really trying my very best to help them, but being interned myself, I am not able to do more at present.[396]

It would not be until early in 1942, as a result of the intervention of a sympathetic Jewish-Canadian visitor to Camp I, that Fischer would be released and sponsored to continue his medical studies at U of T. He described his good fortune in the letter to his brothers in this way:

> There will perhaps be a chance for me of being released in Canada to complete my studies at one of the Canadian Universities. As a matter of fact, a very influential gentleman whom I happened to meet at our camp is very much interested in me and told the immigration authorities that he is willing to pay everything and to take full responsibility for me until I get my degree. He also made an application for release for me. It would be simply wonderful if it works out alright. Being a free man I could do a lot more for our dearest parents.[397]

The helpful visitor was a wealthy Jewish businessman from Toronto by the name of Ben Sadowsky. Fischer turned his attention immediately upon release to the needs of his parents. It was still possible to receive letters from Vienna in the early years of the war. However, Fischer did not learn of his parents' survival for an excruciatingly long period after the end of hostilities. Of the over 200, 000 Jews who had inhabited Vienna prior to the Anschluss, less than 5, 000 remained in the city at the end of the war. Most had either emigrated like Fischer and his brothers, or been subject to the deportations to death camps in the east.[398]

Luckily, Fischer's parents had been amongst the few Jewish survivors of the war in Vienna. According to Beatrice's recollections, Sara Fischer had been chosen by the Kultusgemeinde to control the supply of food in the Jewish Ghetto in Vienna and this role may have saved her life.[399] After the war, through Martin Fischer's organizational efforts, his parents were able to travel to Israel for a happy reunion with their younger sons. In the context of such a long struggle for survival and reunification, it is tragic that Fischer's "selige Mutter" died from complications after surgery in Israel in 1948. He had traveled all the way there to see her through what should have been a relatively minor operation.

Eventually, with the support of Ben Sadowsky's sponsorship, Fischer graduated from medical school at U of T in 1943. In 1944 he married Beatrice Shapiro, a lovely and articulate Jewish woman who was from Woodstock, Ontario. Her father, a tailor, owned a menswear shop. He had moved his family from New York to Woodstock to escape the deadly Spanish Influenza pandemic of 1918. In a letter she sent to Fischer's parents in Vienna in 1945, Beatrice boasted that she had won his heart even though he "wasn't at all interested in girls."[400] Instead, he was focused on his youthful ambition to become a psychiatrist. He succeeded in 1947, when he became a certified specialist in psychiatry with the Royal College of Physicians and Surgeons in Ontario. He joined the Department of Psychiatry at U of T in 1948, the same year his "selige Mutter" died in a Tel Aviv hospital.

Martin Fischer's journey from Vienna to Toronto and its contextual setting in the tragic history of European anti-Semitism might help to explain certain peculiarities of his career as a psychiatrist. Fischer consistently sought to break down barriers to the democratization of psychoanalysis in his efforts to apply it in educational settings. Fischer's career not only culminated in his appearance as the psychiatrist in the award winning film Warrendale, but also in his role as the founder in 1977, and the first President, of the Canadian Art Therapy Association.[401] Erica Fischer recounts that Fischer discovered the therapeutic benefits of art while a young resident at the Lakeshore Psychiatric Hospital, which was an early post-war "asylum" more like a jail than a hospital. Desperate to find something to distract a patient in an acute manic phase who was "bouncing off the walls," Fischer passed him paper and crayons through the bars of his cell. "Just draw," he said. Before he knew it, the patient was screaming for more paper. In their later discussions about the drawings the patient achieved meaningful progress in coping with his symptoms.[402]

Most importantly for the purposes of this study, the wide net Fischer cast as a psychiatrist is seen in his treatment of his friend Jack Seeley. He may have kept Seeley close in order to protect him from himself (we shall learn more about Seeley's difficulties in the next chapter) but they were also professional allies. It may be that the importance Fischer attached to Seeley had a religious motivation. Fischer may have seen in Seeley an opportunity, so frustrated while he was interned during the Holocaust, to save a fellow Jew. In these efforts to defy authority in his "discipline," perhaps Martin Fischer felt he was achieving some form of substitute victory over the "Nazi Terror" in relation to which he had once been so powerless. He may have also been fighting back against subtle forms of anti-Semitism he experienced working amongst the Toronto medical establishment in the post-war era. Eric Fischer recalls that her father always ate alone at lunchtime, feeling excluded by the Gentiles, as only the second Jewish intern at Toronto General Hospital.

Martin Fischer with Patient, 1950s. Photo by Graham Bezant, *Toronto Star*, Getty Images.

# Floating Anxiety

In his interviews with me, Seeley said his reason for entering psychoanalysis as the Forest Hill Village Project came to a climax in 1953 was, "floating anxiety, like most people." It makes sense in the context of where Seeley was in the process of the Forest Hill Village Project that he might have begun his own psychoanalysis at about this time. He had finished his work in the schools of Forest Hill in the spring of 1952 and was moving into the writing–up phase of the project. An entry in the "Minute Book of the Forest Hill Village Home and School Association, 1949–1953," dated January 29, 1952 records that during the winter of 1952 a gift for "Dr. Seeley," was already being planned, "Mrs. Pearl made the suggestion that the Program Committee set aside a sum of money at the end of the year to help meet the expense of a gift for Dr. Seeley."[403] This was followed up on March 25, 1952 with the following entry, which was the last mention of Seeley in the minutes:

> It was moved by Mrs. McMurty and seconded by Mrs. Salsberg that $100.00 be set aside as a nucleus for a gift for Mr. John Seeley at the conclusion of the project in Forest Hill. Passed. Mrs. MacFarlane moved and it was seconded by Mrs. Pape that this amount be put in a separate Seeley gift account and suggested a minimum goal of $200.00 be set so that the new executive could be guided thereby. Passed.[404]

The absence of any further mention of Seeley in the Minute Book during the school year of 1952–1953, is further evidence that by this time Seeley had finished his work in the schools. Perhaps this transition from the busy workday world to the isolation of writing pushed Seeley's anxiety to new levels, and prompted him to seek out a more serious approach with Fischer. This is borne out in Seeley's recollections of that time outlined in a letter to Fischer:

> Only as we confronted the necessity for publication of the Forest Hill Village Project material did the latent anxiety really break through as the trap closed. To secure admiration generally (and to please my colleagues like Bettleheim and Riesman) nothing but a critical, penetrating, piercing, probing analysis

would "do"; nothing else would have reclame and sales, and nothing else would therefore furnish on one side what would please them, BUT, on the other what might give me sufficient security (e.g., by job-offers) to permit me later to be really independent. As against this the publication to the Forest Hill Village people who could and would read it as a critical analysis would threaten my carefully nurtured friendships there.[405]

In addition to the performance anxiety of writing, it seems that Seeley also felt that his efforts to please disparate groups might fall apart in the process. And it would seem that the degree of anxiety these pressures caused him was far greater than he admitted. In fact, Seeley makes reference in letters to Fischer to experiencing levels of anxiety and panic that were "near terror."[406] In the following excerpt he describes the intensity of his anxiety at the time:

It is only at a number of quite identifiable points that I experience marked anxiety to near terror. I am very uncomfortable with any of the authority figures here. When we had a picture taken together for publicity purposes I felt, "as though about to faint," couldn't smile, could hardly pay any attention to the conversation—indeed, hear as though through the usual auditory fog or blanket. I also feel very anxious when I think about the Forest Hill Village project or handle any of its materials. I wrote about two pages last night and that was about all I "could" do.[407]

However, the public face any person puts on their inner experience is always braver than that which is revealed in their more intimate relationships. In a letter to his elder brother Frank dated January 5, 1953; Seeley also played down the severity of the suffering in rebuttal of his mother's suspicion that he had suffered a "nervous breakdown":

As to Mama's shrewd suspicion as to what is going on, I think she had best be told with some clear distinctions drawn. This is no "breakdown," nervous or otherwise. I have had to stop and reorganize my life and that is what I am now doing. Would you tell her that I have been forced to recognize an anxiety state, that I have had to seek help in coping with it, and that I have that help, that we are making rapid progress, that the main task is to understand my childhood and especially my relation to her.[408]

Does Seeley here "protest too much"? Though "nervous breakdown" is not medical terminology, perhaps her "mother's intuition" was not that far off. She certainly knew how to get the best of him, and it was his relation to her that Seeley felt was the key to his problems, as he wrote to Frank:

> To me, the main question seems to be to recall the facts of my life and make them intelligible. Mama is the key figure. You need no longer—for my sake—leave out of discussion any issue, or soften or moderate what you wish to say about it. No knowledge or insight could any longer prove devastating, and it is much more important now to get as much of the truth as soon as possible, than it is to cushion against shock. So feel free to write freely.[409]

The reference to his mother raises a second issue that he desperately needed to address with Fischer, namely, the anger issues with which he struggled. Seeley confessed in a letter to Frank that his outbursts of suppressed rage toward Fischer were quite troubling:

> The analysis continues the same—uneven, hard—won gains that cannot be predicted or hurried. My analyst is a God-given fit to my needs, but, sadly, the recipient of all kinds of projected aggression and hostility. To treat anyone so, is about as difficult an aspect of therapy for me to accept as any. The year ahead is going to be anything but easy for any of us.[410]

No doubt his anger management problems were traceable to repressed desires to retaliate against his mamma's "dutiful whippings." But of course the child is powerless in the first instance and must suppress the rage he feels. This does not mean it goes away. Instead, as we learn from the study of psychoanalysis, it lingers more or less unconsciously in the mind, on the lookout for the slightest sign of danger. As he described in his own intellectualized way in a letter to Frank, Seeley had little hope that he could forgive his mamma at the time he entered "psychoanalysis":

> In 1929, in one of our bitterer quarrels, I quoted Oscar Wilde to Mama, "Children begin by loving their parents; then they judge them; sometimes they forgive them." I partly omitted, partly buried Act II. *Tout comprendre, c'est tout pardoner*, I told myself a hundred times. But I now know that an important part of me would like to do her damage commensurate with what she did to me. There may be a dawn of coolness to follow the night of battle-heat and hate, but I will not now refuse that night. I will embrace it, and see what comes."[411]

Seeley recounted for me being shaken by his "hate" in what might otherwise be viewed as quite a banal session with Fischer. It took place when he and Fischer were meeting at lunch-time (further evidence of the informality of their relationship). The secretary was out, and Fischer had to leave the room to answer the phone in the midst of their session. This enraged Seeley because it reminded him of his mother walking out of his room after delivering a "whipping."

Admittedly, psychiatric indifference often comes as quite a blow. But this time Seeley struck back. He called Fischer to account for being unprofessional, and felt empowered after having done so. It was this experience, Seeley recounted to me, that made him aware of his anger issues.[412]

It also pointed the way toward a more mature and assertive response than withdrawal into revenge fantasies, which only repeat the trauma of childhood. If we recall Seeley's dream, for example, we might interpret biting Frank's "little finger" down to the "bone," as the fulfillment of a wish to do "damage commensurate with what she did to me." Might we even infer an association between "biting to the bone," and the traumatic memory of being whipped by his mama, or flogged by his school masters? In the first scene Seeley's brother Frank is "on his back" and digs "painfully" into his spine which might symbolize Seeley's experience of being whipped, or caned. Contrary to the reality of such child abuse, however, in the dream Seeley is empowered to "bite back." Thus the dream condensation works to disguise but also satisfy Seeley's wish to lash out in anger at his brother with his mamma's "biting whip" (a common simile used, for example, by Kafka in his short story, *Jackals and Arabs*)? Moreover, by castrating her favorite, Seeley satisfies his Oedipal desire to possesses his mother.

It makes sense that, as the most important woman in his life, Margaret also often bore the brunt of Seeley's displaced fury. We know this because she too wrote letters to the Fischer family, some of a friendly day to day nature, and others seeking to inform Martin Fischer of her husband's progress, saying she thought "he should know." Below is an example of the more day to day type of card:

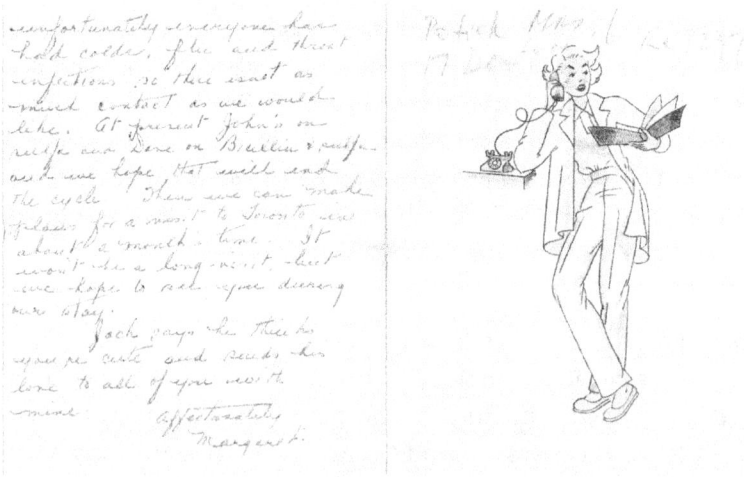

Letter from Margaret Seeley to the Fischers, 1950s. Fischer Papers, Toronto, Ontario.

On the surface Seeley was unfailingly polite and considerate in relations with his wife, but even this was unnerving for her because she felt that he was not always being genuine. She complained that it was as if he was following some "script." Instead, Seeley's anger poured out in other subtle forms of controlling behavior. For example, Seeley once tried to enforce a "time budget" on family life. As Margaret explained:

> I'm not quite sure when the time budget came into being. I think it was some time after his second visit to England to see Frank and Mamma. The time budget annoyed me. Jack clocked himself all day. I discovered at the end of the first month that time spent in love-making (usually for Jack's satisfaction and only "quiet" acquiescence on my part) was charged to me.[413]

At other times, however, the intensity of the rage Seeley directed at Margaret was frightening. He did not mince words in the following letter to Fischer:

> Nobody on earth has a duty to put up with this shit! The answer to any attempt to discuss what was happening was met by, "If I'm all that bad, I'd better go and leave you all to each other," or, "I'd like to die." With unerring accuracy she strikes seriously and effectively. She "might as well be a servant"; she is "put-down," "side-tracked"; I am guilty of "arrogance," "deviousness in argument," and "death wishes." The key woman in my life (the only woman) simply cuts down and destroys my belief in myself. I am not going to play with infantile fantasies of suicide, but if fate were to truncate my life it would help.[414]

Their relationship was not always this stormy. In fact, Margaret wrote to Fischer that she was quite pleased with the progress he made in his psychoanalysis:

> During the past year his expressions of affection changed, I think, he was freer and seemed to feel what he said, and I could respond. Jack is more considerate of me than he was before. He asks what I'd like to do and where I'd like to go, and does little things to add to my comfort.[415]

An example of Seeley's "Time Budget," 1960s. Clara Thomas Archives, York U.

However, there was one issue in their relationship that proved more intractable. Ironically, given that Seeley was an educator, it was parenting. "This is one area where our problems have not been solved," she wrote to Fischer. Margaret grew up in a very traditional, patriarchal, family. She was uncomfortable with Seeley's permissiveness, both with her and the children. She frequently found herself in the position of having to enforce boundaries. Whenever she attempted to do so, however, she felt the children would gang up on her because Seeley would not back her up. Rather than lay ground rules applicable to all, he preferred to treat each child differently. Margaret described this in the following passage about what she saw as favoritism rather than fairness toward one of their sons:

> His intellectual capacities gave Jack further cause for admiration. Jack thought he was beautiful with violet eyes and gold hair. Actually, he was quite a plain baby with blue eyes and brown hair. Where he was bad tempered, his

behavior was excused because of health or lack of sleep. We even went so far as to arrange feeding schedules so that he would be present at only one feeding in a day. Jack took him out or played with him during the 7 pm feeding. I balked and stopped hiding....[416]

Margaret sensed here that power games were still at work in this special treatment of the "gifted" child. For his part, the neo-Freudian "progressive" approach to education which inspired Seeley's experiment with "free discussion" in the classroom seemed to have also guided his parenting style. It is hard to reconcile the image of Seeley as an overly indulgent parent and teacher, with that of him as controlling and angry, and yet Margaret found both of these extremes very difficult. Perhaps there is only the appearance of a contradiction here, for every family knows that the withdrawal of involvement can be just as cruel as the arbitrary imposition of power. Margaret complained of other forms of withdrawal such as the onset of colds that left Seeley bedridden at difficult times like the birth of children, or panic attacks, or the failure to complete household chores. Perhaps Seeley had passive-aggressive tendencies?

In whatever form, it appears that Seeley also projected his anger issues in relationships with colleagues at work. Reva Gerstein, for example, who took his place at the CMHA when he moved to the Department of Psychiatry, and who was close to their mutual friend Murray Ross, said to me that, "there was something destructive" about Seeley. In fact, Gerstein found that when she arrived at the CMHA his name was "taboo."[417] Obviously, Seeley did not entirely succeed in his inner struggle to contain all "badness of impulse," discovered through psychoanalysis.[418] The part of him which aimed to pursue a "criminal and exploitive career," as he described it to Fischer, was never entirely subdued.[419] We have already seen Seeley's issue with authority, which seemed to emanate from his anger in anticipation of its perceived abuse, undermine his relations with important mentor figures early in his career like Everett Hughes and Bruno Bettleheim. In the next chapters, we shall see that his problems with authority figures escalated as his power increased.

But we should perhaps not place all of the blame for these troubles on the internal workings of Seeley's psyche, and also consider the impact of his professional milieu. It is a curious fact that the two men who exercised the most influence on Seeley's educational experiments also faced charges of an excessively authoritarian therapeutic style. Bruno Bettleheim, Head of the Orthogenic School in Chicago was famous for his use of the "slap";

and, Martin Fischer as psychiatric consultant at Warrendale, aroused controversy for his experimentation with "holding therapy" for children in crisis. According to psychoanalytic theory, physically holding a child who is acting out should protect him from self-harm while at the same time providing the kind of physical connection they had not had as babies. In a similar way, resident youth at Warrendale were given bottles at bedtime to provide the kind of care their birth parents failed to provide. The hope was that missing stages in the development of self-esteem and self-regulatory powers could be reenacted and internalized by patients. However, as can be readily seen in the film, holding sessions easily turned into wrestling matches with the potential for harm; and yelling at the child to express his feelings, if anything, was often a disempowering experience. The following description of a screening of the film *Warrendale*, attended by Fischer and Seeley, is quite suggestive:

> The psychiatrists were enraged, especially by the "holding" sessions, and their questions reflected this. After each explosion or question Martin would nod sagely and then nod again for the next question, as any good analyst would do. About twenty minutes into the string of tirades, there was an explosion from the childcare workers and nurses sitting, in equal numbers, behind the doctors: "What do you folks know? You see kids an hour a week! We work with them all day every day of the week and we have never seen anything before as amazing and helpful to us!" They explained why—holding was an especially useful notion, so were the routines around meals and bedtime, the rocking and affection expressed. Martin had hardly to say a word. It was almost as if he were working with the children, Carol and Tony, as he did in a scene in the film: letting them make the discoveries they needed to make for themselves; having earned them, they owned them.[420]

Both Bettleheim and Fischer were experimenting boldly at an early stage in the history of the "medicalization of education." Even if "holding therapy," has since been largely discredited, it may not be fair with the benefit of hindsight, to pass judgement.[421] However, their experiments do call for explanation. Is it possible they developed strong defense mechanisms because of their mistreatment, not at the hands of parents or schoolmasters, but of the Nazi guards? And these defensive instincts played themselves out in their work in these rather physical forms of correction? We may recall that Seeley also suffered from anti-Semitism and its effects on his family history.

It was in fact Bettleheim who wrote that some inmates in a concentration camp had a tendency to "identify with the Gestapo," in order to adapt and survive.[422] He observed, "a great amount of aggression accumulated" in prisoners who prided themselves of being, "as tough as the Gestapo," and who copied "their form of bodily aggressions," in relations with others. Thus Bettleheim and Fischer may have unconsciously revisited their own experience upon their patients; not to perpetuate the trauma, but to redeem it.

In other words, the question is whether in the process of trying to help children "wrestle" with the terrible trauma to which they had been subjected, these men were also in some degree seeking to resolve their own. After all, they had both been "held" in malicious confinement by Nazi and, in the case of Fischer, by Canadian authorities. Fischer's "holding therapy" at Warrendale, and his more psychological "holding" of so many patients in group and informal therapy; at his home, a restaurant, or taxi ride; modeled not only a nurturing parental embrace for so many people seeking to get back on their feet, but may also have reassured Fischer himself that he was using his authority correctly, for the benefit of others, rather than repeating the violence of the "verbrechers." Being alongside, but not on the inside of this same experience, Seeley was able to see its benefits and dangers.

Thus Seeley's personal struggle with anger, and his participation in the educational experiments of Bettleheim and Fischer, combined to heighten his theoretical awareness of the relationship between the exploitive tendencies of the social science expert and the reinforcement these qualities receive in institutional settings. He made this explicit in *Crestwood Heights* where he suggested that the training of teachers in psychoanalytic pedagogy, "would safeguard the process against the perversion to sadistic uses of which it is clearly capable.[423] Indeed, one is reminded of how Mengele applied his psychological knowledge to torment his victims at Auschwitz in the following passage from *Crestwood Heights*: "In the psychological fields it is not unlikely that the knowledge of how to heal may also lead readily into the knowledge of how to destroy."[424] At another point in the book, Seeley further explains the defining characteristics of such exploitation:

> In some cases the patent enjoyment of what would otherwise be thought of as an uncomfortable situation and the near total-unconsciousness of what is being done, hint that some deep-seated need of the expert is indeed being

> satisfied. The lack of distress in mining the gold of guilt in his audience and dredging advantage from its dependency, the uninhibited satisfaction of his own needs for exploit and for exploitation, suggest the building of bastions by the expert against some felt inner passive dependency.[425]

The reader wonders whether Seeley was not here describing the motivations of his friend Martin Fischer, or even himself.

Whatever the source of Seeley's insight, he accurately forewarned of the anti-psychiatry movement that was to come. Scholars who, like Wini Breines, suggested that there were no signs in *Crestwood Heights* of the "social and ideological struggles" that were to surface in the sixties perhaps overlooked this. Most famously, the character of Nurse Ratched in *One Flew Over the Cuckoo's Nest*, a best-selling 1962 novel by Ken Kesey, represented precisely the kind of abuse of power by a mental health professional envisaged by Seeley. The same year Michel Foucault also criticized the "moralizing sadism" of the psychiatrist in his 1962 work *Mental Illness and Psychology*. More importantly, Seeley's work may have directly influenced Erving Goffman, another Jewish-Canadian sociologist, who also did graduate work with Everett Hughes at the University of Chicago. Goffman's criticism of the "total institution" in his 1961 book *Asylums* is considered a leading text in the anti-psychiatry literature: "It is important to keep in mind the influence that psychoanalysis had on sociologists, so well exemplified by John Seeley. It is very likely that Goffman was familiar with this direction in the late 1940s and 1950s."[426]

In all of these works the emancipatory claim of psychoanalysis is called into question. Rather, it is interpreted as a modern form of inquisition, but one which has dispensed with physical torture in favor of ever more refined techniques for inducing psychological dependence and fear. According to Foucault, psychiatry is a transmutation of the "pastoral" power of the confessor which, "cannot be exercised without knowing the inside of people's minds, without exploring their souls, without making them reveal their innermost secrets. It implies knowledge of the conscience and an ability to direct it." Moreover, this "medicalization" of society has taken over the functions of Church and State:

> Power of the pastoral type which over centuries—for more than a millennium—had been linked to a defined religious institution, suddenly spread out into the whole social body. It found support in a multitude of institutions. And, instead of a pastoral power and a political power, more or

less linked to each other, more or less in rivalry, there was an individualizing 'tactic' that characterized a series of powers: those of the family, medicine, psychiatry, education.[427]

Crestwood Heights won fame as a critique of, or apology for, suburbia; but perhaps it deserves a second look as a seminal work in post-modernist thought for the part it played in the development of anti-psychiatry literature, an important sub-genre. Might we even go so far as to suggest that in order to dramatize his observation of anger issues at work in his own clinical style, and that of Fischer and Bettleheim, Seeley helped to invent the "sadistic therapist" trope. The proto-Indo-European roots of the English word "anger" do suggest connotations of "pain" and "wrath," which are associated with the Enlightenment term "sadism." We might even trace such famous characters in contemporary literature as Hannibal Lecter back to Seeley's influence. Ironically, Seeley's critique of psychiatric power was one of a series of events that led to the demystification and deinstitutionalization of psychiatry in the 1960s, a major setback for the mental health revolution he sought.

# The Unpublished Version of *Crestwood Heights*

Perhaps in an effort to distinguish *Crestwood Heights* from other pop sociologies of the period, Seeley planned to define anxiety not only as the central mental health issue troubling the people of Forest Hill, but also as the very essence of mental illness itself:

> For the purpose of the discussion to follow the problem of mental health is the problem of anxiety—its generation, disposal, structuring, control, and effects.[428]

This project, as outlined in the following pages, may have been abandoned as a rough draft in the Fischer Files because of Seeley's own anxieties; or it may have been held back in response to intense pressures from institutional players involved in the publication of the book. These pressures not to offend governmental sponsors and the community will become more evident in the chapters which are to follow, but the provocativeness of the analysis which Seeley planned to present should be evident here.

In the "unpublished version" of *Crestwood Heights* Seeley pointed to a "discrepancy between potentiality and achievement" as the fundamental cause of anxiety in the suburbs. He placed his elaboration of this concept under the subtitle, "ineffectualness." The picture Seeley painted of Forest Hill was of a community "selected" on the basis of a particularly anxiety-driven need to succeed. Seeley meant by "selection" that the influx "of parent-adults with an unusually high neurosis-prevalence, actual and potential," were "drawn into" Forest Hill by an attraction to this "natural area," as opposed to any kind of forced removal to this place:

> It is we believe demonstrable that many neurotic, self-exploitative and anxiety-ridden people will tend to be over-represented in a population

selected as is that of *Crestwood Heights* on the basis of examining the selective apparatus and the selecting process largely by mere impression, it is true, in the observation of the researchers. The direct confidences reposed in them as to states of emotion, the warranted inferences from observed behavior, the impressions of others, the material gathered in the child guidance clinic, and more generally in human relations classes with children and in informal intercourse with them, all seem to support the view that, in comparison with any other community the researchers have lived in or heard of, this one manifests a particularly high level of anxiety generally, and a particularly high frequency of individuals in whom anxiety is sufficiently concentrated as to be notable.[429]

There was nothing really original in Seeley's analysis of why the already anxious were attracted to the suburbs. Anxiety was perhaps implied in the utopianism of the post-war aspiration to return to a "garden of Eden," and in so doing to establish one's higher standing in the community. One had to redeem the suffering of the wartime years. If he had published more of the material in the draft, however, Seeley might have been credited with insight into processes internal to suburban society which, instead of providing an escape or reward, actually intensified people's anxiety. The problem was that, in the shadow of the Holocaust, there might have been significant controversy if Seeley had gone ahead with publication of his analysis of "deracination" and "concentration" factors behind the high levels of anxiety he and his team observed in suburbia.

Although in Seeley's first draft he chooses to avoid explicit reference to the issue of anti-Semitism, the use of the term "deracination" to describe the effects of cultural assimilation in Forest Hill came very close. Seeley defines deracination as the process of uprooting and leaving behind a family's connections to its ancient culture in Europe. He wrote that:

> The radical character of the deracination establishes a sharp distinction between 'me' and what was once "us." This issued in sharply accentuated feelings of loneliness and isolation.[430]

The loneliness that accompanies processes of deracination lays the basis for the intensification of anxiety in the Jewish émigré to Forest Hill. In the absence of support from custom or community, according to Seeley, the suburban parent is "re-infantilized:

> The parent becomes dependent, in the same situation as he was as a child in relation to his parents, on the expert as parental figure to guide him in his actions as father or mother of his children, because the connections to grandparent, to church and community is broken for the émigré. This causes recurrence in the adult of the repressed anxieties of the child because of his or her similarly absolute dependence.[431]

Seeley makes reference in this context to Bruno Bettleheim's concept of an anxiety-provoking "totalitarianism" in the new suburbs. This is a mental form of enclosure invoked by the new parental dependence on the expert in relation to the most intimate aspects of their lives, though Seeley is quick to point out that *Crestwood Heights* is not, "in any way totalitarian in reality." Next, Seeley suggests, the provocation of anxieties in Forest Hill comes full cycle when the anxiety of the parents is felt by the children:

> The basic anxiety of the parent and her uncertainty and variability in the management of the child, both from day-to-day or hour-to-hour and from age-period to age-period, tends directly toward the production of an anxiety-ridden child, or, if her defense takes the form of over-indulgence, a more or less impulse ridden one. In the first case, the anxiety of the child felt directly and evidenced in conduct difficulty call out further waves of anxiety and other emotional disturbance and conflict in the parent. In the second case, the impulsive behavior of the child threatens the parent's internal and external control-systems, thus reactivating anxiety.[432]

The parent thus not only experiences a re-infantilizing form of anxiety in relation to the expert but also in relation to their own children. This is where the term "concentration" emerges in Seeley first draft. The vicious cycles of parent and child anxiety in the upwardly mobile *Crestwood Heights* suburban environment are the effect of what Seeley refers to as a "concentration of anxieties" that has no room for those who might offer a countervailing reality-testing function. Everyone is already too anxious and feeds off everyone else's anxiety.

Some of the ways that the "concentration of anxieties," is self-perpetuating includes; first, a disengaging movement where "Most of the attempts to encourage the friend in distress to "pull herself together," or join X denomination, or "let yourself go" or "try to look on the sunny side of life"—attempts which directly deny the advisers' own experience with anxiety and knowledge about its operation and therapy—are actually attempts to seem helpful without running the risk of involvement. They are at bottom self-protective, and occasionally guilt-charged because vindictive." Second, Seeley suggests a "magnifying to the advisee the inappropriateness of his reaction" to make oneself feel better, was often observed. Third, Seeley says that the naïve confirmation out of one's own experience of the reasonableness of what is really a neurotic judgment may often be offered. In general, the social surface of anxiety is a superficially polite society:

> The side-stepping dance involved in the general ritual of compulsive politeness. The meaning of this general politeness as fear-expression, self-protection, vindictiveness-channel remains to be explored.[433]

Seeley introduced a variation on Riesman's concept of the "loneliness of the crowd," in an attempt to summarize the general character of a community that suffers from this kind of "concentration of anxieties." He called it "isolation-in-interaction":

> The *Crestwood Heights* isolation-in-interaction is in some ways like this (the well-known phenomenon of loneliness in a crowd) and in some ways different. At the overt and ostensible level the interaction goes forward extensively, intensively and frequently in an air of palpable excitement—heightened color, brightened eye, awakened body-set, rapid breathing there is even, frequently a heightened pseudo- or quasi-intimacy-bodily contact, caress, the use of endearing or intimate gesture. But the intimacy sought for never quite comes off. The vital issues are lost in the wilds of abstraction or buried under the petals of politeness. Each one realized his aloneness but thinks it a function of his own peculiar nature since all the others 'seem' to be achieving the intimacy and securing the satisfactions desired. The meeting is over and the people involved feel more isolated than ever—each to himself, and each firm in the belief that this is what distinguishes him from the others. There is something like a social equivalent of coitus interruptus.[434]

"Isolation-in-interaction" patterns are self-reinforcing in the sense that the lonely person is driven further and further back into the private realm to supply the missing sense of connection and intimacy. Yet, everyone at home has anxieties of their own. Not only does it lead one to retreat into home life more and more, it also leads to an inner retreat into what Seeley describes as "self-mining practices which are at the root (or close to the root) of the problem in the first place." Seeley defined "self-mining" as:

> The attempts to suggest to oneself, to manipulate oneself, to convince, compel and drive oneself are sensibly accelerated, with an increasing need for and diminishing feeling of potency and control.[435]

At this point in the argument, it seems clear that everything has been very well set-up for the social science experts; that is the psychiatrist, psychologist, social worker or teacher; to appear on the stage to provide the needed reality testing function that might offer a way out of the vicious cycle of anxiety in the suburbs. This conclusion might have been welcomed by Seeley's superiors at the University and the Canadian Mental Health Association but, instead, Seeley plunged the people of Forest Hill to their final doom by suggesting that the expert's own issues with anxiety only serve to add another layer to the whole trap. In a section of his first draft he entitled, "The Institutionalization of the Self-Mining Drives," Seeley argues that the same vicious cycle of selection for, and concentration of, anxiety-ridden persons operates within the psychiatric community.

It would be repetitive of what is already contained within the published version of *Crestwood Heights* to review in any depth Seeley's blistering attack on the psychiatric profession. Suffice it to say that, according to Seeley, the demands of the psychiatric profession selects for those whose excessive work ethic is proof of an anxiety driven need for social transcendence. This anxiety manifests in an attraction to the position of power the psychiatrist holds as an expert in a field shrouded with an aura of mystery. The whole ritual of psychoanalysis, according to Seeley, is designed to enhance the mystery of the psychiatrist's presence. The doctor says nothing about himself and thereby gradually deepens the dependency of the patient who is asked to expose himself completely. The psychiatric practitioner might argue that this aspect of the process of "re-infantilization," which Seeley sees as part of the general tendency toward the "totalitarian" invasion of private space in suburbia, is a necessary part of the cure. Seeley portrays it rather as an excuse for the invasion. Seeley uses Freudian language in the unpublished version of *Crestwood Heights*, to explain the missionary dimension of "therapeutic imperialism" in the suburbs:

> The expectation is that if one believes in the true message (and its bearers) this will in and of itself achieve certain desired magical results—principally relief from suffering. Thus it might be at a given moment that to accept the Freudian interpretations and their promoters would be regarded as a sufficient condition for escape from the Freud-described hells.[436]

Thus the unpublished version of *Crestwood Heights* anticipates the kind of internally generated levels of anxiety in the suburban situation that would later be described as characteristic of the "total institution." Erving Goffman uses the examples of the concentration camp, the prison, and the asylum to describe this phenomenon. According to Seeley, the suburban population is similarly "selected," because of its "illness." It is subjected to a "stripping process" by "psychiatric" authorities whose constant judgment in regard to time management, dress, manners, and work assignments consigns the "inmates to live with chronic anxiety."[437] The "total institution" model obviously applies most correctly to the women of Forest Hill whose work life and leisure time all happened in the same place. The fact that *Crestwood Heights* did concern itself, by force of the suburban situation, mainly with the women and children of the village therefore comes as no surprise. The suburbs are Goffman's *Asylums* writ large.

# Waspish Tone

Seeley's next challenge, having completed his brief psychoanalytic experiment with Fischer in the fall of 1952, and having begun a first draft, was to negotiate with his colleagues and superiors on a common approach to *Crestwood Heights*. With his work in the schools of Forest Hill finished, Seeley assumed the leadership of another social research project in Indianapolis which was published in 1957 by U of T Press with the title, *Community Chest; A Case Study in Philanthropy*. Seeley tried to reassure his co-authors of *Crestwood Heights* in Toronto, Alex Sim and Elizabeth Loosley, that "my removal to Indianapolis will, I hope delay or complicate things very little." As it turned out, this was overly optimistic.[438]

The battle lines were drawn early between Seeley and Sim over editorial policy, and this vied against the urgency Stokes felt to get the book finished. It would seem that Elizabeth Loosley, the third author, was caught in the middle of a masculine struggle for dominance, and Seeley was not one to shy away from power struggles. There may have been more to the rivalry between Seeley and Sim than mere jockeying for position. Where Seeley had been born into a wealthy Jewish family in London; Sim was born on a farm in rural Ontario in a small town named Holstein. His father was a hard-working, church-going member of this small town. Alex left his father's farm to pursue his education in sociology in the thirties in Toronto and Michigan, but he never really left farming. Even while he worked on the Forest Hill Village Project Staff his family based themselves on a farm on the outskirts of Toronto. He commuted every day from his farm to the city.

Sim could never quite come to accept suburbia as an honest way of life. When he moved on from his job at U of T to pursue a career in the Federal Civil Service, he and his family continued to live on a farm outside of Ottawa. As he put down in handwriting somewhere amongst the many letters and notes archived at the Library of Canada recording his personal experience of the Forest Hill Village Project:

> Why did I write my part of the book? Why does a team of three horses plow a furrow? Is it fear of the "whip", encouragement of the master or rest at the end?
> Of course, everyone wants to write a book like everyone wants to own a farm, everyone that is who doesn't already own one.[439]

In fact, in later life, he was so dedicated to his father's way of life that he wrote a book about him, entitled, *Robert Sim II: His Life and Work, 1876–1956*.[440] Despite their differences, however, it should be pointed out that Seeley kept in close touch with Sim throughout the writing phase of *Crestwood Heights*, and remained friends with him after it was all done. In fact, he never made a move without consulting Sim or the third author, Elizabeth Loosely.

For her part, "Betty" was a very private person. According to an autobiographical family history she wrote entitled, *Memories of the Looselys and Magees: Two Canadian Pioneer Families*, her quiet life followed in the way of her ancestors, especially on her mother's side. She describes the Magees as follows:

> It was all very Irish; the male dominance; the assumption that the duty of children was to look after the 'old folks' (Grandfather Magee was the only one of Great-Grandfather's five children to marry); the emphasis on thrift and saving; the stern, Protestant ethic of work as a virtue; even the adherence to Methodism; the intense concentration on the family—Aunt Jo once cautioned me, "We keep ourselves to ourselves."[441]

Though quiet and reserved, she was unusually independent and well-educated for a woman of her time. She demonstrated this by being counted among the few women who could say they had served in the Royal Canadian Air Force Woman's Division during World War II. She also revealed herself to be somewhat leftist in her political thought:

> In my university and early working years, I would try out my newly acquired C.C.F. theories on Cousin Fred. Fred, an unrepentant capitalist, never took me seriously, although he once gave me a tour of Dofasco on a Sunday morning.[442]

Given this background, Loosley's most revealing comment about her sense of identity was made in a letter to Seeley in the final year of their work together. Apparently Dr. Capon, a member of the Toronto psychiatric elite, made a pejorative comment when he heard that she was to follow up her research position on the Forest Hill Village Project Staff by an appointment as Editor of *Food for Thought*, a publication of the Canadian Association for Adult Education. She indicated her outrage to Seeley in the following way:

> He must be really mad! But even a psychoanalyst, if he looks around him, must realize that even 'nature' hasn't created every female a dumb blonde![443]

Free thinking or not, Betty Loosley was not impolitic enough to take sides in the battle between Sim and Seeley. The first shot, it seemed, was taken by Sim who, in a "Note" to the Staff of the Forest Hill Village Project in 1952, outlined a very different approach to the writing of the book than would eventually be agreed to by Seeley. Sim wanted himself and Seeley to co-author the book, although he does suggest that, "It is my assumption that Jack, as the director and innovator of the project, would appear as the senior author of the book." He proposed that he and Seeley would "write the first and last parts. The remaining chapters would be contributed by the project staff." Sim also suggested that the integration and editing of the whole would be undertaken jointly by himself and Seeley, "The authors will edit the entire work. They will write bridging sections for the Parts II, III and V, and rework the chapters somewhat as Jack and I did Betty's."[444]

Seeley, on the other hand, was quick to correct Sim's proposal in a memo clarifying that he, Sim, *and* Loosley would all be listed together as senior authors, though he accepted Sim's recommendation that the name Seeley should be listed first. In this memo he also outlined the table of contents for the book and the writing process to be followed.

The research-oriented part of the book was to be written mainly by Sim and Loosley. Seeley wrote the brilliant introductory section called "The Stage"; and the devastatingly critical concluding Parts Three and Four of the Book, entitled "Integration" and "Implications" respectively. The administration of the publication process was to be managed by a committee led by Stokes who was already setting things up with the U of T Press. Originally, an agreement had been reached with the U of C Press to act as the American publishing arm of the project, though in the end it was Basic Books who played this role.

Seeley wrote a letter to "Betty" on February 5, 1954 in which he compliments her on being the first to finish her drafts: "so far you are the only member of the team who seems to have turned out anything like what was expected and a great deal more in the time expected."[445] The implication was that Sim was late with the completion of his material. However, this early work by Loosley met with criticism from the leaders of the Forest Hill Schools Board of Education. It was Sim who informed Seeley of these concerns:

> Don Graham has chapter X and XI. He and Vern Trott have read them, and they are both considerably disturbed by the chapter on the School. He does not think a fair picture has been presented, but he does not want to influence us unduly to change our findings. I do not think irreparable damage has been done.[446]

The significance of the concerns expressed by school officials at this point in the story of the writing of *Crestwood Heights*, is that it indicates the kinds of pressures the writers were under from the very beginning of their efforts. Alarmed that he had displeased his friends in Forest Hill, Seeley was quick to write to Don Graham in an attempt to smooth things over. He urged Graham to forward his concerns so they could be considered in the final editing of the work: "As you know the materials are still not beyond correction, and I would want the general sense of this chapter and indeed of the whole book to be as fair as it can be made." Seeley also tried to explain to Graham that the work was meant to be a critical study, "and therefore it should not be expected that it would deal with equal weight with favorable and unfavorable aspects of the community studied. The introduction, I think, does make clear that the book deals largely with people's problems and less with their successes and happinesses."[447]

But since Seeley was out of town, it was left to Sim to meet with Graham to reassure him about the school chapters, and apparently he had some success:

> I had lunch with him alone (Dr. Stokes' idea) rather than with Trott and Betty as was originally planned. He felt much better after—and is coming to see our position much better. I hope and believe he does not feel that the chapter is unduly judgmental. I assured him we all agreed, that you had written 155 comments etc. He has 2 other chapters now. Later when we start revising

we'll see if he can contribute substantially to the factual side. I am conferring with Stokes on tactics so you can be sure caution will be the watchword.[448]

Seeley was quite complimentary to Sim in regard to his progress in writing the first drafts of his sections, as well as in his handling of the school official's issue:

> The progress you are making is simply wonderful. Your handling of Don must have been really remarkable too. I do not believe that you could hope to do as much with Vern, but with Don we should be able to reach clarity either in agreement or disagreement on clear issues. I think for his sake and for ours and for that of the volume this is most important.[449]

By the end of April 1954, Sim and Loosley had themselves begun to look for new jobs. They exchanged letters discussing whether the price for the book should be $8.50 or $5.00. Obviously the pressures on the writers included not only political pressures from school officials but also economic considerations. They needed to finish the book to move on to other jobs and, while they were in transition, they began to hope for a windfall. At this time, they were excited to learn that Seeley's famous friend, David Riesman, had recommended their project to Basic Books, a major American publisher of social science materials including works by Freud, Fromm, and Piaget. Arthur Rosenthal, President of Basic Books, writing to Seeley to express an interest in publishing *Crestwood Heights*, made reference to Riesman's recommendation, "After a discussion of your work, David Riesman said, 'This is a book you should go after and one that Basic Books can do the best publishing job on.'"[450]

The fact that Sim and Loosley were planning to leave the Department of Psychiatry for other jobs, and that Seeley had been the first to go, alarmed Stokes enough about the progress of the publication that he became very adamant that the whole group have a meeting. Stokes wrote to Sim that he felt that such a group meeting was "absolutely essential." He reinforced the urgency he felt by writing to Seeley personally:

> It does seem very important that the research group of the Forest Hill Village Project have a meeting before the personnel dispersement makes the situation even more complicated. The meeting is of particular importance in connection with publication and in connection with content. Whether or not the meeting takes place will depend entirely on your ability to attend. I

would sincerely hope that you may do so and invite you to give the matter your fullest consideration as of priority importance.[451]

The meeting was held on July 2, 1954. As it commenced, Stokes stressed the importance of completion of the project, and sought to downplay criticisms from external readers of the manuscript. According to the minutes, the "University of Chicago Press readers" warned of, "repetitions, lack of evidential material, and the interweaving of description and interpretation."[452] The main point of the critique seems to be that the book loses the thread of its central themes because of its wordiness, "one keeps losing the thread and wandering off on the many excellent, and I would grant, relevant tangential associations which the author presents and overelaborates." According to the Chicago readers, the book is mainly speculative, and intended for a semi-academic audience, "Presumably, from the lack of evidential materials and the general style of writing, the authors are hitting for a much wider market than the academic. My guess is that they might do it, if some of the repetition is taken out."[453] On the other hand, the Chicago readers' were most positive about the beginning parts of the book written by Seeley and Sim. For example, "All readers liked the early chapters and one remarked particularly about the chapter on "Time," and, "The beginning chapters are a delight, generally the writing is pretty clear and dynamic."

Loosely made a revealing comment in a note on a copy of the "Summary of Readers' Reports," from the U of C Press, which she forwarded to Seeley in Indianapolis. The report had criticized the manuscript of *Crestwood Heights* for failing to address the issue of juvenile delinquency:

> Certain omissions were pointed out—in particular the matter of juvenile delinquency. The reader suggested that if this problem did not exist in *Crestwood Heights* the study would lose value to US readers as one of a typical North American Community. This omission sounds pretty silly to me! After all the whole point of there being "no juvenile delinquency" in the Village is that no one there can afford to recognize that it exists—it's quietly absorbed by the School Counselors, Clinic, and private psychiatrists![454]

The meeting with Stokes continued, after its review of the reader's reports, to a discussion of the criticisms offered by Mary Doan, a leader of the Forest Hill Collegiate Home and School Association. The minutes suggest sensitivity on her part about the "tone of criticism." Her feelings were very similar to that of the school officials who had read the manuscript.

She felt that the portrayal of the Forest Hill as "controlled and duped" by an army of mental health workers was unfair: "Some of the text impressed me as picturing a community super-saturated with child-rearing experts, if not already in control, rapidly gaining control of duped parents."[455]

Her perspective was that these so called experts were not nearly as knowledgeable as they were portrayed to be in *Crestwood Heights*. Moreover, she argued that the mothers were far more skillful and knowledgeable in their own right than their portrayal suggested. The vitriol with which she attacked Seeley for misrepresenting his own knowledge of and commitment to child welfare is surprising. In a most revealing anecdote, she recalls Seeley's comments on fundraising for the development of a recreation center in Forest Hill:

> You suggested a pageant of the historical evolution of democratic ideals. You also made a remark which horrified me, and which I intended to mention to Carroll later, because I felt sure she would be equally horrified—but which I didn't. It was to the effect that whatever we decided upon it would have to be bigger and better than any other community could achieve. I considered this a most shocking point of view for a Mental Hygienist to be harboring! I was also shocked and embarrassed when you asked if our Concert Series was finer and better than anyone else's.[456]

She accused Seeley of, "an almost hysterical persecution on the part of the writer, imputing charlatanism to the child rearing experts." In fact, she suggests that it was Seeley who was himself the charlatan:

> As an aside, I am curious to know if you know that your sentence, "It is only when we feel uneasy and feel indeed that something is not quite as it might be that we can sustain the pains that must ensue between the emergence of curiosity and the securing of even a temporary satisfaction to it;" is descriptive of a basic principle central to a local child rearing expert's concept of security. This is another of the clues that you do not seem to me to be as familiar with child rearing concepts as I thought you would need to be, to make some of the allegations you make. When I read in your text material which I interpret as imputing charlatanism to the child rearing experts, and then I read a letter from you in which you subscribe to a principle long ago incorporated in child rearing material, available both to you and to parents, I am baffled indeed.[457]

The local expert whom Doan is referring to here with deference is likely Blatz, and his "security theory." Seeley did not fail to respond to Doan's charges against him. In a return letter he said: "It is no charge at all to say that the authors seem ill at ease in the child-rearing field since this kind of uneasiness is a good beginning point for research into anything." As to her charge that Seeley launched an almost hysterical attack on other child psychologists like Blatz, he responded:

> I do not know whether what you say about me is true or not, but again I feel it would be perilously close to total irrelevancy. The question is not whether all the authors, let alone one of them, were inclined to be critical of child psychologists, but whether or not given this initial bias or interest or curiosity they have reported with reasonable fairness what was going on.[458]

Seeley's response to Doan's comments was supported by Stokes, who appealed to the group to basically ignore them and focus on finishing the book:

> Dr. Stokes felt that value-judgments could not be cut out of the book at this point, nor could statistical material be included now. He felt that the authors should not give so much consideration to criticism from outside, which had to be expected in any case, but rather to what they wanted to communicate themselves.[459]

The minutes close with a statement of general policy to prevent these editorial tensions interfering with the completion of the book: "It was decided that any disagreement that might arise between the authors ought to be settled in such a way that the completion of the book is not endangered."[460] Seeley's handwritten notes, as the meeting came to a close, were:

1) Qualifications on generality
2) Too critical in tone
3) Write without feeling, write without diagnosis

Above these numbered notes are doodles that could be characterized as taking the form of a hangman's platform. Just below them, on the margin in small, lightly penciled writing, Seeley scratched:

J. G.—Jack Griffin
Death[461]

Seeley was probably feeling quite tense about being held to the task by Stokes.

At another level, Seeley's feelings of tension in this important meeting may have arisen in response to the expectations of others in the group that he, as their leader, stand up to Stokes's demands. Sim wrote in a letter to Seeley that he felt that Stokes's secretary had gone too far in the minutes to play down the importance of their discussion of the concerns of Mary Doan and Don Graham: "I was a little disturbed that Elizabeth's minutes tried to minimize the seriousness of their comments and the value I feel we all place on them."[462] Perhaps she had done this at the behest of Stokes who wanted the minutes to reflect his priority on the completion of *Crestwood Heights*.

Sim's discontent only got worse after Stokes suggested that assistance might be sought from another member of the U of T Department of Psychiatry:

> Dr. Stokes mentioned that—if the authors felt it desirable—an outside person might be considered for assisting in cutting and editing, and he suggested that Mr. Gordon Watson might be approached, as he would be highly qualified for such work from a professional as well as a literary point of view.[463]

Watson was a criminologist hired by the Department of Psychiatry as part of Stokes's plan to encourage an interdisciplinary approach. Given the fact that he was therefore well known to the authors, his objectivity might be called into question. Whether genuine or politically motivated, however, Watson mercilessly attacked Sim's part of the book, picking up on the theme that Seeley himself emphasized in his personal interviews with me, namely, that Sim was prejudiced against the upper class and city-dwellers:

> It is difficult for the reader to doubt that the author intensely dislikes these people about whom he is writing; the tone throughout these chapters is bitter, cynical, and contemptuous. The treatment of the most personal and delicate aspects of these people's lives is quite callous. And the impression on the reader is offensive.
>
> The tone being what it is, one of the most difficult tasks for the reader is to control his own reaction against the author—antagonism, which moves one to doubt the reliability of the presentation.[464]

Though there was a time lag between the receipt of Watson's letter and Sim's reaction, the tension between Sim and Stokes became palpable after this incident. In a letter to Seeley sent early in the following year, 1955, Sim revealed his discouragement:

> If Watson does not wish to share his notes with the other authors, that is O.K with me, but that his notes are in fact and by agreement confidential is a new situation to me, and is rather surprising since in deference to Dr. Stokes, deference or reticence, it was I who asked him to do this work. But I am not making this an issue because the MSS is now, to me, something between an amputated limb, a pair of outmoded shoes, and a child (my own but one of many) who had died of a lingering malady.[465]

Seeley was quick to jump on Sim's negative sentiments. For one thing, he wanted to clarify that *Crestwood Heights* was his child, not Sim's:

> I am a little unhappy about your analogies but I am sure I should not interpret them too literally. I would not wish to think of the child I am trying to warm to life at the moment, as being to you something between an amputated limb and a pair of outmoded shoes on a child who had died of a lingering malady. I think it is coming to a happy life.[466]

It would seem that after the Watson intervention, Sim began to drag his feet and Seeley did not hesitate to point this out to Stokes:

> At the moment I am waiting for Betty and Alex's material. As usual Betty has completed hers, but about Alex I am much less certain. As you remember, October 1, 1954, was their deadline.[467]

When by June of 1955 the book was still not finished, Stokes was angry. He wrote sternly to Seeley:

> We would all wish, I think, to clear up the publication of *Crestwood Heights*. It is now seven years since the project started, one year to get it under way, two years of observation and 3 ½ years of preparation for publication. You will appreciate that I am under considerable pressure from the funding bodies to report, and the University, from the point of view of contribution to new knowledge, is properly enquiring as to the present position. Chapter eight seems still to be missing.[468]

Chapter Eight was Seeley's responsibility, so it wasn't just Sim who was slow to finish. Indeed, Stokes's frustration is understandable given that the group had promised to finish the book by the end of 1954. The fact that the pressures he felt from federal and provincial funding authorities were real is suggested by his persistence on this point even up to the time of publication. As the final copies were being readied for the press Stokes intervened in a handwritten telegram to Seeley to ensure that there was proper acknowledgement in *Crestwood Heights* for the governmental funding that had made the Forest Hill Village Project possible:

> Specific acknowledgement of Federal Mental Health Grants and Provincial Support necessary. Trust you are attending to this requirement. Reference in introduction Chapter I does not meet the need.[469]

In this letter Stokes also sets a new expectation that the project be completed by September of 1955. Seeley himself admitted in a return letter that his part was the only thing left to be done, and promised to comply with Stokes deadline of the end of that summer for completion:

> All that is missing then at the present time is the final chapter which is half completed and on which I am currently working and which I hope to have finished very shortly—certainly before the summer is over.[470]

By this point in the writing process, the focus had shifted back to Seeley's parts of the book and Sim lost no time in making things more complicated for his rival. In an early draft of his comments about Seeley's chapters, Sim's major criticism was that it was too "abstract and obscure for the average reader, but not systematic or detailed enough to satisfy a critical academic reader":

> I had to re-read some sections to understand what was being said and to see if I agreed in general and to try and remember if what was said had any resemblance to what I had seen in *Crestwood Heights*.[471]

Sim also felt that, while Seeley's writing was "prophetic and predictive," it strayed from the general intent of the authors to be descriptive. Perhaps of particular interest is Sim's sense that Seeley's attack on the exploitive tendency of the "expert" was too strong:

> There is an eloquence and an element of polemics in the chapter which I think is unfair to the partners concerned even for Dr. Blatz who is I feel your principal target, certainly for the more innocent, more naïve accomplices such as Don Graham, Trott, Maltby and perhaps all of us; they are only tending to do what we believe to be potentially exploitive, or even if what they are doing is deliberately evil it is only part of a tendency, not a ripe social abuse.[472]

But Seeley explained his targeting of Blatz otherwise in a letter to Riesman:

> I am not sure how clear the manuscript made it (to you) that all this concern with the "expert" was not primarily in origin or target, in reference to ourselves ie., not a matter of conscience, which came later, but of observation which came first. We were struck, when we came, with the "We brought our Jim up on Billy Blatz's book, even though we felt terrible and it didn't seem to work too well," type of remark. Later we realized he had predecessors. Only very late did we realize that we had been cast as successors, and only very last of all did it strike me that, in reality, we had courted that casting.[473]

Sim again expressed his concern about the provocativeness of Seeley's final chapters, presumably after having seen a re-worked version:

> I am wondering if Chapter 13 is your last. I am sorry that I have not been able to give you more help with this chapter but, as I recall, my feelings about it fell under two heads: the first had to do with Tone. I felt that we should suggest our conclusions in as tentative a form as possible and (returning to Tone) they should be stated in as modest and humble a manner as possible. There should not be any judgmental reference anywhere either toward the expert or the parent.[474]

In a hand-written note on the draft of chapters 13 and 14, Sim wrote further that the interpersonal difficulties the authors were having barred a full and frank discussion of editorial differences:

> I am attaching a letter and notes of chapter 13 and 14. You will find that I have been critical of ch. 13. That I am at this late date causes me a good deal of embarrassment. When I first read it I felt 'in my bones' that it was not suitable and that I did not agree with its inclusion in the book, but the balance of relations in the group had reached such a point I did not have the courage, or could not find the means to say so without doing so in an aggressive way, or without doing harm to you. The day we had lunch (I apologize for pulling that real estate character into the conversation for I know it was not easy for you) you raised the question very frankly: why was it so difficult for us to write up this material and to operate inter-personally? I think I was evasive at this point ostensibly and practically because it was not the time or place to finish fairly something fairly begun.[475]

These problems with "operating interpersonally" between Seeley and Sim continued after the issues around the manuscript itself were left behind. Instead the focus shifted to disagreement over David Riesman's "Introduction" to *Crestwood Heights*. They arose in the context of the new pressures on the authors that came along with the agreement that Basic Books would be the publisher of the book for the American market. Basic Books President Arthur Rosenthal asked the authors to agree to his proposal that David Riesman provide the "Introduction" to the work and that the subtitle be changed to include the word suburbia. Rosenthal suggested that alternative subtitles might be, *A Psychological Study of Suburbia*, or *A North American Suburb*. These moves were designed to improve the marketing success of *Crestwood Heights* in the United States. Eventually, to appease Rosenthal, the subtitle agreed upon was, *A Study of the Culture of Suburban Life*. The question of Riesman's "Introduction" was, however, more difficult to resolve.

Even before Riesman was asked to write the "Introduction" by Rosenthal, Sim had written Seeley that he would be unlikely to write anything as "effusive" as they might like.[476] Seeley himself also anticipated problems if Riesman were to write the "Introduction" but he was willing to go along with it anyway because of the optics. As he wrote to Sim in January of 1956:

> We are going to have an interesting cognate problem to deal with. Basic Books have asked David Riesman to supply a forward and they have seen it, although I have not. I have, however, talked to Riesman briefly on the telephone about it after it was done. The publishers are willing to accept it even though it may be quite critical and my feeling here is that we, also, ought to accept it sight unseen. I think if it seemed outrageously unfair— though I do not believe that this will be the case—that the most we could do would be to attempt to supply Riesman with whatever explanations might cause him to modify what he had said, but beyond this we should not go, and that having once permitted the publisher to ask him for the foreword we can hardly reject it.[477]

Sim disagreed with Seeley about the unconditional acceptance of Riesman's "Introduction." Not surprisingly, once he saw the piece, he felt it was too critical to be included. In the following excerpt from a letter to Seeley, Sim outlines his objections:

> [T]he suggestions that 'satire', 'waspishness' and 'parody', and 'sardonic awkwardness' are present in the material does not sit with the allusion to the

writers sensitivity, "did not take exploitation for granted," the "researchers own niceness." If the style was at once deadpan, humorless, waspish, the phrases "not quite jargon, not quite literature," if there are no models in sociology, but only in literature of a special sort, there is no one more capable than David to sense from the literary style the agony that we severally yielded to first in the daily act of observing, then in attempting to record what we had seen, and also to analyze it. The phrases he uses to describe the work could be applied to an adolescent.[478]

Seeley took the blame for the harshness of Riesman's critique, suggesting that his relationship with Riesman, as well, may have been strained. He wrote to Sim that the Riesman's "Introduction," had a "curious motivational history which I cannot go into here."[479] In fact, Riesman apparently avoided Seeley's invitation to a meeting to discuss the matter, as proof of the tension between them. Seeley was forced to resort to a letter, which, not daring to really ask for any changes, merely explained his own editorial reasoning in the hope of a softening of tone by Riesman.

What is interesting about the following excerpt from Seeley's appeal to Riesman is the ironic reference to underlying cultural differences between the various writers involved. Remember Sim was very much a White Anglo-Saxon Protestant and was sensitive to Riesman's dismissal of his and Loosley's "waspish tone":

> I thoroughly agree on the "sardonic" of page 8 and the "waspish" of the prior page. We still don't know fully why every one of the people who wrote on the project did so, though we were aware of it, and I took an enormous amount of "barb" out. Fred Flemming who wrote much of the material for this camp chapter was waspish as hell, but so were some of the sweet gentle unsophisticated school-teachers who, in the course of their training, wrote one or another research document for us. Why, why, why? First, I thought, my influence. But it occurred in people I hadn't touched. Later, I concluded it had something to do with the "threat" involved in examining 'own' institutions, but I don't know. Certainly it's there, and at one time it made me feel the book should be withheld on that account alone.[480]

Seeley claimed that it may have been because of him that the book took on such a "waspish" tone. This self-portrayal may be an illustration of the delicate balancing act Seeley felt he had to maintain to "please" others. At the same time that he claimed to understand the latent anti-Semitism in the writing of his "waspish" colleagues in Toronto; that is, at the same time that he donned his *yiddishe Kopf* to empathize with Riesman's position; he also claimed that it was the fact of his appearance as "more English than the English" that elicited a disturbingly "waspish" tone in *Crestwood Heights*.

In any case, Seeley claimed to Sim that the problem was solved as a result of his correspondence with Riesman:

> In effect, by a few small changes, he has cancelled the feeling of the original—of a critic of hauteur standing above or outside our system—to a feeling of standing beside us in general, though not necessarily on our spot.[481]

Still, it would appear Sim was not yet ready to give up the fight to try to get Riesman's "Introduction" removed. In fact, Sim did succeed in having Riesman's "Introduction" taken out of the Canadian edition published by the U of T Press because he was present in Toronto when these final decisions were made. We might question whether in this campaign Sim was acting out of a sort of benign rural anti-Semitism that had found support at the higher levels of the U of T? In any event, when it came to the American edition, the situation was reversed and it was Seeley who was able to use his geographical location to ensure that the Riesman "Introduction" remained intact. All of this is revealed in the following excerpt from a letter Seeley wrote to Sim in March of 1956:

> I spoke to Jeanneret directly and since I knew you were in town in Toronto I asked him to speak to you. It was at this point that I concurred even though I was not wholly convinced of the wisdom of leaving the Riesman Introduction out of the Canadian edition. However, this is settled now. As to the inclusion of the Riesman Introduction in the American edition, I suppose none of us is perfectly happy. Rosenthal whom I saw last week thinks, I believe, that it will add significantly to sales. Curiously enough he originally had Fromm in mind as you will remember I did in the beginning. However, Fromm is notoriously unreliable. I am sure it is impossible to get any further changes in [Riesman's] Introduction. Betty, I believe, thinks it is quite a gain for the book as a whole. I should hate to feel, however, that I had coerced your judgment on this, or indeed any other vital point. Unless I hear from you to the contrary, however, I will do nothing further, letting the matter stand as it is essentially between the publisher and Riesman.[482]

Obviously, Sim never got back to Seeley on this point because the Riesman "Introduction" is found in the Basic Books edition of *Crestwood*

*Heights*. Still, the power struggle over the text was not quite over. All the authors were also quite disappointed with the brevity of Stokes's preface. In a letter, Seeley asked Stokes to expand on the main points of his piece to no avail:

> I think your Preface covers the three points that you intended to make in any case—the difficulties, the worthy society, the relationship to mental health—and I am only sorry when I see it that you did not allow yourself considerably more space and latitude to expand on these ideas. They seem to me worth expansion.[483]

Aldwyn Stokes, 1957. Courtesy of CAMH Archives.

The problem with the "Preface" was that like Riesman, Stokes couldn't seem to bring himself to be very enthusiastic about *Crestwood Heights*. Stokes's main concern seemed to be to offer an apology for the failings of *Crestwood Heights*. With regard to the questioning of the manuscript for its lack of scientific evidence, Stokes's apology is something to the effect that the authors were never trying to be scientific anyway:

> The social scientist, with his disciplined curiosity represents a sober effort at comprehending the human scene. He may contrive a unique method of

exploration or ingeniously devise a new technique of measurement. The present research depends neither on contrivance nor ingenuity, it is basically descriptive.[484]

To reduce Seeley's critique of suburbia and the psychiatric profession in *Crestwood Heights* to mere description was a quite pointed insult, and one which betrayed Stokes's disappointment with the book. Stokes attempted to turn Seeley's controversial critique to advantage by claiming that it was done in the spirit of therapeutic reflection:

> In any human situation, most favorable as it may be, some breakdown in living occurs. To know the causes of personal failure or collapse, attention must be given to the family or social forces that assail the individual.[485]

The issues around which Stokes was developing an increasingly negative assessment of Seeley's work had begun to crystallize in the "Preface." Stokes viewed with concern Seeley's philosophical rejection of systems of power, which Stokes had dedicated his life to building. He also frowned upon the lack of an empirical basis in Seeley's writing. For his part, Seeley had come to feel that this need to "prove" everything was part of the empire-building process itself. In a letter to Seeley accompanying his manuscript for the "Preface," Stokes was as cryptic as the "Preface" itself. Like a true politician, or a gambler, he wanted to hedge his bets on the success of the book: "Herewith my effort at a Preface. Whether it should be regarded as a stirrup-cup or a faulty bit of harness will depend on the success of the hunt."[486]

# Jewish Tempers in the Village

As it turned out, Stokes need not have been so cautious. The book was an immediate success, and has since found a place in the canon of sociological literature as a "classic work of 1950s social science." Stokes was quick to write to Seeley congratulating him for *Crestwood Heights* being, "a sell-out," but still hedging his bets, encouraged the writers not to say anything further:

> The reception of the book has been associated with much less vituperation than I had supposed. Indeed in my view there is no need whatsoever to be on the defensive regarding it and I would advise still that all the authors and people concerned adhere to the 'no comment' principle. I gather the University of Toronto sales record a sell-out.[487]

Within the first week after publication on May 31, 1956, the U of T Press had sold over a thousand copies and had ordered a reprinting. Marsh Jeanneret, Director of the U of T Press, also congratulated Seeley and even suggested that he had, "cast a milestone in Canadian publishing history." He went on in this letter to predict that Seeley "will earn one third of a Governor-General's Award Medal in due course."[488] Seeley was never awarded such a medal, but the publishers' initial enthusiasm reveals the extent to which they judged the book a success. U of T Press Field Representative Hilary Marshall pointed out the extensive press coverage the book received:

> *Crestwood Heights* has so far received a total of 55 feet and 3 inches (in column inches) of <u>free publicity</u> in local papers, which we feel might be a record of one sort or another.[489]

While the publishers were ecstatic with the initial popularity of the book, they were less happy with the position taken by Stokes and Seeley against accepting requests for public comment. The opportunity for involvement was ripe at first because the book had begun to cause quite a stir even before the actual publication date set for May 31, 1956. In a memo to the authors, Hillary Marshall, the field representative for U of T Press wrote:

> You will have heard of, or seen, the stories that were published starting on May 2nd. While distorted they have undoubtedly caused a considerable degree of interest in the book, and there has been almost continuous comment since. When the newspaper stories broke, the CBC news round-up program carried interviews with various villagers. Miss Halpenny broadcast a very short factual account of the book to set the record straight.[490]

To substantiate Marshall's claims we can refer to an article written by Rabbi Slonim, a staff writer for the *Toronto Telegram*, entitled, "Forest Hill Village on Analyst's Couch." Slonim reported that in the weeks prior to publication there had been much "discussion based on hearsay that has agitated the community and twisted the book's meaning out of all proportion." According to Slonim, there were excerpts from the book released prior to publication that were taken out of context and, "some of the Village residents became angry, others fearful, and still others, in an attempt to shake off the stigma of being guinea pigs, have taken the positions of one woman who was heard to remark in a Forest Hill bake shop, 'They don't mean me.'"[491] Given the fact that Slonim was a rabbi, and given that the focus of public concern was the "stigma of being guinea pigs," we might easily suspect that much of the public controversy emanated from the Jewish population. They may have viewed this so-called mental health initiative as a veiled form of anti-Semitism. Indeed, in his memo to Seeley, Marshall acknowledged that the concern was coming from the Jewish community:

> [I]t appears that Jewish tempers are unduly ruffled in the Village by a book they haven't read, and this despite the fact that Rabbi Feinberg preached what appears to have been a first class sermon on the book in which he described it as "earnest, consecrated and uncompromisingly honest."[492]

In a handwritten note reacting to Marshall's report, Seeley asked incredulously, "Why Jewish opinion, why is explanation of the Book needed?" Given his general policy of avoidance in regard to Jewish issues, Seeley's surprise about this may be understandable, if not a bit disingenuous. Apparently, he was not the only one. There is no clue in the *Toronto Star* coverage of *Crestwood Heights* as to whether in fact it was mainly the Jewish community that reacted strongly to the news of the upcoming publication of the book, nor is there any indication of the nature of the concerns.

The newspaper stories about the publication of *Crestwood Heights* referred to by Marshall and Slonim that got the whole commotion started were on the front page of the *Toronto Daily Star*, on May 3, 1956. Sprawled in big black lettering was the title, "Find Mental Problems Prevalent in New Suburban Areas: Forest Hill Mothers are Indignant over 'Crestwood Heights', A Book which Blasts Way They Raise Their Children."[493] The news stories claimed that parents in Forest Hill were alarmed that the study revealed "an estimated 5% of Forest Hill's 2,000 school children were in need of clinical aid for acute mental disturbances and that 20 percent required individual treatment of some kind." In addition, the newspaper emphasized rhetorical comments made in the book such as the one describing Forest Hill mansions as "looking like department stores and appearing rather cold and lacking in life." Much to the chagrin of the mothers interviewed, the paper also highlighted the book's observation that children were typically not allowed to play in their own living rooms.

To further foment controversy, the photographs splashed across the front page pictured young mothers, with cat's eye glasses and curls, seemingly encouraging their children to romp with dolls and rocking horses in the living room. Mothers are quoted in the article as objecting to the study by saying, "the only thing wrong with my children is that they're too normal." Even School Board officials are caught expressing concern about the book because it was displayed at the American Psychiatric Association Convention in Chicago before any of them had seen a copy. The School Board officials backtracked, however, with the claim that any concerns about *Crestwood Heights* were offset by the positive benefits to the community that had accrued from the Forest Hill Village Project over the previous five years.

The publishers informed Seeley and the other authors about the controversy the publication was causing in the local press. In addition, Marshall wrote on May 15 urgently requesting that Seeley be available for public comment around the date of publication:

> I am writing to you particularly as I wonder whether there is any chance of your being in Toronto anywhere between May 30th and June 2nd. We could give the book a tremendous start with a TV and/or radio interview. We must

(and will) get it moving fast before people start away to their cottages and summer camps.[494]

*Crestwood Heights* hits the front page of the *Toronto Daily Star*, May 3, 1956.

In red ink Seeley wrote in the margin of Marshall's letter—"NO"! Perhaps, Seeley's "removal to Indianapolis" also had something to do with his determination to escape the easily anticipated fall-out from the publication of *Crestwood Heights*? Since Seeley did not respond immediately, Marshall wrote again on May 16 in an attempt to convince him to come to Toronto:

> I have just finished talking to Ross McLean, the CBC producer of Tabloid— an extremely popular Television program. He is very anxious indeed to have you appear on his program on Wednesday May 30th, and you can imagine what terrific publicity this could be for *Crestwood Heights*. Besides this, of course, the newspapers (*Star* in particular) would like to interview you, and it could well be that the Press would arrange other entertainments (?) for you![495]

What "other entertainments" were being implied one would not want to venture speculation on, but it may be understandable that Stokes was against such additional publicity given that he could already claim victory to his superiors without the risk of contributing to any unnecessary public disorder. It is more difficult, however, to understand why Seeley avoided jumping into the fray. After all, he had a long-term professional interest in the book's success. Nevertheless, in a letter he wrote to Sim on this matter, Seeley explained why he did not want to get involved in the media campaign:

> Will you let me know what your own posture and attitude will be towards the inquiries and demands for explanation and defense that will doubtless begin to flow in as soon as the book is out? My own attitude, since I am now deeply involved in other matters, since the work was done a long time ago, and since I have neither time nor desire to get drawn into a whole lot of new enterprises on its account will be "no comment." I think this attitude would serve us best severally and jointly but would be glad to have an expression of your views on it.[496]

Sim wrote back to Seeley that he was "rather disturbed that you will not be available for defense and indeed of the last section." This suggests that Sim shared the concern of Ontario's medical elite about Seeley's provocative critique of the psychiatrist's "sadistic" tendencies. However, Sim said, he would nevertheless have to abide by the "no comment" position himself because, "my present position as a civil servant will preclude participation in controversy."[497] Seeley did, however, decide to write a short letter to the *Daily Star* attempting to diffuse the tensions, if not by way of an apology to the people of Forest Hill with whom he had worked:

> For the sake of countless of our friends in *Crestwood Heights* and for the sake of objectivity and justice please note that the authors nowhere state Crestwood children are spoiled nor that Crestwood homes are generally cold. They do not regard the forthcoming book as a blast or an unflattering portrait nor do they imply Crestwood is different from many other communities and criticism based on the contrary assumption is already more than a little off the beam. Let the book speak for it-self when published and let the good people of a good community then assess its intent, justice and relevance.[498]

Upon receipt of requests for further comment from Marshal and for public appearances on television and radio, Seeley solidified his decision not to become involved in the media campaign. First he confirmed the "no comment" policy that he and Sim had already agreed on with Elizabeth Loosely. Her instincts, both as a librarian and as a woman of her time, were certainly not to seek out the limelight. She wrote to Seeley about how she had been hounded by the local press:

> He asked me if I'd ever run into any hostility while interviewing and I said I couldn't honestly say that I had—we'd all had unusual cooperation and intelligent understanding of what we were doing. I mentioned the seminar group where the research process had been explained and that the study was as serious and conscientious as we could make it and that I wasn't interested in the sensational repercussions.[499]

Seeley wrote to Marshal confirming that the authors had all agreed to adhere to a "no comment" policy:

> I can fully see the advantage of moving with, if not heightening the tide of publicity which you have—if I may mix the metaphor—set into flow or helped. On the other side, I think there are at least five weighty reasons why the authors would not wish to be involved even if that involvement should be financially or otherwise to their benefit.[500]

Seeley went on in the letter to explain that the authors felt that it would be inconsistent with the book's outlook if they did not restrict themselves to scholarly discussion amongst their peers. Seeley also pointed out that the authors agreed on a "no comment" approach in order to handle potential differences between themselves. Finally, Seeley added:

> I should say for myself that such spontaneous or impromptu appearances as are involved, say in a press conference or a TV or radio interview, are not the kind of thing I do well or with comfort and I should rather wish to avoid that kind of involvement.[501]

This final point is surprising because one might think that Seeley's outstanding verbal facility would incline him to welcome such opportunities. On the other hand, in his private letters to Fischer he had indicated that he was feeling particularly anxious during his time in Indianapolis. This may have been linked to his separation from Fischer, and also to his feelings of being somewhat estranged from his former colleagues in Toronto. He may have feared that his general state of anxiety would have been aggravated by the pressures of appearing on television and radio.

Instead, Seeley decided it was safer to respond to the controversy in writing. He informed Marshal that he would write a comment as part of a series of articles in the *Toronto Star* about *Crestwood Heights*:

> Despite all of this I should inform you that a Mr. Johnson from the *Toronto Star* telephoned yesterday, stating that he was intending to do a series of four articles which would essentially restate parts of what was said in the book and asking whether I would write the fifth article of the series. I told him that one of us would be willing to write about 500 or 800 words of comment.[502]

Of the many defensive remarks Seeley made in his letter to the *Star*, the most interesting were twofold; first, Seeley wanted to address the claim that *Crestwood Heights* had argued that the schools were "dangerously dominating" Forest Hill Village. As we have already seen, Seeley, Sim and Loosley were very concerned about the objections to the manuscript that had been raised by Don Graham and other Forest Hill school officials. Seeley sought to clarify that *Crestwood Heights* had merely put forward the view that schools were assuming more social functions and that they might be in danger of getting beyond democratic control. Moreover, rather than suggesting schools were becoming oppressive institutions, the authors had developed great respect for the teachers and school administrators they had worked with: "We respected the men and women and students in the schools. If they needed any further tribute they paid it to themselves when they permitted us to study them in the cold white light of detachment."[503]

Seeley also wrote that the main point of the book was for experts to be more straightforward with laypersons. This aim was not helped, Seeley wrote, by journalistic attacks which only feed expert anxieties about whether they are understood, and may only serve to force them into more cryptic messages. In closing his letter, Seeley seemed to conjure an image of himself as just such an expert, forced to descend from the "cold white light" of Platonic detachment into the shadowy cave of public debate against his will: "I join only most reluctantly, feeling virtually coerced."[504]

Seeley certainly wasn't encouraged to join battle by Stokes, who rewarded him for the successful completion of the project, albeit somewhat belatedly, with a "contingent" and part-time position back in Toronto with the Department of Psychiatry: "You will know how much your colleagues here would welcome you back into a fellowship of good thinking and good doing. I just wanted you to know that if the post appeals to you, and it certainly has tremendous opportunities and very worthwhile relationships, a contingent appointment with the Department of Psychiatry as Associate would be definitely arranged."[505]

Seeley accepted this offer, which allowed him to return from the United States with some honor, as he explains in a rather cordial letter to Sim:

> The rumors you hear are correct. After looking at umpteen jobs—some with a great deal of money but very little scientific interest attached and some with a lot of scientific interest but not a very great deal of money—I decided chiefly, I believe, on sentimental grounds that the overriding consideration would be to take a job that would bring me back to Canada. At least three were offered but in terms of what I wanted I chose the one at the Alcoholic Research Foundation of Ontario together with a return as an Associate in the Department of Psychiatry, but without any onerous duties.[506]

But what Seeley portrayed in public, as we know, was sometimes quite different from what he felt in private. The bravado he put on in this letter about his return from Indianapolis masked his real feelings. These are revealed in a letter he wrote to Fischer at the time:

> I dreaded coming back to Canada in August. But I talked to Don Graham Monday night and everything seemed most cordial, then saw Stokes just a few minutes ago and he invited me to stay with them if I came up for a conference about the book in June. So where are my ghosts? I anticipated that neither would willingly speak to me, and felt accordingly.[507]

We can only speculate about why Seeley felt such dread about his return. Perhaps he felt that his former colleagues would harbor animosity over his precipitous flight to Indianapolis? Perhaps he feared that the conflicts that had surfaced around the time of the publication of *Crestwood Heights* with men like Donald Graham might come back to haunt him? We must not forget that according to Reva Gerstein, who replaced Seeley at the Canadian Mental Health Association, his name was unmentionable amongst the senior staff of the group who had been responsible for launching his career.

Margery King, who had worked in a Secretarial capacity with the CMHA at the time of the Forest Hill Village Project, felt that Seeley had offended his colleagues by "taking the project off in his own direction."[508] He did this in two significant ways; first, in his final critical analysis of the "implications" of the Forest Hill study, he attacked the "destructive" tendencies of the psychological "experts" which are rooted in their tactics of anonymity and the pretense of objectivity:

> If an expert talks about destructive tendencies, in a social situation in which his talk is a function of *his* destructive tendencies, without permitting or causing his audience to see what he says in the context of his own need as well as theirs, his indirect teaching is of a first order degree of falsity.[509]

Indeed, it was likely in order to address such issues, that Seeley and Fischer sought to breakthrough artificial boundaries in their personal psychoanalytic experiment. Secondly, Seeley concluded in *Crestwood Heights* that the intervention of the CMHA in collaboration with the U of T Department of Psychiatry in Forest Hill had not worked:

> We have no assured indication, from the experience of *Crestwood Heights*, as to what would improve the mental health facilities of a good school. The only objective evidence would seem to point towards no better mental health, or perhaps worse, among children in this community.[510]

Needless to say, this was not what Hincks or Griffin wanted to hear. We may do well to recall that Seeley anticipated such a reaction when it came to his efforts to "secure admiration generally (and to please my colleagues like Bettleheim and Riesman)." As he reported to Fisher, he felt that "nothing but a critical, penetrating, piercing, probing analysis would "do"; nothing else would have reclame and sales." But, as he feared, this did come at an initial cost to his relations with members of the Gentile Establishment in

Toronto. As Seeley's letter to Fischer upon his return to Toronto indicates, however, the strains were short-lived and Seeley resumed cordial relations with Griffin as was the case with Line.[511]

As to Stokes, while Seeley may have also managed to maintain relations, he would never be invited to return to work full-time at the U of T Department of Psychiatry. Stokes was an understanding psychiatrist and an adroit politician; but his courtesy toward Seeley was likely quite superficial and designed to cover-up his deep feelings of disappointment in the man in whom he had once placed high hopes. Indeed, Seeley's projections about trouble at work were not altogether ungrounded. There is an intriguing undated letter written by Stokes to Seeley found amongst the "Fischer Papers" which sheds light both on why Seeley was so anxious to leave Toronto for Indianapolis in the first place, and why he feared coming back.

The letter attempts to explain why an application by Seeley to be made a *permanent* employee of the U of T Department of Psychiatry was rejected:

> You will recall that I promised to let you know by the end of October what the prospects were of changing or modifying your work opportunities in Toronto. Since our dining together I have spoken with Murray Ross and Jean MacFarlane and in a general way with other colleagues. It is clear that, at the moment, there is no possibility of providing a full time University Post. Perhaps in recent years you have moved into logical analysis at the expense of scientific empiricism. You may be right to do so, but I would argue otherwise. Logical analysis implies self-contained systems, symbolic abstractions and a contained harmony; scientific empiricism implies phenomenal realities, open systems and an acceptance of discordant fluctuating variables. Symbolic logic cannot be well communicated to the scientific empiricist who knows, "in his bones" that reality is an infinite matrix. Opposite positions are bound to arise with conflict unless a mind position is maintained, with excursions, where appropriate, into logic on the one hand and experimentations on the other. Your tremendous abilities lie in the mind position but, I think at the moment you are using one arm only in your fight for truth (which in this human vale of tears can only be relative). Whether or not I have expressed myself well or confusedly, you well know what I am trying to say.[512]

Stokes's concern was with the lack of empirical foundation in Seeley's work. This may be taken at face value, or interpreted as symbolic of a deeper divide that had emerged between Stokes and Seeley as the psychoanalytic turn in Seeley's thought became increasingly evident. Seeley's emphasis on self-reflection over empirical research may have been perceived by Stokes as a failure to show sufficient commitment to the "medical" priorities of the corporation.

Luckily, however, there was still one option open for Seeley to pursue on his return to Toronto. Already in the spring of 1956 as he was wrestling with the final stages of publishing *Crestwood Heights*, Seeley wrote to his last friend in high places in Toronto, Murray Ross, then Vice-President at U of T. Ross had long-promoted Seeley's career since he spotted him amongst the crowd of other orphans at the YMCA in the early days of the Depression. Quite fortuitously, Ross was chosen to preside over the establishment of York, a "new" university in Toronto.[513] Seeley was quick to ask Ross for a full-time position that would enable him to write a second book on psychoanalytic pedagogy based on the Forest Hill Village Project materials. In a letter, Seeley claimed that the Human Relations Classes had been the chief scientific achievement of the Project, but that this topic had been sidelined by the ethnographic focus of *Crestwood Heights*. If he were offered an academic post at the "New University," he promised Ross that he would write this second book, and undoubtedly he planned to submit this to the U of C and formally be awarded a Doctorate:

> I am left, now, with an unfinished task, the completion of which I judge to be of some importance. In the course of the Forest Hill Village Project we conducted, as you know, a study within a study: actually a study in education or preventive psychiatry. Under stringent scientific controls we set up in the suburban school system a series of free discussion groups with normal children. Our leading hypothesis was that children exposed to such an experience would differ from matched children not so exposed, in a statistically significant way—and in the direction of better mental health or attitude improvement. Our data not only demonstrate that such is the case, but that differential gains in school-performance were shown by the experimental children as well. These findings are of considerable significance both to educators and psychiatrists. Everyone who has seen or heard of the material wants to see it turned into a book.[514]

# Protégé

As we turn to the penultimate chapter in Seeley's Canadian adventures, it is important to contemplate the extent to which he was dedicated to the ideal of York as a small tutorial-style university. Seeley saw in this model the correct form for the pursuit of a "psychoanalytically enlightened education." Seeley believed deeply in the importance of the relationship between teacher and pupil, an idea that traverses Western philosophy of education from Plato to Freud. This kind of relationship was not possible in the large lecture hall. Even prior to his attempt to realize this vision at York, he continued his experimentation in "psychoanalytic pedagogy" with Clayton Ruby, an ambitious youth who sought Seeley out as an intellectual mentor.

Ruby was a student in the Forest Hill elementary school system while the FHVP was on-going. Like many others, he has no specific memories of the Project and how it might have affected him. Perhaps the intellectual climate in which the FHVP emerged nonetheless played a part in his desire to seek out a mentor in the field of "social psychiatry," which he was interested in studying further at University. While still a high school student at Forest Hill Collegiate, Ruby said he heard that Seeley was involved in this area of research and made contact with him.

Ruby came to greatly admire Seeley's intellect. He described Seeley as "a classic polymath" whose scores on standard IQ tests were "un-measurable." He recalls Seeley playing bridge, knowing every intricacy of the game, and between hands worrying over the eternal paradoxes of mathematics. Ruby said that Seeley was "the kindest, wisest man," he's known.[515]

According to Ruby, during his last years of high school he started meeting Seeley in Oxford-style tutorial sessions, "not connected to classes." During these tutorials Ruby said he and his tutor "talked about everything on earth."[516] However, they shared a particular interest, as Ruby indicated was his motivation for making contact with Seeley, in "psychoanalytic pedagogy." In fact, Ruby said that at the time he bought for himself the complete works of Freud. The following excerpt from a letter to Seeley illustrates their exchange of references to ideas and books, especially about Freud:

> Incidentally, I find Norman O. Brown's view of Freud to be very congenial. Do you think he overstates the centrality of 'repression'? The importance he places on it makes the whole of Freud more meaningful, for me at least.[517]

The fact that Ruby valued Seeley's psychoanalytic insights, and that they were the stuff of student intellectual life during the sixties, can be seen in the following excerpt from a letter to Seeley in which Ruby asks him to help a friend: "Please try to get him to look at himself psychoanalytically as only you can do. From what he's said to me, I think he's about to become open to this kind of thing now."[518]

It is interesting to note that, though fascinated with Freud's work, there are signs that their discussions encompassed the kind of critical anti-psychiatry perspectives of which Seeley's writings, especially *Crestwood Heights*, were a forerunner. For example, at one point in his discussions with Seeley about a paper he was writing, Ruby makes the following observation: "Irrational authority seems to me the basic problem anywhere I look even in psychotherapy, mostly: what Lyward calls the "usurped life."[519] In other places, Ruby joins with Seeley in a critique of the exaggeration on method over content which characterizes "Modern Learning," as it is often referred to:

> I returned to the book I was reading – *Felix Frankfurter Reminisces*. He makes an interesting comment on page 40; interesting because we have both held this to be true: "I have so little patience with all this talk about method, pedagogic methods, and curricula. It's all the bunk unless you have men of stature and depth and quality. Because as Holmes said somewhere, "If you believe in great things, you may make other people believe in them."[520]

Rick Salutin, another protégé of Seeley's who has risen to prominence in Canada as a journalist, novelist and playwright, was part of a circle of students, along with Ruby and others, who engaged with Seeley in the kind of psycho-social discussions that were *de rigeur* in the sixties. Though Seeley has fallen through the cracks in Canadian scholarship, it is a compliment to the perception of Ruby and Salutin that they recognized early that he was an important pioneer in the field.

One excerpt from the letters Salutin and Seeley exchanged is of particular interest because of the reference to *Crestwood Heights*. In this passage

Salutin is commenting on student culture at Brandeis University where he was studying toward his BA in Near Eastern and Jewish Studies during the winter of 1962. Brandeis was founded as a "non-sectarian" University in 1948 by the American Jewish community to create educational opportunities for Jews and other ethnic and racial minorities, and women, who at the time faced discrimination. The university is named after Louis Brandeis, the first Jewish Justice of the Supreme Court.[521] It would seem that from Salutin's perspective, Brandeis suffered at that time from a similar sense of *ennui* that Seeley observed in Forest Hill:

> There is nothing here for people to hold onto. There is no gravity. The intellectual atmosphere poses the question about purpose and existence but provides no answer and the silence itself is taken as the response. So a girl like Carol today looks at herself and goes to pieces. Maybe it has something to do with not being prepared to face the responsibility of having a human life (your own) in your hands because of protective parents. (This place is *Crestwood Heights* College).[522]

Clayton Ruby ca. 1950s. Photo by Rick Eglinton, *Toronto Star*, Getty Images.

But it wasn't always so serious between Seeley and his protégés, after all they were young men with a healthy skepticism regarding the "powers that be." For example, Ruby and James L. Newman blamed the latter for obstructing their co-authored sociological "Inquiry into Social

Participation, Failure and Related Phenomena" at Forest Hill Collegiate, from which they recently graduated. They took the opportunity in a brief addenda at the end of the paper, likely submitted as coursework at York, to poke fun at Seeley whom they clearly enjoyed and trusted enough to do so:

> "How about discussing Dr. Seeley? He's way off with that *Crestwood Heights*. There is nothing abnormal about Forest Hill students. In fact, I don't think anybody in here is crazy except maybe Dr. Seeley. Research has led him to incorrect facts." Bells ringing, uproarious and violent laughter while interviewers escape, feverishly clutching tape recorder and notes, hoping to lose themselves in the crowded hostile halls.[523]

In sum, it might be said that Seeley and Ruby conducted a psychoanalytic experiment much like that of Seeley and Fischer, or Riesman and Fromm. As in both of these other cases the benefits resonated outward in Canadian society. For example, we might think of Ruby's career long defense of the legal right of "freedom of expression," as related to his mentor's call for "free discussion" in the classroom. In one famous case Ruby successfully defended the publication rights of a gay magazine, *The Body Politic*. He made the argument at trial that according to the standards of witnesses for the Crown, Socrates himself would have to be banned from teaching in Ontario because of his homosexuality.[524]

Ruby fought many important legal battles, but another that may be particularly worthy of mention was his negotiation of a settlement compensating the Dionne Quintuplets. We might recall Seeley's rivalry with Blatz, the psychologist whose clinical segregation of the Quints caused them so much suffering. Certainly Seeley's neo-Freudian sensitivity to the needs of the child, as embodied in the "free-discussion" classes at Forest Hill Collegiate, might have spared them the "goldfish bowl" trauma they suffered under Blatz's more "directive" clinical style. No one has ever sought redress for Seeley's educational experiment! The reader might even go so far as to speculate whether Ruby's legal defense of the Quintuplet's served as a double-attack aimed not only at governmental exploitation, but also at the dangers posed by the abuse of expert knowledge in the field of psychology which Seeley so presciently identified in *Crestwood Heights*.

The question of Jewish heritage also reemerges in this story of mentorship maturing into friendship between these prominent Canadian intellectuals; as was also the case between Seeley and Fischer, Fromm and Riesman. Ruby said that he did not know much about Seeley's Jewish heritage. He understood that Seeley's family had been "refugees from Germany who had settled in England." Ruby did recollect Seeley speculating about overhearing his grandmother "rambling in Yiddish in the attic." But in the early days of their work together, Ruby said that he did not pry into this area because Seeley was "sensitive about religion."

For his part, Ruby's father was one of many children born to poor Jewish immigrants from Poland who managed to eke out their survival farming a "few acres of rock" in Quebec. Louis Ruby therefore "had no money" of his own and was forced to "go out and work," Eventually he found his way to the "Big City" (as Seeley so often referred to Toronto in *Crestwood Heights*) where he rose to prominence in the local publishing business. In fact, we have already encountered the tabloid *Flash,* of which Louis Ruby was the publisher, "together with large numbers of local area newspapers and magazines about horses, horse-breeding and racing," according to Ruby.

*Flash* was one of many "cheap locally produced newspapers" like *Hush, The Rocket, True News Times,* and *Justice Weekly* that had their origins in the Depression-era.[525] While its content was, "filled with stories of murder, scandal, celebrity gossip and illicit sexuality," *Flash* was the only Toronto paper which openly accused the Forest Hill school system of "Anti-Semitic Segregation" in 1950. This is not surprising given that *Flash* and other such tabloids from this period all spoke with a, "determined anti-Nazi voice," and, "denunciations of anti-Semitism were much more common within their pages than in those of the mainstream Toronto dailies."[526] *The Toronto Daily Star* and other mainstream newspapers were controlled by Gentiles and reflected their social values. The tabloid press was likely the only field of journalism open to Jewish businessmen and writers in Toronto at the time.

It is thought-provoking to witness the emergence of further important persons in Seeley's life, namely Ruby and Salutin, who are of Jewish heritage. Ruby said that in the summer of 1960, he and Seeley were talking in the kitchen and the question arose. Seeley told Ruby that during a recent visit with his brother Frank "Friedberg-Seely" in New York it was finally confirmed for him that he was Jewish. According to Ruby, he "welcomed the knowledge." Given the complexity of Seeley's unique "origin story" which left him without any certainty as to who his parents were, and Lilly Friedeberg-Seeley's determined "de-Judaization" of the family for the sake of naturalization and a "fashionable atheism," it must have come as a relief to him. On the other hand, it must be pointed out that prior to this Seeley had already acknowledged the question of his Jewish identity in private conversation with his brother Frank and Martin Fischer. It may be important to consider whether it was quite a different thing in the early fifties to publically explore one's Jewish identity issues given the lingering effects of anti-Semitism, especially as the "Director of the Forest Hill Village Project."

The "rather singular" omissions regarding Jewish issues that Seeley observed in the 1950s both in his own family and Forest Hill, may be explicable in part because of the "delayed impact" of the Holocaust. The lingering mistrust, if not explosive anger, associated with recent memories of such virulent anti-Semitism inclined Jews to avoid the topic. In addition to his own uncertainties, Seeley's tendency to remain silent on these issues during the fifties except in his closest relationships, may have also had something to do with Ruby's observation that he "was not interested in politics." Very much as Plato described in the *Seventh Letter*, Seeley experienced an inner tension between his dedication to the intellectual life which inclined him to turn away in disgust from the "evils of the time", and an activist's desire for reform. Assuming something in common between religion and politics, Seeley might very well have assumed an atheistic position early in his career, as he described in his version of *Strange Journey,* in order to set aside contentious religious issues. He was having enough difficulty managing inner conflicts during this period:

> When I encountered the active living hope incarnate of extending the light and cool of "Science" into human affairs in the form of "the Social Sciences," I had found, I believed, the successor to and superior of previous religions, as the devotion-worthy and "last, best hope" of humankind. Light for heat; and courteous discussion for bitter debate.[527]

Unfortunately, there was no escape route from workplace politics. Unlike Plato, Seeley had responsibility for a large family which made it imperative that he join the fray. Ironically, Seeley always approached his job with the "religious sense of mission" instilled in him by his Jewish grandmother amongst others, including his Christian nanny and the local "Meenster" in Lorneville whom he looked up to as a boy.[528] This was certainly the case when, in 1959, his friend Murray Ross selected him as "senior author of *Crestwood Heights,*" to be his lead man in the development of a faculty, curriculum and sociology department at the "new" university.[529]

# Uprising at York University

Seeley liked to say that there was a running joke amongst the staff at York that if a Professor was "caught with more than one student in his class he would be fired."[530] He had managed to convince his friend and superior Murray Ross of this vision, at least in the early days. Before long, however, population pressures resulted in increasing demand for university spots in Metropolitan Toronto and Ross was forced to abandon the small liberal arts university ideal. In fact, York would grow to become Canada's third largest University with over 45,000 students. For Seeley the small tutorial university ideal was so intimately connected to the educational philosophy he had already begun to devise during the Forest Hill Village Project, he could not accept compromises on its integrity. He was enraged by Ross's willingness to stray from the script he had written for him in his inaugural vows as President of York University. But Seeley should have realized where Ross's true loyalties lay.

Ross was part of what has sometimes been referred to in the Canadian media as the "Maritimer Mafia." Ross was promoted to prominence by President of U of T Sydney Smith, "because Smith wanted to work with a fellow Cape Bretoner."[531] Both Smith and Ross were the descendants of poor Scottish settlers in Cape Breton. Smith's ancestors were Loyalists who found their way to Port Hood, where they worked as fishermen. Ross's ancestors were farmers and blacksmiths from Pictou County who made their way to Sydney, Nova Scotia. Ross's father worked as a sales clerk who made no more than $9,000 a year.[532]

These men were deeply committed to demonstrating their worth amongst the high-born of Upper Canada. They were very sensitive to the difference between themselves and men like U of T Chancellor Vincent Massey, scion of wealthy industrialists. As outsiders themselves, they were as jealous of the positions of power they had achieved in Ontario as were Jewish emigrants like Fischer and Seeley. Moreover, their Anglophile roots made it easier for them to step over their Jewish competitors in the climb up the corporate ladder.

When Ross was promoted to President of York University he was careful to secure his position by arranging that another Maritimer be appointed Chairman of the Board of Governors of the "new" university. When Ross was asked by Colonel Eric Phillips, Smith's successor at U of T who also "had roots in the Maritimes," for a nominee; he responded, "Perhaps Bob Winters."[533] Of course, Winters' was the son of a fisherman from Lunenburg Nova Scotia. Though a Liberal, in contrast to Smith who ended his career as Minister of External Affairs in the Conservative Diefenbaker government, Winters' was a formidable player in the corporate world. He served in various portfolios as a member of the Liberal cabinet under St. Laurent and Pearson. When the Conservatives won the election of 1957 he was forced to set aside his political ambitions temporarily in favor of various corporate boardrooms. He was even referred to in this context by George Grant, another famous York U professor, in *Lament for a Nation:*

> Our rulers, particularly those who enjoy wielding power, move in and out of the corporations, the civil service, and politics. Robert Winters, who could not stomach the inconveniences of opposition, must content himself with running Rio Tinto and York University.[534]

Murray Ross. Photo by Annette Buchowski, *Toronto Star*, Getty Images.

In their role as guardians at the gates of high society, class traitors like Ross, Smith, and Winters' were concerned during the early period of the Cold War with signs of social unrest. In fact, Ross's writings as a scholar focused on the need for Western educators to ensure the competitiveness of their institutions *vis-a-vis* "Education in the U.S.S.R." (the latter being the title of a series of articles Ross wrote for the *Toronto Star* in 1958). In a speech to the Canadian Club entitled, *Soviet Challenge: Canadian Response*, a copy of which is held at the York University Archives that happens to be heavily edited by Seeley, Ross declared that education was the key to winning the Cold War:

> We Canadians are beginning to realize that we have not translated into action our certain knowledge that our future as a democracy depends on the improvement and development of our educational program.[535]

Ross must have developed his skills as a Cold Warrior under the tutelage of Sydney Smith, who had kept a close eye on communist activity at the U of T. "Without a doubt," Smith wrote to the President of the University of Alberta in 1947, "the Canadian Communists have a well-formulated and long-term policy with respect to establishing cells within Universities."[536] Smith is perhaps most famous for stifling dissent in his 1944 decision, as President of the University of Manitoba, to expel a student for publishing an anti-war poem in the *Manitoban Literary Supplement*. The poet claimed that, "if those who made the wars were forced to fight in them, there would be fewer wars." Smith was concerned that this publication might "affect recruitment among the university's students," and make the University "appear in a bad light."[537] For his part, Winters' led the right wing of the Liberal Party in its losing battle with the notoriously statist Pierre Trudeau for the leadership of the Liberal Party in 1967.

The point of this brief digression into Ross's background as a Cold Warrior is that Seeley, as an anti-establishment academic figure interested in "free discussion" and Freud, represented exactly the kind of threat for which these men were on the lookout. Indeed, Seeley's activism was becoming increasingly radical during his time at York. During the spring of 1963, Seeley wrote a letter to the editor of the *Globe and Mail* in which he identified a "crisis in Canadian universities," which pointed the finger at his erstwhile friend Murray Ross in a very thinly disguised way:

A community of scholars, like a religious community, must be a community where goodness, truth, and beauty go before all and unite all in a common dedication that makes power and politics subordinate, if not irrelevant. But Canadian Universities are mostly not like that. At best they are vast corporations; at worst, petty tyrannies using methods of internal government that would shame the worst political party or commercial organization. Liberal education is for free men; it must be mediated by men who are free.[538]

In a later *Globe and Mail* book review entitled *The Sad State of the Multiversity*, Seeley went so far as to say, "a revolution is required."[539]

In addition to these media forays, in which he demanded an "independent inquiry" into governance issues at York, Seeley also participated in meetings with "dissident" students and faculty to organize resistance to the expansionist policies that Ross was pursuing.[540] It is important to note, as does historian John T. Saywell, that Seeley was not alone in his objections to Ross's manipulative administrative style. Saywell gives the example of political science professor Dennis Smith who, of the many discontent faculty that left York during the crisis, said, "My reason for leaving is the character of the President, Murray G. Ross." Similarly, sociology professor Walter Coughlin left because of the "disturbed climate in faculty and student circles engendered by broken promises, misrepresentation, suspicion, contradiction and manipulation on the part of the President."[541] My father, also a member of the "Maritimer Mafia" from Truro Nova Scotia (of whom more will be said in the Epilogue), suggested that like himself Ross was a "political animal," who was "good at manipulating people" without any undue strain on his nerves.[542] It was all part of the rough and tumble of growing-up in an outpost of the British Empire which, as it turns out, was an excellent training ground for ambitious young men.

Ross admitted in his memoirs only that he was perhaps too "authoritative" in the early years, but was quick to point the finger at Seeley for being "unnecessarily difficult."[543] Yet, if we return to the "Ross and Seeley rhetoric" of 1959, which was Seeley's reason for leaving his comfortable position as research director of the Alcoholism and Drug Addiction Foundation, we can see why. In the "Notes" Ross sent to Chair of the York Board of Governors W. A. Curtis; "preaching for a call," as Saywell put it; Ross not only "suggested the tutorial be the basis of instruction" at the "new University," but also that the curriculum "be a concentration of a few well integrated courses," and that, "emphasis be given to the Social Sciences."[544]

We might recall Seeley's memo's written for the Department of National Defense in which he called for the social sciences to serve in the role of psychoanalytic tutor for all the rest.

It would be surprising then, if this were not a vision of education designed with Seeley in mind. The latter's gift for grand schemes of social engineering, already demonstrated in the Forest Hill Village Project, was again on display. But by the time of the "uprising" in 1963 it was evident to Seeley and many others that Ross had only used this vision, and Seeley himself, to advance his own career. None of it was possible in the "multiversity" Ross was building around them. Perhaps in contradiction to his anti-political rhetoric, Seeley began to mobilize students and staff to defend his ideals. According to Saywell, he went so far as to collect "anonymous articles from faculty," which gave vent to "vicious attacks on the President," and submitted them to the student newspaper, *Pro Tem*.[545]

But like Don Quixote charging the windmills, such resistance was futile. Seeley did not have a chance against a tight-knit group of corporate operators like the "Maritimer Mafia." For Ross, this type of public criticism amounted to an "uprising" and a, "conspiracy to attack me overtly and to have me removed from office."[546] It would seem that once Seeley had crossed Ross in this way, it was the last straw. Ross is reputed to have threatened long-term consequences for Seeley if he persisted in the campaign against his leadership at York. This conversation is reported by historian John T. Saywell as follows:

> In their last meeting, surrounded by construction debris, Murray said to Seeley, "I may be a liar and a bastard. I may be everything you people say I am. But I'm here like these buildings, and those who don't like it better go."[547]

To explain the crisis, Ross suggests in his *Memoirs* that Seeley's oppositional behavior had gone beyond the sometimes helpful role of the conscientious objector. He referred to Seeley's campaign against his leadership of the University as "paranoid," and suggested that it had not been rationally motivated:

> Unfortunately, what may have been legitimate faculty complaints got out of hand and led to personal, abusive and perhaps libelous attacks that prevented rational discussion of the issues.[548]

In support of Ross, the York University Board of Governors even went so far as to hire a private investigator to look into Seeley's "conspiracy."

According to Ross, this had been Winter's way of dealing with the situation: "... then there is a report by a private investigator who investigated the charges from a different perspective. All cleared me but were less generous to Seeley."[549] Of course, Ross does not stoop so low as to actually reveal what was in the private investigator's report. However, in an unpublished draft of his *Memoirs* there remains a key passage that was later crossed out. It provides an important clue as to what the Board of Governors had concluded about Seeley's motivations. To grasp the significance of this passage the reader is made aware by Ross of Doctor Ray Farquharson, a member of the York University Board of Governors who had been head of the medical school at the University of Toronto, and who had "many years of medical experience." Ross reports that Farquharson spent some time talking with Seeley in an effort to understand the nature of his grievances. Ross then dropped a bombshell. He said that that the Board had relied on Farquharson's "medical" opinion in formulating its response to the "Seeley Incident":

> [T]he Board relied heavily on Ray Farquharson's judgment. This was that, "Seeley is a sick man." It helped the Board find its way through the dilemma with which it was faced.[550]

Ross ends his account by pointing out that on the basis of this "medical" judgment; albeit that of a lone medical practitioner who also happened to serve on the Board with Ross; the University Board of Governors made the decision to deal "quickly and summarily" with Seeley. Unfortunately, the alleged conclusions of Farquharson, and the "private investigator's report," are nowhere to be found in the York University archives.

This should come as no surprise at this point in our inquiry into Seeley's "Strange Journey." Whenever the issue has come down to the location of what might be termed a "smoking gun," the trail of historical documents always seems to mysteriously run dry. We might recall the missing "Maltby Report," the inaccessible files of the Psychoanalytic Society in regard to the rejection of Martin Fischer, the missing pages of letters exchanged between Frank and John Seeley in regard to the "Wolff Child"; and, of course, the controversial censure on the publication of posthumous therapy "process notes"—designed no doubt as much to protect the power and reputation of the psychiatric profession as that of the patient. One is reminded of the ancient policy of Thutmosis III to smash the obelisks and erase all images carved in stone of his stepmother,

Hatshepsut. The powerful are never content to merely impose their version of events in the present, but insist on their right to preserve it for all time.

Nevertheless, the archives do contain some revealing documents in regard to the reasons for Seeley's "resignation" from York. These include a most accusatory performance appraisal of Seeley's work submitted to the Office of the President by then Dean of the Faculty of Arts and Science at York University, R. O. Earl in 1963. Administrators never fail to use this tactic, to threaten an employee with "termination" on grounds of incompetence or impropriety, when their interests are threatened. Right on cue, Earl reported to Ross that not only had Seeley never done any teaching at York during the three years in which he had served as Special Assistant to the President and Head of the Sociology Department, he had also not produced anything toward the completion of the curriculum-writing project for which he had been hired:

> It does not appear that any report of research on a curriculum for York University has been made by Professor Seeley, in spite of repeated requests and reminders.[551]

In an accompanying letter, Dean Earl also raised another ominous sounding concern which suggested that there was a more serious level of suspicion in high places about Seeley's behavior than simply that he had been remiss in the performance of his duties:

> My concern, so far, has been on the ground of propriety; but impropriety has its penalties and if I did not do something about this case now both you and I would be in difficulty. Everyone here knows everything that goes on and I have even been asked about you, in this respect, by a person high in administration in the University of Toronto (I said I did not understand the situation). Some here appear to be afflicted by unwarranted, unworthy and wild surmises. These must be dispelled.[552]

It seems that Farquharson was not alone in his research, as Ross had claimed; but, in another instance of clash between today's standards and those of the past; Seeley's mental health issues, whether or not at all relevant, were being used against him by the York Administration. Seeley never directly addressed what may have been behind these "wild surmises" in any of the voluminous letters he later exchanged with Earl during the winter and spring of 1963 before he left York.

In the aftermath of the "uprising," as Murray Ross referred to it, Seeley fled to the United States where he first took up a position at the Massachusetts Institute of Technology and then moved to Brandeis University. This pattern of ostracism continued in Seeley's career to the very end of his life, as Ross duly notes with an air of vindication:

> As for Seeley, he went on to Brandeis University where he repeated his York experience. He attacked the president of Brandeis as incompetent and bureaucratic and threatened to resign. A friend sent me clippings from the Boston Post about this uprising. They were, if one interchanged the names of York and Brandeis, identical to earlier reports in the *Globe and Mail* about Seeley and my-self. From Brandeis, Seeley went to the Center for the Study of Democratic Institutions in California where I assumed he had finally found his proper milieu. However, again problems overtook him, and for reasons of which I have no knowledge, he and the institute parted company. I am not certain of his occupation since, but it seems likely that the important jobs he desired and for which he had the potential have not come his way.[553]

As we have already witnessed, at the beginning of our story, Seeley also failed in his later attempts to return "home" to work in Canada. We are brought back now to where we began, with the "Seeley Question;" that is the question of Seeley's final banishment from academia in Canada by OISE. Unfortunately, if we turn to the letters of reference submitted to OISE in regard to Seeley's application, which are housed at Library and Archives Canada, we do not get much closer to the truth. The letters do reveal that there was no doubt as to Seeley's stature as an academic of international repute. Dieter Misgeld, a German-educated Professor of Philosophy at OISE, himself a student of distinguished scholars Jurgen Habermas and Hans-Georg Gadamer, spoke for the Faculty Association when he said that on the basis of the letters it could be concluded that, "Seeley is an enormously prestigious scholar and a 'brilliant' academic."[554] On the basis of this achievement, the Department of Sociology of Education at OISE was ready in April of 1974 to unanimously recommend that Seeley be appointed as a full professor.

Yet, in an unprecedented move, the Director of OISE, R.W. B. Jackson, requested in May that further information about Seeley be collected from his previous supervisors at U of T and York University. Misgeld, who later lead an investigation on behalf of the OISE Faculty into the procedural irregularities around Seeley's appointment, said, "I do not know why and do not understand why the Directors Personnel Advisory Committee (DPAC) deemed this important." Was this where the Minister of Education's decision to pass on "negative information" about Seeley to the Director OISE came into play? We will never know because the additional letters of reference requested by the Director are missing from the archives. All we have is the following account of them from Misgeld: "One of the letters solicited on this basis is the only letter containing a critical assessment of Seeley as an academic and colleague."[555]

Of course, given that this letter is lost (or burnt?), we do not know who wrote it or what it said. However, in some of the other letters of reference which do remain, we get hints of the controversy that swirled around Seeley's work. The following excerpt from the reference letter of Professor Leonard Duhl, M.D., of the University of California, Berkeley might serve as an example:

> There are some who have been critical of Jack's activities. In my experience, in those settings where colleagues have understood the vast ability to contribute and are truly pre-occupied with the important questions of scholarship, and science in the world there are few difficulties. It is only in those places where small minded people cannot follow the beauty of this man's personality and mind that issues arise.[556]

Similarly, Claude Bissell who, though not a direct "supervisor" of Seeley's, had chaired the U of T Mental Health Committee that helped to finance the Forest Hill Village Project, and later went on to become President of the University, said that he knew only two things about Seeley: "He is a brilliant person; he has a talent for stimulating controversy, which may be a good thing."[557] Obviously, Seeley had his detractors, but their objections are subtly phrased.

Given that the historical document that might reveal the motive behind the decision by the OISE Board of Governors in 1974, namely the "one critical letter" referred to by Dieter Misgeld, is predictably missing; we are forced to read between the lines in the following excerpt from a document in the files marked <u>CONFIDENTIAL</u>:

> May 9/74—Letters sent to following individuals: Dr. Murray Ross, and Dr. A. B. Stokes, From Robin H. Farquhar (RHF), Assistant Director of OISE, seeking comments on Mr. Seeley's suitability.

May 14/74—Telephone conversation by RHF with Dr. Murray Ross; May 21/74—Receipt of letter from Dr. Stokes. Formal Notice given of Directors Personnel Advisory Committee (DPAC) meeting call for May 27th, 1974.[558]

Misgeld scrawled in ink beside each of these dates in the "Schedule of Events re: Recommendation from the Department of Sociology in Education for the Appointment of Mr. John Seeley"; the following questions: "Why?", "Why?" "Why?" Again, it would seem, the authorities played the mental health card, which at the time was something that worked for them rather than against them; showing that at least the spirit of the pre-war eugenicist determination to exclude the "unfit" still applied; and that Seeley had been right in *Crestwood Heights* to argue that all the money and educational measures organized in support of mental health were of little effect when the chips were down.

In an interesting piece of investigative journalism by Jim Bledsoe on the question of Seeley's rejection by OISE in 1974 entitled, "Stilletto for Seeley: An Academic Thriller," published in *This Magazine*, it was reported that a close confidant of Murray Ross and a member of the OISE Board of Directors by the name of Roby Kidd, had made a decisive intervention at the Board Meeting during which the decision against approving the hire of Seeley was made. Kidd had reported to the meeting that, "Seeley had never done the great sociological work that we all had expected from him. We had expected such great things from 'Jack' and he'd never quite done them."[559] In addition, Bledsoe reports, Kidd, "let out the crunch: that Seeley had had 'problems' and that there was reason for concern."[560] Such an ominous-sounding warning can take on a particularly damaging meaning in an educational context. Obviously it had the desired effect, though it could easily have been a ploy to achieve that end rather than having been based on any valid evidence of impropriety on Seeley's part. In the end, whatever the sources of the "controversy" around Seeley's reputation; the DPAC committee decided to recommend to the OISE Board of Governors in May of 1974, "that the regular appointment of Mr. John Seeley to the rank of Full Professor *not* be approved." In his own words, Seeley had been, in effect, "exiled from Canada."

# Epilogue

It must be inferred from the OISE documents that Seeley's mentors Aldwyn Stokes and Murray Ross both turned on him in the end. It cannot have been a coincidence that the final decision to overturn Seeley's appointment came within days of the "receipt" of their letters and phone calls. The feelings of betrayal ran deep within all three men. For Stokes and Ross, Seeley had failed to live up to expectations as a corporate team player. Even his academic writing was criticized by his superiors and peers for a failure to complete work, and a lack of academic integrity. His failure to complete his PhD was likely an important factor behind the limitations of his research. Perhaps because of his tendency to oppose authority he could not bring himself to be an authority. On the other hand, given his struggles with mental health it was remarkable what Seeley did achieve as a writer. Nevertheless Seeley's marginalization in Canadian academia as a troubled man who could not find a way to fit in either as a Jew or a member of the Gentile establishment, culminated in this final act of ostracism.

For Seeley, rejection by OISE was just another in a long line of such experiences in his relations with authority figures more interested in power than in him. In fact, it was perhaps out of his own bitter experience with violence and the abuse of power that Seeley was able to so perceptively critique the "expert" in *Crestwood Heights*. Of course, he received no credit for this from Stokes and Ross or other members of the Gentile intelligentsia. They were never comfortable, it would seem, with Seeley's social fluidity. Was he a scion of a wealthy "Victorian Family" from England, comfortable like they were with eugenics and other forms of social hierarchy; or, was he a poor Jewish orphan with a cut-throat desire to scratch his way to power? Was he a "brilliant" sociologist at the cutting edge of academic research, or an imposter? In the end they decided that they could not trust him.

Indeed, Seeley's supporters believed that it was the radical nature of his views that led to his expulsion from the academic world of a province still steeped in the conservative traditions of a former British colony. To them he was a Socratic figure martyred for his refusal to compromise on his ideals. This sentiment is very well captured in a published essay entitled, *John Seeley: Poet and Revolutionary*, written by a former colleague of Seeley's with the Department of Psychiatry, Donald Coates. His view of the "Uprising" at York was that Seeley

> held a profound belief in the form of university government itself as an educational instrument. This led to both disillusionment and exile a very few years later when, in a showdown between student activists and institutional authority, he was accused of attempting to undermine the authority of senior university officials.[561]

It is also worthy of note that Coates highlights the theory and practice of group psychotherapy in the classroom as Seeley's most significant "revolutionary" achievement. It is certainly true that, either because Seeley left Ontario (or was banished) and never published the results of his studies on the Human Relations Classes; or because of institutional resistance at the U of T, the CMHA and the Board of Education; Seeley's educational experiments with psychoanalysis had no lasting effect either within the school system or in educational theory:

> While *Crestwood Heights* emerged as a book of seemingly dispassionate observation on the life of a single community, it must be remembered that *Crestwood Heights* in its inception was action research in almost pure form. There are those, Tom Mallinson for one, who regret that this side of *Crestwood Heights* went unreported. In truly majestic vision, the local change that was encouraged was seen as just the first step, the seed from which would grow a national mental health revolution in Canada. This was idealism, fanciful and freewheeling. No one, not even the charismatic Trudeau, has since had such a vision of change for Canada.[562]

Coates's assessment of *Crestwood Heights* places Seeley in his best light. He would certainly have enjoyed being compared to Trudeau with whom he had actually formed something of a professional relationship. He loved to recount how Trudeau would meet him in the Parliamentary cafeteria with his young sons draped over his shoulders to consult on issues of mental health and education. Now one of those sons, Justin Trudeau, is Prime

Minister of Canada, and one who has in this capacity been an active advocate of mental health promotion. It may not be a stretch to suggest that Seeley's pan-Canadian vision of a mental health revolution was kindred in spirit to Trudeau's conception of Canada as a mentor state to the world community. It was a time of grand visions, but we have since lost at least some of the naiveté that characterized the hippie era.

Indeed, it would be too simplistic from the perspective of our time to leave off with a description of Seeley as naïve or uniquely well-intentioned, as had acolytes like Michael Rossman:

> In perpetual naivete, he sought to extend justice and reason in a world in which, though he grasped the facts of malice and insanity and despite of his experience of them, he could never quite comprehend their nature and force. The cowardice and betrayal of his colleagues continued to surprise him; time and again he foretold the routine bureaucratic disaster, yet was always amazed when it came. Totally involved in cultivating an integral sensibility, he could not grasp how others not so committed could escape the obviousness of its conclusions, nor what a genuine rarity was his way of being in the moral world.[563]

Rather, we know that virtually from the time of his early childhood, there was a dark quality to Seeley's "fate," a theme which frequently recurred in his letters to Fischer.[564] To some, he was an angry and difficult man. He certainly harbored a terrible hostility toward authority figures, but for good reason. It must have been very cold and lonely to set off on your own as a young boy on a ship across the Atlantic. At that moment Seeley was unsure of everything. He no longer knew who his father was, whether he was Christian or Jewish, English or German. The teacher at Henfield to whom he had turned as a substitute father figure had sexually abused him. He even doubted whether the woman who had cruelly disowned him at the dock was really his mother. To his credit, he maneuvered the trials and errors of this first oceanic voyage to the new world with the skill of Odysseus. But his efforts foundered finally on the rocks and windswept fields of North York where his own issues played a part in his dismissal.

When he left York U, the Canadian chapter in his life, with which this book has been concerned, came to a close. But his career in the United States in the years that followed continued to be eventful, and not just for its continuing pattern of dismissal and reinvention, as Murray Ross reductively narrated. For example, he wrote a sequel to *Crestwood Heights*, the thought-provoking title of which was *The Americanization of the Unconscious*, in which he portentously likened the unconscious of the New World to his own:

> [O]nly in America does one turn and turn, the corporate image before all the available transforming mirrors of this frame of reference and that. Other peoples glory in their singularity, but since the singularity of America is its variation, how could America fail to glory precisely in that?[565]

Seeley's glory was the contribution he made to the invention of this "other-directed" American character and culture in his life and his books. Seeley embodied what was best and worst in it. On the one hand, his mellifluous ability to fit seamlessly into any social situation might make him a hero of the new era of identity politics. He was equally at home with Jew or Gentile, gang or faculty member, child or adult, rich or poor. His sensitivity to the problems of anxiety amidst plenty, and his bold initiatives in the field of mental health policy to address them, also set an example for our time.

On the other hand, his identity confusion represented the *reductio ad absurdum* of the modern "Renaissance Man." At various times in his life he claimed to be a Sociologist, Teacher, Professor, Psychoanalyst, and Administrator without the possessing the credentials customarily expected for professionals in those fields. Seeley even took on patients as a "child psychoanalyst." He boasted of this in a "talk to celebrate his 80th birthday," held at the U of T. In one case he claimed to have cured a boy of his food phobia:

> Then he asked with a lot of affect, "Would you dab this on me?" While I hesitated, he removed his shirt and, with a single flick of his zipper, his shorts; he had been barefoot, so he was bare now except for his underpants. To my hesitation, he rejoined, "ok, let's do it in the alley." (There is an alley that runs past my office – a busy place). I assented and we went. To critical looks from male truckers and female parents I dabbed the paste practically all over him from head to toe. A sort of ecstatic content settled on him as he found himself finally encased in food (except for his eyes and genitals) like a sausage in a sausage roll."[566]

If there was ever potential for the abuse of power by a social science expert, he was it. Yet, Seeley was self-reflective enough to recognize the danger that he himself represented. His warning in *Crestwood Heights* about the "sadistic therapist" anticipated the anti-psychiatry movement of the sixties. Seeley also issued a prescient warning in the *Americanization of the Unconscious* about the dangers posed for the culture at large:

> It has also the possibility of becoming a manipulative society in which the minor clumsy attempts depicted by Vance Packard in *The Hidden Persuaders* are perfected to the point where resistance is virtually meaningless; a society in which, moreover, the threats of manipulation from without are countered but fatally compounded by self-manipulation.[567]

Seeley sought a corrective for this tendency in philosophy. As he wrote in the *Americanization of the Unconscious*, we need a new "rational ethic" that is, "derivative of the full-grown science of man," and which derives its authority, "from what is abiding and universal rather than local and transient." Seeley was a Platonist. Perhaps to compensate for the mass of contradictions at the core of his own personality, Seeley took refuge in an idealist faith in truth and in the ability of a guardian class of "psychoanalytically enlightened" teachers to lead us toward it. In the discovery of such a scientific morality, Seeley argued, humanity will "remake himself in the image of his gods." However much this conclusion may point toward communism, and the *Americanization of the Unconscious* does include essays on, "The Psychiatrist as Reluctant Revolutionary," and "Parents—the Last Proletariat"; Seeley himself turned increasingly toward the Episcopalian Church as he grew older.

This return to religion at the end of his life brings us back to the issues raised by Seeley's Jewish heritage. It is striking that Seeley deepened his commitment to Christianity even after he discovered he was Jewish. This may be explicable in terms of his early immersion in Christian communities as a school-boy in England, and a Cub-Scout leader in Depression era Toronto. It may also fall within a certain pattern of dissimilitude, or "other-directedness," which has been noted in Seeley's character.

The question of Seeley's heritage was difficult to address not only because of his behavior, but also because I am not Jewish. I am a descendent of New England planters who migrated to Nova Scotia prior to the American Revolution in the eighteenth century. How could I hope to understand the life of someone with such a different background to my own? This was a question posed to me by Harold Troper during my doctoral exam at the University of Toronto (In fact, all of the members of my doctoral committee were reputable Jewish historians; David Levine, author of *The Dawn of Modernity*; Cyril Levitt, author of *The Riot at Christie Pits*; and Harold Troper, author of *None is Too Many*). Troper asked how I had been able to write ("quite well" he suggested) about a character in Jewish history, being an outsider to the culture. This question brought to mind certain episodes from my own childhood. When I was a boy living in Antwerp, Belgium, I went on many school trips to nearby Breendonk, to visit the ruins of a concentration camp. For some reason the story told to me about German soldiers torturing Jewish prisoners by putting out the butts of their cigarettes on arms and bodies, stayed with me. It was an image of being set fire to, of being burnt alive, which the word Holocaust is meant to convey.

Perhaps because of these experiences, I wrote a short story that was submitted in a high school writing contest in Sarnia, Ontario entitled *Dachau*. It was about the thoughts and memories appearing in the theatre of a boy's mind as he made his final walk to the gas chamber. I told this story to my committee and speculated that there may be many people who themselves feel marginalized, as had Seeley, that identify with the history of Jewish people.

To my surprise, just a few years after I completed my doctorate, my father's DNA test revealed Jewish ancestry on his side of the family. When I shared this with Levine, he said: "Maybe that is why you wrote about Seeley?" The mind does wander to the possibility that some unconscious archetypal sympathy may be at work in my interest in a figure in Jewish history. Seeley himself, despite his confusion about his Jewish identity, often found his way toward other Jews in his search for companionship.

Or, was there something else? As had been the case with Seeley's gravitation toward Riesman or Fischer, perhaps my unconscious cultural affinity with Seeley was secondary to my interest in him as an intellectual role model, a father figure. For I too had lost my father to the demands of an international business career. As a senior Vice-President of Polymer, George Firman (or "Firm") Bentley was a distant figure. In his time the company reached a new zenith in the production of synthetic rubber after its original establishment by the Canadian Government during World War II. According to Mathew Bellamy's history of the company, *Profiting the Crown*:

> By 1983 Polymer's rubber operations were again the largest in the free world, with major production facilities in six different countries. A new class of senior managers—made up of men like Firm Bentley, Pierre Choquette and Charles Ambridge—sent out directives to the various divisions emphasizing the need for growth in high value-added areas that offered attractive profit margins.[568]

To meet the requirements of this expansionary business plan, my father was constantly travelling to Akron Ohio, Strasburg, Moscow and Beijing, to list some of the places I recall. I followed "Firm" to postings in Antwerp and Brussels Belgium, where I spent my early school days, but it nevertheless seemed that he was always leaving me behind. If he was not on his way out the door to catch a flight, he withdrew into a drunken stupor. No doubt he was self-medicating to ease the anxiety of corporate responsibilities, but there was a history of alcoholism in his family of "Master Mariners" from Nova Scotia. The plane had replaced the schooner, but the behavior of the Bentleys from Port Greville on the Bay of Fundy did not change.

Such memories make me wonder about the silence in my family about my father's alcoholism and my own struggle with related symptoms of OCD. Aside from the genetic inheritance, how much of what I have suffered can be traced back not only to my father's lifestyle, but also to the seafaring life of his ancestors? My grandfather, "Wicks," was the last surviving child of Lena Merriam, who died in childbirth when he was but a year old. His father George E. Bentley remarried, and he was raised by his step-mother Ida along with the nineteen other children born to the Master Mariner before he was finished manning his ships.

The Bentleys of Port Greville, ca. 1910 (My grandfather, "Wicks," second from left, bottom row; and his father George E. Bentley, second from right, bottom row). Courtesy of the Mariners Museum, *Newport News*, Virginia.

My grandfather left school after grade eight to work on my great-grandfather's ships and eventually to take a job in Boston, but before long he had volunteered for the Canadian Expeditionary Force. "Wicks" had to wash out his eyes with boracic acid every day because of recurring inflammation after the gas attacks at the second Battle of Ypres, and would eventually die from the long-term effects of his wounds. No wonder, like me, he sought out the more stable career of a grocer after such a tumultuous childhood. I recall a nightmare my father reported to me; that one dark night a car turned to shine its headlights into my grandfather's store, and to his horror, revealed a macabre "dance of the devils."

Somewhere in Seeley's story, as I said at the beginning of this "Strange Journey," I hoped to find a solution to this problem of mental illness and addiction, still so shrouded in silence and stigma. Unfortunately, however, Seeley's faith in the "institutionalization of affection," as he put it in the *Americanization of the Unconscious*, does not seem to have been entirely borne out by his personal experience, or research. Of course, Freud never thought that psychoanalysis could "cure" mental illness, or promote happiness. All it could do, he said, would be to enable the individual neurotic to "work and to love." Even this appears to have been quite ambitious in retrospect.

Perhaps the problem in Seeley's time was that anti-depressants and other recently developed medicinal solutions to mental health problems were not available, and as a result, too much of the burden for treatment was placed on the benefits of "talk" therapy. In my own experience, even after twenty years of self-examination under the tutelage of a psychiatrist, there remained an impenetrable core of terrible anxiety that was not relieved until I began to take escitalopram. I only stumbled into taking SSRIs at the age of 45 because of my family doctor's insistence that I do so as I struggled to contain an outbreak of severe hypochondria in relation to a series of, what turned out to be false, heart tests. Suddenly, my anxiety subsided as did the vicious cycle of "obsessional" thinking. My psychiatrist nearly fell off his chair when I said I was ready to terminate therapy.

This is not to say that I could have done without the many years of psychotherapy. What Alcoholics Anonymous had done for my father, psychotherapy did for me. Perhaps, his example led the way. Seeley as father-figure taught me not to give up on the educational importance of psychotherapy, although it is true that once I started taking medication, I largely gave up on it in practice. But I had twenty years of experience with the exploration of the mysterious workings of the unconscious behind me. I knew that this skill was most invaluable, especially in relationships; and I had learned of the almost drug-like catharsis of truly "free discussion." Indeed, if there is anything to be found in the story of John R. Freideberg Seeley which can help us to prevent mental illness, it is that we must stretch our tolerance for open discussion, even in surprising places like the classroom.

"But the classroom teacher is not a therapist," say the critics of the "medicalization of education." "The teacher's role is only to ensure that students master the curriculum," they say. If only it were that simple! While it is true that the history teacher should help students find meaning in say, the shooting out of the clock towers on the eve of the French Revolution; it is also true that, as Seeley said to me, "I don't think you can call it teaching if you do not know your students." The psycho-drama of relationship-building is part of the teaching process whether we like it or not; and conversation that is free, tolerant, and open is the key to a good relationship. Though our relationships are not enough; they are certainly fundamental in the prevention and treatment of mental illness.

It seems fitting to conclude with a dream of my own about the learning process in three parts, which I presented to my psychiatrist, like a gift, early in our relationship.

In the first scene, I am in his office; but it is an empty clinical consulting room with white walls. There is no one there but me. Out the window I see a laughing moon.

In the second scene, my psychiatrist appears as a teacher in a classroom invigilating a math test which I write with trepidation. The laughing moon has become a black and white clock hanging over the door.

In the final scene, I walk into a warm colorful den with book-lined wooden walls. Historical artifacts decorate the panels and desk. My therapist is seated comfortably in a leathered chair. His eyes are remarkably blue, like cat's eyes. As our conversation begins, he transforms into a beautiful woman.

The End.

# Endnotes

1. Interviews with John R. Friedeberg Seeley, March 2007, Los Angeles, California. As will be more fully explained later, this was the phrase Seeley used to describe his own reasons for entering psychoanalysis.
2. Nick Midgely, "'The Matchbox School': Anna Freud and the Idea of a 'Psychoanalytically Informed Education,'" *Journal of Child Psychotherapy* 34, no. 1 (2008): 24.
3. Duhl to Harvey, *Letter of Reference*, April 19, 1974, Library and Archives Canada, File Professor John Seeley, OISE, 1972–1977, Q5-24868.
4. Schwartz to Harvey, *Letter of Reference*, April 19, 1974, Library and Archives Canada, File Professor John Seeley, OISE, 1972–1977, Q5-24868.
5. Wini Breines, "Gender and Some Social Science," *Sociological Inquiry* 56, no. 1 (January 1986): 70.
6. Lionel Trilling, *A Gathering of Fugitives* (Boston: Beacon Press, 1956), 86.
7. Seeley, Sim, and Loosely, *Crestwood Heights: A Study of the Culture of Suburban Life* (New York: Basic Books, 1956), viii.
8. Ibid.
9. Ibid., 439.
10. Max Weber, *The Protestant Ethic and the Spirit of Capitalism* (1905), http://xroads.virginia.edu/~HYPER/WEBER/WeberCH5.html, accessed September 29, 2018.
11. J. R. Seeley, A. Sim, and E. Loosely, *Crestwood Heights: A Study of the Culture of Suburban Life* (New York: Basic Books, 1956), 6.
12. Murray G. Ross, *The Way Must be Tried* (Toronto, Stoddart Publishing Co., 1992), 22.
13. Seeley, Sim, and Loosley, *Crestwood Heights*, xi.
14. Ibid., 4.
15. Brian J. Low, "'The Hand that Rocked the Cradle': A Critical Analysis of Rockefeller Philanthropic Funding, 1920–1960," *Historical Studies in Education* 16, no. 1 (2004): 33–62.
16. Editorial, "The Seeley Question," *The Globe and Mail*, December 13, 1974.
17. Ibid.
18. John R. Seeley, *Strange Journey*, Seeley Papers, Los Angeles, California.
19. Ibid.
20. Interviews with Seeley, March 2007, Los Angeles, California.
21. Interview with Beatrice Fischer, September 10, 2008.
22. Fischer's Notes, Fischer Papers, Toronto, Ontario.
23. Fischer's Notes, Fischer Papers, Toronto, Ontario.
24. Lilly Etta Friedeberg-Seeley to the Home Office, August 2, 1929, UK National Archives Kew, Surrey (HO 334/128/1141).

25 Roger Gravil, "The Anglo-Argentine Connection and the War of 1914–1918," *Journal of Latin American Studies* 9, no. 1 (May 1977): 63–64.
26 Home Office Memorandum re: Lilly Etta Friedeberg Seeley (German), June 19, 1929, UK National Archives, Kew, Surrey (HO 334/128/1141).
27 Certificate of Release, the President of Police, Berlin, October 2, 1925, UK National Archives Kew, Surrey (HO 334/128/1141).
28 Home Office Memorandum re: Lilly Etta Friedeberg Seeley (German), June 19, 1929, UK National Archives, Kew, Surrey (HO 334/128/1141).
29 Museum of the Jewish People—Beit Hatfutsot, https://www.bh.org.il/.
30 Home Office Memorandum re: Lilly Etta Friedeberg Seeley (German), June 19, 1929, UK National Archives, Kew, Surrey (HO 334/128/1141).
31 Home Office Minutes, June 6, 1929, UK National Archives, Kew, Surrey (HO 334/128/1141).
32 Home Office Minutes, July 11, 1929, UK National Archives Kew, Surrey (HO 334/128/1141).
33 Home Office Minutes, July 22, 1929, UK National Archives Kew, Surrey (HO 334/128/1141).
34 Metropolitan Police, Scotland House, Memorandum to Home Office, January 4, 1932, UK National Archives Kew, Surrey (HO 334/128/1141).
35 Home Office Minutes, November 30, 1925, UK National Archives, Kew, Surrey (HO 334/128/1141).
36 Seeley to the Home Office, July 10, 1929, UK National Archives Kew, Surrey (HO 334/128/1141).
37 Seeley to Frank, Fischer Papers, Forest Hill, Ontario.
38 Scotland Yard Memo to Home Office, January 4, 1932, UK National Archives, Kew, Surrey (HO 334/128/1141).
39 Seeley to Fischer, December 12, 1954, Fischer Papers, Toronto, Ontario.
40 Seeley to Frank, April 1953, Fischer Papers, Toronto, Ontario.
41 Seeley to his mother, December 10, 1954, Fischer Papers, Toronto, Ontario,
42 Borchardt-Pincus-Peise family website, https://www.myheritage.com/person-1544744_224678941_224678941/else-wolff-born-friedeberg, accessed May 8, 2018.
43 Interviews with John R. Seeley, Los Angeles, March 2007.
44 Lilly Friedeberg-Seeley to the Home Office, May 21, 1929, UK National Archives Kew, Surrey (HO 334/128/1141).
45 Seeley to Frank, January 5, 1953, Fischer Papers, Toronto, Ontario.
46 Seeley to Frank, January 5, 1953, Fischer Papers, Toronto, Ontario.
47 Seeley to Fischer, December 12, 1954, Fischer Papers, Toronto, Ontario.
48 Seeley to Fischer, Fischer Papers, Toronto, Ontario.
49 John R Seeley, "A Poem for Mother's Day," 1952, Fischer Papers, Toronto, Ontario. Seeley, Untitled poem, Fischer Papers, Toronto, Ontario.
50 Seeley, Untitled poem, Fischer Papers, Toronto, Ontario.
51 Seeley to Frank, April 1953, Fischer Papers, Toronto, Ontario.
52 Seeley to Frank, Fischer Papers, Toronto, Ontario.
53 Seeley to Fischer, Undated (sometime around 1970), Fischer Papers, Toronto, Ontario.
54 Sandra Martin, "'Obituary': John Seeley, 94, Sociologist and Psychoanalyst," *The Globe and Mail*, January 26, 2008.
55 Interview with Beatrice Fischer, April 10, 2008.
56 Seeley to Frank. January 5, 1953, Fischer Papers, Toronto, Ontario.

57  John R. Seeley, "Educational Autobiography," Term Paper Submitted at the University of Chicago, 1952, Seeley Papers, Los Angeles, California.
58  Interviews with Seeley, March 2007, Los Angeles, California.
59  John R. Seeley, "Strange Journey," Seeley Papers, Los Angeles, California.
60  John R. Seeley, "Strange Journey," Seeley Papers, Los Angeles, California.
61  John R. Seeley, "Strange Journey," Seeley Papers, Los Angeles, California.
62  Alex Renton, "School of Hard Knocks," *The Guardian*, April 8, 2017, https://www.theguardian.com/books/2017/apr/08/school-boarding-secrets-crimes-alex-renton-kipling-rowling-dahl-churchill.
63  Ben Godard, "Former Housemaster at Private Herefordshire School Jailed," http://www.herefordtimes.com/news/14676629.Former_housemaster_at_private_Herefordshire_school_jailed_for_nine_years_after_grooming_seven_pupils_into_sexual_activity/.
64  John R. Seeley, "Educational Autobiography," Seeley Papers, Los Angeles, California.
65  Interviews with Seeley.
66  Kenneth Bagnell, *The Little Immigrants: The Orphans Who Came to Canada* (Toronto: Macmillan, 2000), 100.
67  Lilly Seeley to the Home Office, June 21, 1929, UK National Archives Kew, Surrey (HO 334/128/1141).
68  Norman Ward to Seeley, Air Ministry, Whitehall, April 8, 1929, UK National Archives, Kew, Surrey (HO 334/128/1141).
69  Seeley to the Home Office, July 10, 1929, UK National Archives Kew, Surrey (HO 334/128/1141).
70  Lilly Friedeberg-Seeley to the Home Office, August 2, 1929, UK National Archives Kew, Surrey (HO 334/128/1141).
71  Seeley to Frank, Fischer Papers, Toronto, Ontario.
72  Seeley to Frank, Fischer Papers, Toronto, Ontario.
73  Schnell R. L. "'The Right Class of Boy': Youth Training Schemes and assisted emigration to Canada under the Empire Settlement Act, 1922–1939," *History of Education* 24, no. 1 (1995): 86.
74  Fischer's Notes, Fischer Papers, Toronto, Ontario.
75  Library and Archives Canada, Juvenile Immigration Records, Microfilmed Series, RG76-C-4, R1206-158-4-E.
76  Seeley, *Strange Journey*.
77  Schnell, "The Right Class of Boy," 76.
78  Ibid., 89.
79  Eldon Historical Society, *The Family's of Eldon County, Ontario*, unpublished.
80  Ibid.
81  Interviews with Seeley.
82  Seeley, *Strange Journey*.
83  Ibid.
84  Library and Archives Canada, Juvenile Inspection Report Cards, Microfilmed, RG76-C-4-C, R1206-161-4-E.
85  Interviews with Seeley.
86  Interviews with Seeley, March 2007, Los Angeles, California.
87  Ibid.
88  H. S. M. Carver, *Personnel Selection in the Canadian Army*, National Defence HQ (Unpublished, 1945), 99.
89  Interviews with Seeley.

90 Re: Captain Herbert John Ronald Friedeberg-Seeley, Library and Archives Canada, Access to Information, Privacy and Document Delivery Services Division, Personal Records Division, Reference PRA2010-06622/A1.
91 Carver, *Personnel Selection in the Canadian Army*, 138.
92 Ibid., 39.
93 T. Copp and B. McAndrew, *Battle Exhaustion, Soldiers and Psychiatrists in the Canadian Army, 1939-1945* (Montreal & Kingston: McGill-Queen's University Press, 1990), 40.
94 Ibid., 34.
95 Interviews with Seeley.
96 Carver, *Personnel Selection*, 35.
97 Ian Dowbiggin, *Keeping America Sane: Psychiatry and Eugenics in the United States and Canada, 1880-1940* (London: Cornell University Press, 1997), 140.
98 Angus McLaren, *Our Own Master Race, Eugenics in Canada, 1885-1945* (Toronto: Oxford University Press, 1990), 110.
99 Ian Dowbiggin, "'Prescription for Survival': Brock Chisolm, Sterilization, and Mental Health in the Cold War Era," in J. Moran and D. Wright, eds., *Mental Health and Canadian Society: Historical Perspectives* (McGill-Queen's University Press: 2006), 140.
100 Clarence Hincks, "Sterilize the Unfit," *Maclean's* (February 15, 1946).
101 Sol Cohen, "The Mental Hygiene Movement, the Development of Personality and the School: The Medicalization of American Education," *History of Education Quarterly* 23, no. 2 (Summer 1983): 123–149.
102 Gerald E. Thomson, *Remove From Our Midst These Unfortunates: A Historical Inquiry Into the Influence of Eugenics, Educational Efficiency as well as Mental Hygiene Upon the Vancouver School System and Its Special Classes, 1910-1969* (PhD Diss., University of British Columbia, 1999), 78.
103 Thomson, *Remove These Unfortunates from Our Midst*, 78.
104 Mclaren, *Our Own Master Race*, 112.
105 John D. Griffin, *Mental Hygiene*, CBC Radio Broadcast, May 23, 1938. CAMH Archives—F11 JDM Griffin Fonds, Box 3, File 1.
106 "University Club," *The Hamilton Spectator*, January 21, 1938.
107 C. Annau, "'Eager Eugenicists': A Reappraisal of the Birth Control Society of Hamilton," *Social History* 27, no. 53 (1994): 100.
108 John D. Griffin, "Clinical for Psychological Medicine," HSC, November 1936. CAMH Archives—F11, Dr. JDM Griffin fonds, Box 4, File 1.
109 John D. Griffin, Mental Health and Hygiene inn Canada, February 21, 1939. CAMH Archives, F11 Griffin Box 3, File 2.
110 Annau, *Eager Eugenicists*, 127.
111 Edward Shorter, ed., *TPH: History and Memories of the Toronto Psychiatric Hospital, 1925-1966* (Toronto: Wall and Emerson Inc., 1996), 86.
112 Shorter, *TPH: History and Memories of the Toronto Psychiatric Hospital*, 84.
113 McLaren, *Our Own Master Race*, 119.
114 Ibid., 113.
115 Mona Gleason, *Normalizing the Ideal: Psychology, Schooling, and the Family in Postwar Canada* (Toronto: University of Toronto Press, 1999) ,40.
116 J. Raymond, *The Nursery World of Dr. Blatz* (Toronto: University of Toronto Press, 1991), 31.
117 Pierre Burton, *The Dionne Year: A Thirties Melodrama* (Toronto: McLelland and Stewart, 1977), 125–126.

118 Interview with Reva Gerstein, August 20, 2008.
119 Mary J. Wright., "Flashbacks in the History of Psychology in Canada: Some Early Headline Makers," *Canadian Psychology* 43, no. 1 (2002): 21–34.
120 J. B. Djuwe and S. Sussman, *Pioneers of Mental Health and Social Change 1930–1989* (London: Third Eye Publications, 1989), 61.
121 T. Richardson, *Century of the Child: The Mental Hygiene Movement and Social Policy in the United States and Canada* (New York: State University of New York Press, 1989), 118.
122 Dowbiggin, "Prescription for Survival," 182.
123 Copp and McAndrew, *Battle Exhaustion*, 31.
124 John Farley, *Brock Chisolm, The World Health Organization and the Cold War* (Vancouver: UBC Press, 2008), 31.
125 David Twiston Davies, *Canada from Afar: The Daily Telegraph Book of Canadian Obituaries* (Toronto: Dundurn Press, 1996), 16–17.
126 Alan Irving, *Brock Chisolm: Doctor to the World* (Markham: Fitzhenry and Whiteside, 1998), 48.
127 Col. M. S. to G. Radcliffe Esq., Secretary, the Eugenics Society of Canada, November 25, 1939, Library and Archives Canada, Directorate of Personnel Selection, [textual record] 1944–1964, RG24-C-3, R112-166-3-E, Vol. 3, File 1.
128 G. Radcliffe to the Honorable Norman Rogers, Minister of National Defence, December 26, 1939, Library and Archives Canada, Directorate of Personnel Selection [textual record] 1944–1964, RG24-C-3, R112-166-3-E.
129 George A. Ferguson, "Psychology in Canada, 1939–1945," *Canadian Psychology* 33, no. 4 (October 1992): 692–705.
130 Preliminary Memorandum on the Use of Psychological Methods in Wartime, Submitted to the National Research Council, September 15, 1939, Library and Archives Canada, Directorate of Personnel Selection [textual record] 1944–1964, RG24-C-3, R112-166-3-E, Vol. 1, File 9.
131 Carver, *Personnel Selection in the Canadian Army*, 36.
132 Blom and Sussman, *Pioneers of Mental Health and Social Change*, 70–71.
133 Copp and McAndrew, *Battle Exhaustion*, 35.
134 Interviews with Seeley.
135 Ibid.
136 Memorandum: Griffin to Brigadier Warner, Department of National Defense, Ottawa, January 26, 1945, Library and Archives Canada, "Suicide and attempted suicide cases—policy," 1944–1945, RG24, Vol. 2053, File No. HQS-54-27-1-86.
137 Memorandum: Griffin to Brigadier Warner, Department of National Defense, Ottawa, January 26, 1945, Library and Archives Canada, "Suicide and attempted suicide cases—policy," 1944–1945, RG24, Vol. 2053, File No. HQS-54-27-1-86.
138 A.G. Letter R786, Feb 5, 1945, Library and Archives Canada, "Suicide and attempted suicide cases—policy," 1944–1945, RG24, Vol. 2053, File No.HQS-54-27-1-86.
139 DGMS Letter A038, March 14, 1945, Library and Archives Canada, "Suicide and attempted suicide cases—policy," 1944–1945, RG24, Vol. 2053, File No. HQS-54-27-1-86.
140 Seeley to Fischer, Undated (sometime in the 1960s), Fischer Papers, Forest Hill, Ontario.
141 Memorandum, Confidential, Re-Orientation and Readjustment, Civilian Advisory Committee—D. P. Select. Summary of Minutes, Library and Archives Canada, Senior

Advisory Committee on Demobilization and Rehabilitation [textual record] 1940–1946, RG32-D-4 > sss 7-4, R234-32-4-E, Vol. 32, File 108-6.
142 Confidential, Re-Orientation and Readjustment, Civilian Advisory Committee—D.P. Select. Summary of Minutes, Library and Archives Canada, Senior Advisory Committee on Demobilization and Rehabilitation [textual record] 1940–1946, RG32-D-4 > sss 7-4, R234-32-4-E, Vol. 32, File 108-6.
143 Memorandum, Confidential, Re-Orientation and Readjustment, Civilian Advisory Committee—D. P. Select. Summary of Minutes, Library and Archives Canada, Senior Advisory Committee on Demobilization and Rehabilitation [textual record] 1940–1946, RG32-D-4 > sss 7-4, R234-32-4-E, Vol. 32, File 108-6.
144 Ibid.
145 Brock Chisolm to Brigadier M. Noel (V.A.G.2) September 6, 1944, Library and Archives Canada, Senior Advisory Committee on Demobilization and Rehabilitation [textual record] 1940–1946, RG32-D-4 > sss 7-4, R234-32-4-E, Vol. 32, File 108-6.
146 Seeley to Brock Chisolm, May 20, 1945, Seeley Papers, Los Angeles, California.
147 Seeley, DND Memo, The No-Fraternization Rule, May 18, 1945, Seeley Papers, Los Angeles, California.
148 Ibid.
149 Ibid.
150 Ibid.
151 Ibid.
152 Ibid.
153 Ibid.
154 Re: Captain Herbert John Ronald Friedeberg Seeley, Library and Archives Canada, Access to Information, Privacy and Document Delivery Services Division, Personal Records Division, Referenc e PRA2010-06622/A1.
155 Seeley to Frank, January 5, 1953, Fischer Papers, Toronto, Ontario.
156 Memorandum to A. G., Civilian Advisory Committee, Minutes of Sixth Meeting, March 31, 1945, Library and Archives Canada, Senior Advisory Committee on Demobilization and Rehabilitation [textual record] 1940–1946, RG32-D-4 > sss 7-4, R234-32-4-E, Vol. 32, File 108-6.
157 Summary of Minutes, Demobilization Policy, Basic Principles, DP Select, Col Line, Library and Archives Canada Senior Advisory Committee on Demobilization and Rehabilitation [textual record] 1940–1946, RG32-D-4 > sss 7-4, R234-32-4-E, Vol. 32, File 108-6.
158 Ibid.
159 University of Toronto President Sydney Smith to Colonel Bill Line, June 20, 1945, Seeley Papers, Los Angeles, California.
160 Seeley, Memo: A Psychological Service for the University, Seeley Papers, Los Angeles, California.
161 Ibid.
162 Seeley to Minister of Health Paul Martin, July 21, 1945, Seeley Papers, Los Angeles, California.
163 Re: Captain Herbert John Ronald Friedeberg Seeley, Library and Archives Canada, Access to Information, Privacy and Document Delivery Services Division, Personal Records Division, Reference PRA2010-06622/A1.
164 By Way of Canada: US Records of Immigration across the US-Canadian Border, 1895–1954, (St. Albans Lists), www.archives.gov/publications/prologue/2000/fall/US-Canada-immigration-records-1.html, accessed September 15, 2009.

165 David Riesman to Murray Ross, November 20, 1959, Clara Thomas Archives and Special Collections, York University, John R Seeley Papers, 1954–1971, F0405, 1975—012/012.
166 Niel McLaughlin, "'Critical Theory Meets America': Riesman, Fromm, and The Lonely Crowd," *The American Sociologist* (Spring 2001): 12.
167 Mclaughlin, "Critical Theory Meets America," 7.
168 Allan Bloom, *The Closing of the American Mind* (New York: Simon and Schuster, 1987), 145.
169 Ibid., 19.
170 Ibid., 21.
171 Ibid.
172 Bloom, *Closing of the American Mind*, 148.
173 David Riesman, *The Lonely Crowd* (New Haven: Yale University Press, 2000), xiv.
174 Ibid., xxii.
175 Seeley to Sim, October 14, 1954, Seeley Papers, Los Angeles, California.
176 Seeley to Head of University of Toronto Press, Marsh Jeanneret, August 16, 1955, Seeley Papers, Los Angeles, California.
177 Pierre Birnbaum, "The Absence of Encounter: Sociology and Jewish Studies" in Andreas Gotzman, Christian Wiese, eds., *Modern Judaism and Historical Consciousness: Identities, Encounters, Perspectives* (Boston: Brill, 2007), 244.
178 Gary Alan Fine, ed., *A Second Chicago School: The Development of Postwar American Sociology* (Chicago: University of Chicago Press, 1995), 233.
179 Interviews with Seeley, March 2007, Los Angeles, California.
180 John R. Seeley, "Social Structure and Personality Structure in a Small United States City," University of Chicago Library, Special Collections Research Center Burgess, Ernest W. Papers Addenda, 1910–1966, Box 18.
181 Interviews with Seeley.
182 Seeley to Fischer, October 21, 1953, Fischer Papers, Toronto, Ontario.
183 Ibid.
184 Ibid.
185 Ibid.
186 Review of *Love is not Enough,* undated, Seeley Papers, Los Angeles, California.
187 Ibid.
188 Bruno Bettleheim, *Symbolic Wounds: Puberty Rites and the Envious Male* (Glencoe, Illinois: The Free Press, 1954), 11–12.
189 Seeley to Bruno Bettleheim, January 5, 1953, Fischer Papers, Toronto, Ontario.
190 Bettleheim, *Symbolic Wounds*, 255.
191 Seeley to Bettleheim, January 5, 1953, Fischer Papers, Toronto, Ontario.
192 Ibid.
193 Interviews with Michael Seeley, March 2020.
194 Hughes to Seeley, October 16, 1958, University of Chicago Library, Special Collections Research Center, Hughes, Everett Cherrington Papers, 1910–1966, Box 57.
195 Ibid.
196 Ibid.
197 Riesman Reference for Seeley addressed to Murray Ross, November 20, 1959, Clara Thomas Archives and Special Collections, York University, John R Seeley Papers, 1954–1971, F0405, 1975—012/002.
198 Seeley to Hughes, October 20, 1958, University of Chicago Library, Special Collections Research Center, Hughes, Everett Cherrington Papers, 1910–1966, Box 57.
199 Ibid.

200 Seeley to Hughes, January 14, 1959, University of Chicago Library, Special Collections Research Center, Hughes, Everett Cherrington Papers, 1910–1966, Box 57.
201 Ibid.
202 Seeley to Hughes, December 15, 1970, University of Chicago Library, Special Collections Research Center, Hughes, Everett Cherrington Papers, 1910–1966, Box 57.
203 Seeley to Hughes, October 11, 1982, University of Chicago Library, Special Collections Research Center, Hughes, Everett Cherrington Papers, 1910–1966, Box 57.
204 John R. Seeley, "Mental Health for Canada," October 1947, Library and Archives Canada, Canadian National Committee for Mental Hygiene [textual record] 1918–1949, MG28-I391, R3858-2-G-E, File 435-5-16.
205 Ibid.
206 Ibid.
207 Interviews with Seeley, March 2007, Los Angeles, California.
208 Seeley, "Mental Health for Canada."
209 Ibid.
210 Meeting Minutes, Board of Directors of the National Committee for Mental Hygiene, October 17, 1947, File 1, Vol. 3, Library and Archives Canada, Canadian National Committee for Mental Hygiene [textual record] 1918–1949, MG28-I391, R3858-2-G-E, File 435-5-16.
211 Harvey Weinstein, *A Father, A Son and the CIA* (Toronto: James Lortimer & Co, 1988), 118.
212 Meeting Minutes, Board of Directors of the National Committee for Mental Hygiene, October 17, 1947, File 1, Vol. 3, Library and Archives Canada, Canadian National Committee for Mental Hygiene [textual record] 1918–1949, MG28-I391, R3858-2-G-E, File 435-5-16.
213 Memo: The Forest Hill Village Project of the National Committee for Mental Hygiene, 1948–1949, April 1948, Seeley Papers, Los Angeles, California.
214 Alex Sim, "The Person in the Process," The William Line Seminar, 1972, Toronto, Centre for Addiction and Mental Health Archives, Fonds, 1918–1984 CAONOOO8.
215 Bruce Byrnes, "Forest Hill Helps Boys, Girls to Solve their Mental Quirks," *Toronto Evening Telegram*, October 21, 1951.
216 *Toronto Evening Telegram*, September 25, 1949.
217 K. S. Tisshaw, "'Ultra-Modern Village School': Newest Forest Hill Unit has Complete Facilities for Intercommunication," *Civic Administration* (February 1950): 14.
218 Minutes, Meeting of the Board of Education for the Village of Forest Hill, March 15, 1948, Toronto District School Board Archives.
219 Seeley to Everett Hughes, December 19, 1970, University of Chicago Library, Special Collections Research Center, Hughes, Everett Cherrington Papers, 1910–1966, Box 57.
220 Harvey G. Simmons, *Unbalanced: Mental Health Policy in Ontario, 1930–1989* (Toronto: Wall and Thompson, 1990), 42.
221 Memo from Stodghill to Cameron, March 30, 1948, Library and Archives Canada, Mental Health Division [textual record] 1946–1974 RG 29-3, R227-103-5-E, File 435-7-11.
222 Ibid.
223 Memorandum from Josie to Dr. Stogdill, April 2, 1948, Library and Archives Canada, Mental Health Division [textual record] 1946–1974 RG 29-3, R227-103-5-E, File 435-7-11.
224 Memorandum from Josie to Dr. Stogdill, April 19, 1948, Library and Archives Canada, Mental Health Division [textual record] 1946–1974 RG 29-3, R227-103-5-E, File 435-7-11.

225 Ibid.
226 Ibid.
227 Josie's Notes, April 1948, Library and Archives Canada, Mental Health Division [textual record] 1946–1974 RG 29-3, R227-103-5-E, File 435-7-11.
228 Stodghill to Hincks, June 26, 1948, Library and Archives Canada, Mental Health Division [textual record] 1946–1974 RG 29-3, R227-103-5-E, File 435-7-11.
229 Hincks to Stodghill, June 30, 1948, Library and Archives Canada, Mental Health Division [textual record] 1946–1974 RG 29-3, R227-103-5-E, File 435-7-11.
230 Martin to Meakins, March 1, 1949, Library and Archives Canada, Mental Health Division [textual record] 1946–1974 RG 29-3, R227-103-5-E, File 435-7-11.
231 Martin to Meakins, July 13, 1948, Library and Archives Canada, Mental Health Division [textual record] 1946–1974 RG 29-3, R227-103-5-E, File 435-7-11.
232 Ibid.
233 Martin to Meakins, July 13, 1948, Library and Archives Canada, Mental Health Division [textual record] 1946–1974 RG 29-3, R227-103-5-E, File 435-7-11.
234 Alex Sim, "The Person in the Process," The William Line Seminar, 1972, Toronto, Centre for Addiction and Mental Health Archives, Fonds, 1918–1984 CAONOOO8.
235 G. E. Thomson, "'Not an Attempt to Coddle Children': Dr. Charles Hegler Gundry and the Mental Hygiene Division of the Vancouver School Board, 1939–1969," *Historical Studies in Education / Revue d'histoire de l'éducation* 14, no. 2 (2002): 42.
236 Pauline M. H. Mazmdar, *Eugenics, Human Genetics and Human Failings: The Eugenics Society, Its Sources and Its Critics in Britain* (London: Routledge, 1992), 180.
237 "Annual Meeting and Election of Officers and Council," *Eugenics Review* 36, no. 2 (July 1944): 52–58, http://europepmc.org/articles/PMC2986150/pdf/eugenrev00256-0014.pdf.
238 Louise Ellis, "'Aldwyn Stokes': The Man and His Contribution to Canadian Psychiatry," *Canadian Psychiatric Association Bulletin* (April 2000): 1.
239 Interview with Douglas Frayn, October 20, 2009.
240 Douglas Frayn, *Psychoanalysis in Toronto* (Toronto: Ash Publications, 2000), 14.
241 Stokes to Cameron, March 5, 1952. University of Toronto Archives, Department of Psychiatry Fonds, A 1986-0032, Box 3, File 55.
242 Edgar Jones, "Aubrey Lewis, Edward Mapother and the Maudsley," *Medical History* 22 (2003): 33.
243 Aldwyn Stokes, "Eugenic Aspects of Social Psychiatry," September 10, 1948, University of Toronto Archives, Department of Psychiatry Fonds, A 1986-0032, Box 3, File 55.
244 Aldwyn Stokes, "The Biosocial Aspects of Psychiatry," Meeting of the Academy of Medicine, January 7, 1949, University of Toronto Archives, Department of Psychiatry Fonds, 1947–1968, A 1986-0032, Ref A1986-0032/001, File 8: BIOSOCIAL.
245 Seeley to Everett Hughes, October 20, 1958, University of Chicago Library, Special Collections Research Center, Hughes, Everett Cherrington Papers, 1910–1966, Box 57.
246 Stokes to Cameron, July 19, 1950, Archives of Ontario, National and Provincial Health Grant Research Project Files, 1948–1973, RG10-22, File 117.
247 Minutes, Meeting of the Scientific Advisory Committee (CNCMH) June 21, 1948, Library and Archives Canada, Canadian National Committee for Mental Hygiene [textual record] 1918–1949, MG28-I391, R3858-2-G-E, File 435-5-16.
248 Ibid.
249 Memorandum from Seeley to Stokes re: Forest Hill Village Project, June 30, 1949, Seeley Papers, Los Angeles, California.

250 Ibid.
251 Library and Archives Canada, Alexander Sim Fonds, File 9, Crestwood Heights: Research Interviews Forest Hill Village, MG30-D260-R2332-0-7-E.
252 Seeley to Fischer, October 21, 1953, Fischer Papers, Toronto, Ontario.
253 Interviews with Seeley, March 2007, Los Angeles, California.
254 Seeley, Sim, and Loosley, *Crestwood Heights,* 427.
255 "Confidential Memo Re: Bob Metcalf, Nicholas Hermes April 9th, 1953," Fischer Papers, Toronto, Ontario.
256 Library and Archives Canada, Alexander Sim Fonds, File 9, Crestwood Heights: Research Interviews Forest Hill Village, MG30-D260-R2332-0-7-E.
257 Interview with Margot (Hill) Wojciechowski, September 28, 2010.
258 Griffin, J. D., *In Search of Sanity: A Chronicle of the Canadian Mental Health Association, 1918–1988* (London: Third Eye, 1989), 11.
259 Minutes from a Meeting of the Liaison Officers, Forest Hill Village Project, February 17, 1949, Centre for Addiction and Mental Health Archives.
260 Dr. Isabel Laird, "Mental Health in Education," Archives of Ontario, RG-10-22, File 138, 605-5-1979. 1955, B440019.
261 Tom Mallinson to John R. Seeley, January 16, 1956, Seeley Papers, Los Angeles, California.
262 Shorter, *TPH: History and Memories of the Toronto Psychiatric Hospital,* IX.
263 Fischer's Notes, Fischer Papers, Toronto, Ontario.
264 Norm Bell, "A Note on Emotionally Disturbing Triads," January 12, 1952, Seeley Papers, Los Angeles, California.
265 Ibid.
266 Ibid.
267 Ibid.
268 Ibid.
269 Library and Archives Canada, Alexander Sim Fonds, File 9, Crestwood Heights: Research Interviews Forest Hill Village, MG30-D260-R2332-0-7-E.
270 Minutes, Meeting of the Forest Hill Village Project Staff and Liaison Officers, February 14, 1949, Center for Addiction and Mental Health Archives.
271 Seeley, Sim, and Loosley, *Crestwood Heights,* 14–15.
272 John R. Seeley, "Interim Report on the Uppertown Experiment," January 13, 1953, Seeley Papers, Los Angeles, California.
273 Seeley and Mallinson, "A Controlled Experiment in Group-Directed Discussion with Children (An Aspect of a Community Research Study)," Archives of Ontario, National and Provincial Health Grant Research Project Files, 1948–1973, RG10-22, File 115.
274 Seeley to Mallinson, April 27, 1954, Simon Fraser University Archives, Thomas J Mallinson Fonds, F124-1-0-0,1.
275 Michel Foucault, *Discipline and Punish: The Birth of the Prison* (Vintage Books: New York, 1977), 308.
276 Minutes, Meeting of the Forest Hill Village Project Staff and Liaison Officers, February 14, 1949, Center for Addiction and Mental Health Archives.
277 Ibid.
278 Ibid.
279 Ibid.
280 Ibid.
281 Ibid.
282 Interview with Michael John Seeley, March 26, 2020.

283 John R Seeley, "Getting Along with Others," February 7, 1952, Seeley Papers, Los Angeles, California.
284 Minute Book of the Forest Hill Village Home and School Association, 1949–1953, January 24, 1950, Forest Hill Village Collegiate Library.
285 Seeley, Sim, and Loosley, *Crestwood Heights*, 265.
286 Minute Book of the Forest Hill Village Home and School Association, 1949–1953, January 24, 1950, Forest Hill Village Collegiate Library.
287 Staff Memorandum no. 50-3-1, September 15, 1950, Seeley Papers, Los Angeles, California.
288 Seeley, Sim, and Loosley, *Crestwood Heights*, 286.
289 Ibid.
290 Ibid., 287.
291 Ibid., 247.
292 Ibid., 337.
293 Will Herberg, *Protestant, Catholic and Jew: An Essay in American Religious Sociology* (Garden City: Doubleday, 1960), 74–81.
294 G. R. Searle, *Eugenics and Politics in Britain, 1900–1914* (Leydon: Noordhoff International Publishing, 1976), 42.
295 Searle, *Eugenics and Politics in Britain*, 42.
296 McLaren, *Our Own Master Race*, 76.
297 Interviews with Seeley.
298 Jack Lipinsky, *Imposing Their Will: An Organizational History of Jewish Toronto, 1933–1948* (Montreal: McGill-Queen's University Press, 2011), 215–16.
299 "Toronto is Third Largest Jewish Community in British Commonwealth," *Daily News Bulletin* (New York: Jewish Telegraphic Agency, 1954), 5.
300 Peter Cheney, "Shouts and Whispers," *The Globe and Mail*, April 19, 2008.
301 Charlotte Gray, "Powerful History of Elitism Uninhibited by Progress," *Toronto Star*, December 10, 1994.
302 Mary Doan to Seeley, October 28, 1954, Seeley Papers, Los Angeles, California.
303 Library and Archives Canada, Alexander Sim Fonds, File 9, Crestwood Heights: Research Interviews Forest Hill Village, MG30-D260-R2332-0-7-E.
304 Leon Whiteson, "Looking at Toronto," *Toronto Star*, July 4, 1981.
305 Mary Doan to Seeley, October 28, 1954, Seeley Papers, Los Angeles, California.
306 Library and Archives Canada, Alexander Sim Fonds, File 9, Crestwood Heights: Research Interviews Forest Hill Village, MG30-D260-R2332-0-7-E.
307 Ibid.
308 Interview with Sharon D'Errico, May 15, 2012.
309 Library and Archives Canada, Alexander Sim Fonds, File 9, Crestwood Heights: Research Interviews Forest Hill Village, MG30-D260-R2332-0-7-E.
310 Interviews with Seeley, March 2007, Los Angeles California.
311 Memorandum from Seeley to Stokes, Forest Hill Village Project—Report, June 30, 1949, Seeley Papers, Los Angles California.
312 Franklin Bialystok, *Delayed Impact: The Holocaust and the Canadian Jewish Community* (Montreal: McGill-Queen's University Press, 2000), 73–74.
313 Bialystok, *Delayed Impact*, 6.
314 Ibid., 71.
315 Ibid., 72.
316 Interview with Ernie Erdos, November 21, 2010.

317 "'Wait, See' Attitude on Forest Hill C. I. Education Experiment," *Toronto Daily Star*, October 14, 1950.
318 Ibid.
319 Ibid.
320 Ibid.
321 Library and Archives Canada, Alexander Sim Fonds, File 9, Crestwood Heights: Research Interviews Forest Hill Village, MG30-D260-R2332-0-7-E.
322 Adara Goldberg, *Holocaust Survivors in Canada: Exclusion, Inclusion, Transformation, 1947–1955* (Winnipeg: University of Manitoba Press, 2015), 140.
323 Library and Archives Canada, Alexander Sim Fonds, File 9, Crestwood Heights: Research Interviews Forest Hill Village, MG30-D260-R2332-0-7-E.
324 "'Wait, See' Attitude on Forest Hill C. I. Education Experiment."
325 Seeley, Sim, and Loosley, *Crestwood Heights*, 332.
326 Interviews with Seeley.
327 Thomas Mallinson, *An Experimental Investigation of Group-Directed Discussion in the Classroom* (PhD Diss., Department of Psychology, University of Toronto, 1955), 39.
328 Ibid.
329 Martin Sable, "'George Drew and the Rabbis': Religious Education in Ontario's Public Schools," *Association for Canadian Jewish Studies* 6 (1998): 36–37.
330 Veronica Strong-Boag, "Home Dreams: Women and the Suburban Experiment, 1945–1960," *The Canadian Historical Review* (1991): 487.
331 Strong-Boag, "'Home Dreams,'" 42.
332 Mary Louise Adams, *The Trouble with Normal: Postwar Youth and the Making of Heterosexuality* (Toronto: University of Toronto Press, 1997), 20.
333 Strong-Boag, "Home Dreams," 55.
334 Wini Breines, "Gender and Some Social Science," *Sociological Inquiry* 56, no. 1 (January 1986): 70.
335 Adams, *The Trouble with Normal*, 26.
336 Staphanie Coontz, *The Way We Never Were: American Families and the Nostalgia Trap* (New York: Basic Books, 1992), 34, 298.
337 Library and Archives Canada, Alexander Sim Fonds, File 9, Crestwood Heights: Research Interviews Forest Hill Village, MG30-D260-R2332-0-7-E.
338 Ibid.
339 Ibid.
340 Ibid. This excerpt had been clipped by Alex Sim and copies sent to Jack Seeley and Betty Loosely during the last year of their work on the writing of Crestwood Heights.
341 Riesman, *The Lonely Crowd*, 89.
342 Library and Archives Canada, Alexander Sim Fonds, File 9, Crestwood Heights: Research Interviews Forest Hill Village, MG30-D260-R2332-0-7-E.
343 Ibid.
344 Ibid.
345 Ibid.
346 Ibid.
347 Ibid.
348 Ibid.
349 Ibid.
350 Seeley to Fischer, 1963, Fischer Papers, Forest Hill, Ontario.
351 John R. Seeley, "Eulogy at the Funeral of Dr. Martin Aaron Fischer," January 13, 1992, Fischer Papers, Forest Hill, Ontario.
352 Ibid.

353 Ellis, "Aldwyn Stokes," 1.
354 Charles Levi, "The Jewish Quota in the Faculty of Medicine, University of Toronto: Generational Memory Sustained by Documentation," *Historical Studies in Education* 15, no. 1 (2003): 131–38.
355 Frayn, *Psychoanalysis in Toronto,* 154–55.
356 Fischer's Appointment Book, Fisher Papers, Toronto, Ontario.
357 Joyce, A.S, Tosca, G.A., Ogrodnicczuk, J.S., "Group Psychotherapy in Canada," *International Journal of Group Psychotherapy* 65, no. 4 (2015).
358 Sharon Carton, "The Poet, the Biographer and the Shrink: Psychiatrist-Patient Confidentiality and the Anne Sexton Biography," *University of Miami Entertainment and Sports Law Review* 10, no. 1 (1993).
359 Seeley to Fischer, October 10, 1966, Fischer Papers, Toronto, Ontario.
360 Interview with Beatrice Fischer, December 15, 2010.
361 Interviews with Beatrice Fischer.
362 Seeley to Fischer, Fischer Papers, Toronto, Ontario.
363 Ibid.
364 Interview with Erica Fischer, November 9, 2009.
365 John R. Seeley, "Eulogy at the Funeral of Dr. Martin Aaron Fischer."
366 Fischer to Aufreiter, March 13, 1958, Fischer Papers, Toronto, Ontario.
367 Interview with Beatrice Fischer, July 20, 2009.
368 Daniel Smith, "Shock and Disbelief", *The Atlantic*, February 2001.
369 Fischer Resignation Letter, Fischer Papers, Toronto, Ontario.
370 Grainne Neilson, *The 1996 CMA Code of Ethics Annotated for Psychiatrists* (Canadian Psychiatric Association, 2002), 11.
371 D. Wright and R. Saucier, "Madness in the Archives: Anonymity, Ethics, and Mental Health History Research," *Journal of the Canadian Historical Association / Revue de la Société historique du Canada* 23, no. 2 (2012): 65–90.
372 *Curriculum Vitae,* Refugee Camp I, St. Paul, Ile-aux-Noix, Quebec, Fischer Papers, Toronto, Ontario.
373 Memorial Book for the Victims of National Socialism at the University of Vienna in 1938, http://gedenkbuch.univie.ac.at/index.php?id435&no_cache1&L2.
374 *Curriculum Vitae,* Refugee Camp I, St. Paul, Ile-aux-Noix, Quebec. Fischer Papers, Forest Hill, Ontario.
375 Interview with Dr. Douglas Frayn, October 18, 2008.
376 Martin Fischer, "Information Required for Biographical Directory of Canadian Psychiatrists," submitted to the Canadian National Mental Health Association, Fischer Papers, Toronto, Ontario.
377 Ernest Jones, *Sigmund Freud: Life and Work* (London, Hogarth Press, 1953–1957), 255.
378 Interviews with Beatrice Fischer.
379 *Curriculum Vitae,* Refugee Camp I, St. Paul, Ile-aux-Noix, Quebec, Fischer Papers, Toronto, Ontario.
380 Memorial Book for the Victims of National Socialism at the University of Vienna.
381 Edzard Ernst, "A Leading Medical School Seriously Damaged: Vienna 1938," *History of Medicine, Annals of Internal Medicine* (American College of Physicians, 2004), http://www.annals.org/content/122/10/789.full.
382 *Curriculum Vitae,* Refugee Camp I, St. Paul, Ile-aux-Noix, Quebec, Fischer Papers, Toronto, Ontario.
383 Memorial Book for the Victims of National Socialism at the University of Vienna.
384 Interview with Erica Fischer, November 11, 2009.

385 Martin Fischer, "Application for Release: According to the Home Office Statement of July 23, 1940 concerning the question of releasing of German and Austrian Civilian Internees," Category C, Fischer Papers, Toronto, Ontario.
386 Fischer, "Application for Release."
387 Eric Koch, *Deemed Suspect: A Wartime Blunder* (Toronto: Methuen, 1980), 7.
388 Ibid., 9.
389 Ibid., 14.
390 Fischer, "Application for Release."
391 Koch, *Deemed Suspect*, 98.
392 Ibid.
393 Fischer to Internment Operations, August 3, 1940, Fischer Papers, Toronto, Ontario.
394 Fischer to his Brothers, Samuel and David, October 31, 1941, Fischer Papers, Toronto, Ontario.
395 Martin Fischer, Letter from Camp I, December 15, 1940, Fischer Papers, Toronto, Ontario.
396 Fischer to Brothers, October 31, 1941, Fischer Papers, Toronto, Ontario.
397 Ibid.
398 United States Holocaust Memorial Museum, "The Holocaust," *Holocaust Encyclopedia*, http://www.ushmm.org/wlc/en/index.php?ModuleId=10005143.
399 Interview with Beatrice Fischer, November 24, 2008.
400 Interview with Beatrice Fischer, October 1, 2009.
401 https://www.canadianarttherapy.org/wp-content/uploads/2018/04/CATA-fact-sheet-April-2018.pdf.
402 Interview with Erica Fischer, March 16th, 2020.
403 Minute Book of the Forest Hill Village Home and School Association, 1949–1953, January 29, 1952, Forest Hill Collegiate Library.
404 Minute Book of the Home and School Association, March 25, 1952, Forest Hill Collegiate Library.
405 Seeley to Fischer, October 25, 1955, Fischer Papers, Forest Hill, Ontario.
406 Seeley to Fischer, January 14, 1954, Fischer Papers, Toronto, Ontario.
407 Ibid.
408 Seeley to Frank, January 5, 1953, Fischer Papers, Toronto, Ontario.
409 Seeley to Frank, June 7, 1953, Fischer Papers, Forest Hill, Ontario.
410 Seeley to Frank, Fischer Papers, Toronto, Ontario.
411 Seeley to Frank, Fischer Papers, Toronto, Ontario.
412 Interviews with Seeley, March 2007, Los Angeles, California.
413 Margaret to Fischer, Fischer Papers, Toronto, Ontario.
414 Margaret to Fischer, Fischer Papers, Toronto, Ontario.
415 Margaret to Fischer, Fischer Papers, Toronto, Ontario.
416 Margaret to Fischer, Fischer Papers, Toronto, Ontario.
417 Interview with Reva Gerstein, August 20, 2008.
418 Seeley to Fischer, Fischer Papers, Toronto, Ontario.
419 Seeley to Fischer, October 21, 1953, Fischer Papers, Toronto, Ontario.
420 http://browndalestaffkids.multiply.com/notes, *Browndale Staff and Kids*, Allan King, Film-Maker, 17/06/2006, 11:31:00 AM.
421 Jean Mercer, "Coercive Restraint Therapies: A Dangerous Alternative Mental Health Intervention," MedGenMed. 2005; 7(3): 6 https://www.ncbi.nlm.nih.gov/pmc/articles/PMC1681667/
422 Bettleheim, Bruno, "Individual and Mass Behaviour in Extreme Situations." *Journal of Abnormal and Social Psychology* 38 (1943).

423　Seeley, Sim, and Loosley, *Crestwood Heights,* 427.
424　Ibid., 366.
425　Ibid.
426　Black Hawk Hancock, Roberta Garner: Theorizing Goffman and Freud: Goffman's Interaction as a Social-Structural Underpinning for Freud's Psychoanalytic Self," *Canadian Journal of Sociology* 40, no. 4 (2015): 423.
427　Foucault, "The Subject and Power," in P. Rabinow and N. Rose, eds., *The Essential Foucault, Selections of Essential Works of Foucault, 1954–1984* (New York: The New Press, 1994). 132.
428　John R. Seeley, "Crestwood Heights and Mental Health," Fischer Papers, Forest Hill, Ontario.
429　Ibid.
430　Ibid.
431　Ibid.
432　Ibid.
433　Ibid.
434　Ibid.
435　Ibid.
436　Ibid.
437　Erving Goffman, *Asylums: Essays on the Situation of Mental Patients and Other Inmates* (New York: Anchor, 1961), 56.
438　Seeley to Sim and Loosley, re: Termination of FHV Project, December 18, 1953, Seeley Papers, Los Angeles California.
439　Library and Archives Canada, Alexander Sim Fonds, File 9, Crestwood Heights: Research Interviews Forest Hill Village, MG30-D260-R2332-0-7-E.
440　Robert Sim and Robert Alexander Sim, *Robert Sim: His Life and Work 1876–1956*, (Toronto: Sim Post, 2002).
441　Elizabeth Wyeth Magee Loosley, *Memories of the Loosleys and Magees: Two Canadian Pioneer Families*, Unpublished memoir, Metropolitan Toronto Public Library.
442　Ibid.
443　Loosley to Seeley, May 21, 1956, Seeley Papers, Los Angeles, California.
444　Alexander Sim, Memo to the Forest Hill Village Project Staff, "A Note on Editorial Policy," September 2, 1952, Seeley Papers, Los Angeles, California.
445　Seeley to Loosley, February 5, 1954, Seeley Papers, Los Angeles, California.
446　Sim to Seeley, February 17, 1954, Seeley Papers, Los Angeles, California.
447　Seeley to Don Graham, February 24, 1954, Seeley Papers, Los Angeles, California.
448　Sim to Seeley, March 22, 1954, Seeley Papers, Los Angeles, California.
449　Seeley to Sim, March 25, 1954, Seeley Papers, Los Angeles, California.
450　Rosenthal to Seeley, April 29, 1954, Seeley Papers, Los Angeles, California.
451　Ibid.
452　Minutes: Forest Hill Village Project Staff Meeting, Thursday, July 1, 1954, Seeley Papers, Los Angeles, California.
453　Chicago Readers' Report Summary, Undated, Seeley Papers, Los Angeles, California.
454　Ibid.
455　Mary Doan to Seeley, October 28, 1954, Seeley Papers, Los Angeles, California.
456　Ibid.
457　Ibid.
458　Ibid.
459　Minutes: Forest Hill Village Project Staff Meeting, Thursday, July 1, 1954, Seeley Papers, Los Angeles, California.

460 Ibid.
461 Seeley's Notes, Seeley Papers, Los Angeles, California.
462 Sim to Seeley, July 7, 1954, Seeley Papers, Los Angeles, California.
463 Minutes: Forest Hill Village Project Staff Meeting, Thursday, July 1, 1954, Seeley Papers, Los Angeles, California.
464 Gordon Watson to Seeley, November 23, 1954, Seeley Papers, Los Angeles, California.
465 Sim to Seeley, July 7, 1954, Seeley Papers, Los Angeles, California.
466 Ibid.
467 Seeley to Stokes, September 21, 1954, Seeley Papers, Los Angeles, California.
468 Stokes to Seeley, June 17, 1955, Seeley Papers, Los Angeles, California.
469 Telegram received by Seeley from Stokes, February 20, 1956, Seeley Papers, Los Angeles, California.
470 Seeley to Stokes, June 30, 1955, Seeley Papers, Los Angeles, California.
471 Sim to Seeley, November 1955, Seeley Papers, Los Angeles, California.
472 Ibid.
473 Seeley to Riesman, February 6, 1956, Seeley Papers, Los Angeles, California.
474 Library and Archives Canada, Alexander Sim Fonds, File 13, Crestwood Heights: 1955–57, Correspondence and Memoranda MG30-D260-R2332-0-7-E.
475 Ibid.
476 Sim to Seeley, January 6, 1956, Seeley Papers, Los Angeles, California.
477 Seeley to Sim, January 17, 1956, Seeley Papers, Los Angeles, California.
478 Sim to Seeley, February 10, 1956, Seeley Papers, Los Angeles, California.
479 Seeley to Sim, March 19, 1956, Seeley Papers, Los Angeles, California.
480 Seeley to Riesman, February 6, 1956, Seeley Papers, Los Angeles, California.
481 Seeley to Sim, February 27, 1956, Seeley Papers, Los Angeles, California.
482 Seeley to Sim, March 19, 1956, Seeley Papers, Los Angeles, California.
483 Stokes to Seeley, March 19, 1956, Seeley Papers, Los Angeles, California.
484 Stokes to Seeley, March 16, 1956, Seeley Papers, Los Angeles, California.
485 Ibid.
486 Ibid.
487 Stokes to Seeley, June 7, 1956, Seeley Papers, Los Angeles, California.
488 Jeanneret to Seeley, June 8, 1956, Seeley Papers, Los Angeles, California.
489 Hillary Marshall, Field Representative for U of T Press to the Editor of *Publishers Weekly*, June 19, 1956, Seeley Papers, Los Angeles, California.
490 Marshall to Seeley, May 16, 1956, Seeley Papers, Los Angeles, California.
491 Rabbi Slonim, "Forest Hill Village on Analyst's Couch," *Toronto Telegram*, May 26, 1956.
492 Marshall to Seeley, May 16, 1956, Seeley Papers, Los Angeles, California.
493 "Find Mental Problems Prevalent in New Suburban Areas: Forest Hill Mothers are Indignant over 'Crestwood Heights': A Book which Blasts Way They Raise Their Children," *Toronto Daily Star*, May 3, 1956, Seeley Papers, Los Angeles, California.
494 Marshal to Seeley, May 15, 1956, Seeley Papers, Los Angeles, California.
495 Marshal to Seeley, May 16, 1956, Seeley Papers, Los Angeles, California.
496 Seeley to Sim, November 4, 1955, Seeley Papers, Los Angeles, California.
497 Sim to Seeley, November 21, 1955, Seeley Papers, Los Angeles, California.
498 Seeley to the Editor of the *Toronto Daily Star*, May 8, 1956, Seeley Papers, Los Angeles, California.
499 Loosely to Seeley, May 4, 1956, Seeley Papers, Los Angeles, California.
500 Seeley to Marshall, May 18, 1956, Seeley Papers, Los Angeles, California.

501  Ibid.
502  Ibid.
503  Seeley to the Editor of the *Toronto Star*, June 1956, Seeley Papers, Los Angeles, California.
504  Ibid.
505  Stokes to Seeley, July 25, 1956, Seeley Papers, Los Angeles, California.
506  Seeley to Sim, July 20, 1957, Seeley Papers, Los Angeles, California.
507  Fischer's Notes, Fischer's Papers, Los Angeles, California.
508  Interview with Margery King, September 10, 2008.
509  Seeley, Sim, and Loosely, *Crestwood Heights*, 366.
510  Ibid.
511  Interview with Michael John Seeley, March 26, 2020.
512  Stokes to Seeley, Fischer Papers, Forest Hill, Ontario.
513  John T. Saywell, *Someone to Teach Them: York and the Great University Explosion, 1960–1973* (Toronto: University of Toronto Press, 2008), 10.
514  Seeley to Murray Ross, April 20, 1956, Clara Thomas Archives and Special Collections, York University, John R Seeley Papers, 1954–1971, F0405.
515  Interview with Clayton Ruby, February 20, 2010.
516  Ibid.
517  Ruby to Seeley, January 19, 1964 Clara Thomas Archives and Special Collections, York University, John R. Seeley Papers, 1954-1971, F0405, 1975 – 012/ 009, File 47-67.
518  Ruby to Seeley, June 1, 1964, Clara Thomas Archives and Special Collections, York University, John R. Seeley Papers, 1954-1971, F0405, 1975 – 012/ 009, File 47-67.
519  Ruby to Seeley, September 23, 1963, Clara Thomas Archives and Special Collections, York University, John R. Seeley Papers, 1954-1971, F0405, 1975 – 012/ 009, File 47-67.
520  Ibid.
521  Brandeis University, https://www.brandeis.edu/, accessed March 24, 2020.
522  Salutin to Seeley, February 6, 1962, Clara Thomas Archives and Special Collections, York University, John R. Seeley Papers, 1954-1971, F0405, 1975 – 012/ 011, File 47-67.
523  James L. Newman, Clayton C. Ruby, "Forest Hill Collegiate; A Study of Social Participation, Failure, and Related Phenomena", Clara Thomas Archives and Special Collections, York University, John R. Seeley Papers, 1954-1971, F0405, 1975 – 012/ 009, File 47-67.
524  Fred Blazer, "Clayton Ruby's People Power," *Maclean's*, October 22, 1979, https://archive.macleans.ca/article/1979/10/22/clayton-rubys-people-power.
525  Will Straw, "'Traffic in Scandal': The Story of Broadway Brevities," *University of Toronto Quarterly* 4 (Fall 2004): 34.
526  Straw, "'Traffic in Scandal': The Story of Broadway Brevities," 34.
527  Seeley, *Strange Journey*.
528  Ibid.
529  Murray G. Ross, *The Way Must be Tried*, 22
530  Interviews with Seeley.
531  Martin L. Friedland, *The University of Toronto: A History* (Toronto: University of Toronto Press, 2002), 444.
532  Canada Census, 1911, Ancestry.ca., November 21, 2014.
533  Friedland, *The University of Toronto*, 371.
534  George Grant, *Lament for a Nation* (Toronto: McLelland and Stewart Limited, 1965), 9.
535  Murray Ross, Soviet Challenge: Canadian Response. Speech at the Canadian Club, Clara Thomas Archives and Special Collections, York University, Murray Ross Fonds, 200-082/003, Inventory # 398,

536 Friedland, *The University of Toronto*, 397.
537 Michiel Horn, "Students and Academic Freedom in Canada," *Historical Studies in Education* 11, no.1 (1999): 1–32.
538 John R. Seeley, "Letter to the Editor," *The Globe and Mail*, May 29, 1963.
539 John R. Seeley, "The Sad State of the Multiversity," *The Globe and Mail*, March 1968.
540 Saywell, *Someone to Teach Them*, 28.
541 Saywell, *Someone to Teach Them*, 28.
542 Interview with George Firman Bentley, March 26, 2020.
543 Ross, *The Way Must be Tried*, 29.
544 Saywell, *Someone to Teach Them*, 25.
545 Ibid., 27.
546 Ross, *The Way Must be Tried*, 29.
547 Saywell, *Someone to Teach Them*, 30.
548 Ross, *The Way Must be Tried*, 20.
549 Ibid., 32.
550 Murray G. Ross, final draft of *The Way Must Be Tried*, Clara Thomas Archives and Special Collections, York University, Murray Ross Fonds, 200-082/003, Inventory # 398, p. 45.
551 R. O. Earl, The Functions and Performance of Professor John R. Seeley, memo dated Sept 16, 1964, Clara Thomas Archives and Special Collections, John R. Seeley Papers, 1954–1971, F0405, 1975-012/012 (95).
552 Earl to Seeley, January 21, 1963, Clara Thomas Archives and Special Collections, 1975 -012/012 (95).
553 Ross, *The Way Must be Tried*, 33.
554 Misgeld Memo, Library and Archives Canada, File Professor John Seeley, OISE, 1972–1977, Q5-24868.
555 Ibid.
556 Duhl to Harvey, *Letter of Reference*, April 19, 1974, Library and Archives Canada, File Professor John Seeley, OISE, 1972–1977, Q5-24868.
557 Ibid.
558 Schedule of Events re: Recommendation from the Department of Sociology of Education for the Appointment of Mr. John R. Seeley, Library and Archives Canada, File Professor John Seeley, OISE, 1972–1977, Q5-24868.
559 Jim Bledsoe, "'A Stiletto for Seeley': An Academic Thriller," *This Magazine* 9, no. 54 (November-December 1975).
560 Ibid.
561 Donald B. Coates, "'John Seeley': Poet and Revolutionary," *Canada's Mental Health* 16, no. 6 (November-December 1968): 33–36. Courtesy of CAMH Archives, D. B. Coates fonds, E36.
562 Ibid.
563 Michael Rossman, "The Fool of Sociology," *Sociological Inquiry, Journal of the National Sociology Honor Society* 46, nos. 3–4 (1976): 161–62.
564 Seeley to Fischer, Fischer Papers, Toronto, Ontario.
565 John R. Seeley, *The Americanization of the Unconscious* (New York: International Science Press, 1967), 4.
566 John R. Seeley, "Tales and Tallies: Reflections of a Life-Long Activist/Theoretician," April 19th, Fischer Papers, Toronto Ontario.
567 Ibid., 16.
568 Mathew J. Bellamy, *Profiting the Crown: Canada's Polymer Corporation, 1942–1990* (Montreal: McGill-Queen's University Press, 2005), 188.

# Bibliography

## Archival Sources

Archives of Ontario
National and Provincial Health Grant Research Project Files
Centre for Addiction and Mental Health Archives
D. B. Coates Fonds
J. D. Griffin Fonds
Canadian Mental Health Association (CMHA) Fonds
Clara Thomas Archives & Special Collections, York University
John R. Seeley Papers
Forest Hill Collegiate Library
Library and Archives Canada
Alexander Sim Fonds
Canadian Association of University Teachers (CAUT) Fonds
Department of National Defense Fonds
Directorate of Personnel Selection [Textual Records]
Division of Mental Health [Textual Records]
National Archives, United Kingdom
Naturalization Papers for Lilly Etta Friedeberg-Seeley
Office of Registry of Colonial Slaves and Slave Compensation Commission
Simon Fraser University Archives
Thomas J. Mallinson Fonds
Toronto District School Board Archives
University of Toronto Archives
Department of Psychiatry Fonds
University of Chicago Library, Special Collections Research Center
Everett C. Hughes Papers
Ernest W. Burgess Papers

## Private Papers

Beatrice Fischer
John R. Friedeberg Seeley

## Interviews

George Firman Bentley, March 26, 2020
Sharon D'Errico May 15, 2012
Ernie Erdos, November 21, 2010
Beatrice Fischer, March 2008
Erica Fischer, November 11, 2009
Dr. Douglas Frayn, October 18, 2008
Dr. Reva Gerstein, August 20, 2008
Bob Graham, October 8, 2008
Cyril Greenland, July 2, 2007
Dr. Margery King, September 10, 2008
Eric Koch, July 8, 2011
Clayton Ruby, February 15, 2009
Rick Salutin, October 28, 2008
John R. Seeley, March–December 2007
Michael John Seeley, March 26, 2020
Robert Sim, May 3, 2010
Margot Wojciechowski, September 28, 2010

## Secondary Sources

Adams, M. L., *The Trouble with Normal: Postwar Youth and the Making of Heterosexuality.* Toronto: University of Toronto Press, 1997.

Annau, C., "Eager Eugenicists: A Reappraisal of the Birth Control Society of Hamilton." *Social History* 27, no. 53 (1994).

Axelrod, P., "Beyond the Progressive Education Debate: A Profile of Toronto Schooling in the 1950's." *Historical Studies in Education / Revue d'histoire de l'éducation* 17, no. 2 (2005).

Bagnell, K., *The Little Immigrants: The Orphans Who Came to Canada.* Toronto: Macmillan, 2000.

Bellamy, Mathew J., *Profiting the Crown: Canada's Polymer Corporation, 1942–1990.* Montreal, McGill-Queen's University Press, 2005.

Bettleheim, Bruno, "Individual and Mass Behaviour in Extreme Situations." *Journal of Abnormal and Social Psychology* 38 (1943).

Bettleheim, B., *Symbolic Wounds: Puberty Rites and the Envious Male.* Glencoe, Illinois: The Free Press, 1954.

Bialystok, F., *Delayed Impact: The Holocaust and the Canadian Jewish Community.* Montreal & Kingston: McGill-Queen's University Press, 2000.

Bledsoe, J., "A Stiletto for Seeley: An Academic Thriller." *This Magazine* 9, no. 54 (November–December 1975).

Bloom, A., *The Closing of the American Mind.* New York: Simon and Schuster, 1987.

Breines, W., "Gender and Some Social Science." *Sociological Inquiry* 56, no. 1 (January 1986).

Burton, P., *The Dionne Years: A Thirties Melodrama.* Toronto: McLelland and Stewart, 1977.

Carton, Sharon, "The Poet, the Biographer and the Shrink: Psychiatrist-Patient Confidentiality and the Anne Sexton Biography." *University of Miami Entertainment and Sports Law Review* 10, no. 1 (1993): 117–164.

Carver, H. S. M., *Personnel Selection in the Canadian Army.* National Defence HQ. Unpublished, 1945.

Channing, W. E., *Complete Works of W. E Channing.* London: Christian Life Publishing Company, 1884.

Chenier, E., "The Criminal Sexual Psychopath in Canada: Sex, Psychiatry and Law at mid-Century." *CBMH/BCHM* 20, no. 1 (2003).

Cohen, S., "The Mental Hygiene Movement, the Development of Personality and the School: The Medicalization of American Education." *History of Education Quarterly* 23, no. 2 (Summer 1983).

Collins, A., *In The Sleep Room: The Story of the CIA Brainwashing Experiments in Canada.* Toronto: Lester and Orpen Dennys, 1988.

Coontz, S., *The Way We Never Were: American Families and the Nostalgia Trap.* New York: Basic Books, 1992.

Copp, T., and McAndrew, B., *Battle Exhaustion, Soldiers and Psychiatrists in the Canadian Army, 1939–1945.* Montreal & Kingston: McGill-Queen's University Press, 1990.

Davies, D. T., *Canada from Afar: The Daily Telegraph Book of Canadian Obituaries.* Toronto: Dundurn Press, 1996.

Djuwe, J. B., and Sussman, S., *Pioneers of Mental Health and Social Change 1930-1989.* London: Third Eye Publications, 1989.

Donaldson, S., *The Suburban Myth.* New York: Columbia Press, 1969.

Dowbiggin, I., *Keeping America Sane: Psychiatry and Eugenics in the United States and Canada, 1880-1940.* London: Cornell University Press, 1997.

Dowbiggin, I., "Prescription for Survival, Brock Chisolm, Sterilization, and Mental Health in the Cold War Era," in J. Moran and D. Wright, eds., *Mental Health and Canadian Society: Historical Perspectives.* Montreal: McGill-Queen's University Press, 2006.

Dyck, E., "Prairie Psychedelics: Mental Health Research in Saskatchewan, 1951-1967," in J. Moran and D. Wright, eds., *Mental Health and Canadian Society: Historical Perspectives.* Montreal: McGill-Queen's University Press, 2006.

Edzard, E., "A Leading Medical School Seriously Damaged: Vienna 1938." *History of Medicine, Annals of Internal Medicine* (2004), http://www.annals.org/content/122/10/789.full.

Ellenberger, H. F., *The Discovery of the Unconscious: The History and Evolution of Dynamic Psychiatry.* New York: Basic Books, 1970.

Ellis, L., "Aldwyn Stokes: The Man and His Contribution to Canadian Psychiatry." *Canadian Psychiatric Association Bulletin* (April 2000), http://ww1.cpa-cpc.org:8080/publications/archives/Bulletin/2000/April/History3.asp.

Farley, J., *Brock Chisolm, The World Health Organization, & the Cold War.* Vancouver: UBC Press, 2008.

Ferguson, G. A., "Psychology in Canada, 1939-1945." *Canadian Psychology* 33, no. 3 (October 1992): 692-705.

Fingard, J., and Rutherford, J., "Social Disintegration, Problem Pregnancies, Civilian Disasters: Psychiatric Research in Nova Scotia in the 1950s," in J. Moran and D. Wright, eds., *Mental Health and Canadian Society: Historical Perspectives.* Montreal: McGill-Queen's University Press, 2006.

Foucault, M., *Discipline and Punish: The Birth of the Prison.* Vintage Books: New York, 1977.

Frayn, D., *Psychoanalysis in Toronto.* Toronto: Ash Publications, 2000.

Freud, A., *Psycho-Analysis for Teachers and Parents.* New York: W. W. Norton & Co., 1935.

Friedland, Martin L., *The University of Toronto: A History.* Toronto: University of Toronto Press, 2002.

Gallagher, B., and Wilson, A., "Sex, Power and Political Identity." *Advocate* 8, no. 4 (August 1984).

Garfinkel, P. E., "Psychiatry in the New Millennium," *Can J Psychiatry* 45 (2000): 40-47.

Gitlin, T., "Foreword," in Riesman, David, *The Lonely Crowd.* New Haven: Yale University Press, 2000.

Gleason, M., *Normalizing the Ideal: Psychology, Schooling, and the Family in Postwar Canada.* Toronto: University of Toronto Press, 1999.

Goffman, E., *Asylums: Essays on the Situation of Mental Patients and Other Inmates*. Garden City, New York, Anchor, 1961.

Gold, J., Lalinec-Michaud, J., and Bernazzani, O., *Pioneers All: Women Psychiatrists in Canada: A History*. Ottawa: Canadian Psychiatric Association, 1995.

Goldberg, A., *Holocaust Survivors in Canada: Exclusion, Inclusion, Transformation, 1947–1955*. Winnipeg: University of Manitoba Press, 2015.

Gotzman, A., and Wiese, C., eds., *Modern Judaism and Historical Consciousness: Identities, Encounters, Perspectives*. Boston: Brill, 2007.

Grant, G., *Lament for a Nation: The Defeat of Canadian Nationalism*. Toronto: McLelland and Stewart Limited, 1965.

Gravil, R., "The Anglo-Argentine Connection and the War of 1914–1918." *Journal of Latin American Studies* 9, no. 1 (May 1977).

Greenacre, P., "The Impostor." *Psychoanalytic Quarterly* 27, no. 3 (1958).

Griffin, J. D., *In Search of Sanity: A Chronicle of the Canadian Mental Health Association, 1918–1988*. London: Third Eye, 1989.

Hancock, B. L., and Garner, R., "Theorizing Goffman and Freud: Goffman's Interaction as a Social-Structural Underpinning for Freud's Psychoanalytic Self." *Canadian Journal of Sociology* 40, no. 4 (2015).

Herberg, W., *Protestant, Catholic and Jew: An Essay in American Religious Sociology*. Garden City: Doubleday, 1960.

Hincks, C., "Sterilize the Unfit." *Maclean's Magazine*, February 15, 1946.

Irving, A., *Brock Chisolm: Doctor to the World*. Markham: Fitzhenry and Whiteside, 1998.

Jones, E., "Aubrey Lewis, Edward Mapother and the Maudsley." *Medical History* 22 (2003).

Jones, E., *Sigmund Freud: Life and Work*. London, Hogarth Press, 1953–1957.

Joyce, A.S, Tosca, G.A., Ogrodnicczuk, J.S., "Group Psychotherapy in Canada," *International Journal of Group Psychotherapy* 65, no. 4 (2015).

Koch, E., *Deemed Suspect: A Wartime Blunder*. Toronto: Methuene, 1980.

Levi, C., "The Jewish Quota in the Faculty of Medicine, University of Toronto: Generational Memory Sustained by Documentation." *Historical Studies in Education* 15, no. 1 (2003).

Lifton, R. J., *The Nazi Doctors: Medical Killing and the Psychology of Genocide*. New York: Basic Books, 1988.

Lipinsky, J., *Imposing Their Will: An Organizational History of Jewish Toronto, 1933–1948*. Montreal & Kingston: McGill-Queen's University Press, 2011.

Loosley, E. W. M., *Memories of the Loosleys and Magees: Two Canadian Pioneer Families*. Unpublished memoir.

Low, B. J., "'The Hand that Rocked the Cradle': A Critical Analysis of Rockefeller Philanthropic Funding, 1920–1960." *Historical Studies in Education* 16, no. 1 (2004).

Mallinson, T., *An Experimental Investigation of Group-Directed Discussion in the Classroom*. PhD Diss., Department of Psychology, University of Toronto, 1955.

Mazmdar, Pauline M. H., *Eugenics, Human Genetics and Human Failings: The Eugenics Society, Its Sources and Its Critics in Britain*. London: Routledge, 1992.

McLaren, A., *Our Own Master Race: Eugenics in Canada, 1885–1945*. Toronto: Oxford University Press, 1990.

McConnachie, K., *Science and Ideology: The Mental Hygiene and Eugenics Movements in the Inter-War Years, 1919–1939*. PhD Diss., University of Toronto, 1987.

McKay, I., *Rebels, Reds, Radicals: Rethinking Canada's Left History*. Toronto: Between the Lines, 2005.

McLaughlin, N., "'Critical Theory Meets America': Riesman, Fromm, and The Lonely Crowd." *The American Sociologist* (Spring 2001).

Midgely, N., "'The Matchbox School': Anna Freud and the Idea of a 'Psychoanalytically Informed Education.'" *Journal of Child Psychotherapy* 34, no. 1 (2008).

Miller, J., *The Passion of Michel Foucault*. New York: Simon and Schuster, 1993.

Phillips, C. E., "Education in Canada, 1939–46." *History of Education Journal* 3, no. 1 (Autumn 1951).

Plato, *The Republic of Plato*. Oxford: Oxford University Press, 1951.

Pols, H., "'Anomie in the Metropolis': The City in American Sociology and Psychiatry, 'Osiris.'" *Science and the City* 18 (2003).

Pols, H., "'Between the Laboratory and Life': Child Development Research in Toronto, 1919–1956." *History of Psychology* 5, no. 2 (2002).

Pols, H., "'Between the Laboratory, The School, and the Community': The Psychology of Human Development, 1916–1956." *Canadian Journal of Community Mental Health* 19, no. 2 (Fall 2000).

Rabinow, P., and N. Rose, eds., *The Essential Foucault, Selections of Essential Works of Foucault, 1954–1984*. New York: The New Press, 1994.

Raymond, J. M., *The Nursery World of Dr. Blatz*. Toronto: University of Toronto Press, 1991.

Richardson, T., *The Century of the Child: The Mental Hygiene Movement and Social Policy in the United States and Canada*. New York: State University of New York Press, 1989.

Riesman, D., *The Lonely Crowd*. New Haven: Yale University Press, 2001.

Ross, Murray G., *The Way Must Be Tried: Memoirs of a University Man*. Toronto: Stoddart Publishing Co., 1992.

Rossman, M., "The Fool of Sociology." *Sociological Inquiry, Journal of the National Sociology Honor Society* 46, nos. 3–4 (1976).

Sable, M., "'George Drew and the Rabbis': Religious Education in Ontario's Public Schools." *Association for Canadian Jewish Studies* 6 (1998).

Saywell, John T., *Someone to Teach Them: York and the Great University Explosion, 1960–1973*. Toronto: University of Toronto Press., 2008.

Schnell R. L., "'The Right Class of Boy': Youth Training Schemes and Assisted Emigration to Canada under the Empire Settlement Act, 1922–1939." *History of Education* 24, no. 1 (1995).

Schull, J., *Ontario Since 1867*. Toronto: McLellland and Stewart, 1985.

Searle, G. R., *Eugenics and Politics in Britain, 1900–1914*. Leydon: Noordhoff International Publishing, 1976.

Seeley, J. R., Sim, A., Loosley, E., *Crestwood Heights: A Study of the Culture of Suburban Life*. New York: Basic Books, 1956.

Seeley, J. R., *Americanization of the Unconscious*. New York: International Science Press, 1967.

Shorter, E., ed., *TPH: History and Memories of the Toronto Psychiatric Hospital, 1925-1966*. Toronto: Wall and Emerson Inc., 1996.

Sim, R. (sr), and Sim, R. A., *Robert Sim: His Life and Work 1876-1956*. Toronto: Sim Post, 2002.

Simmons, H. G., *Unbalanced: Mental Health Policy in Ontario, 1930-1989*. Toronto: Wall and Thompson, 1990.

Straw, W., "'Traffic in Scandal': The Story of Broadway Brevities." *University of Toronto Quarterly* 73, no. 4 (Fall 2004).

Strong-Boag, V., "'Home Dreams': Women and the Suburban Experiment in Canada 1945-1960." *Canadian Historical Review* 72, no. 4 (1991).

Sutton, N., *Bruno Bettleheim: The Other Side of Madness*. London: Duckworth Press, 1995.

Thomson, G. E., *Remove From Our Midst These Unfortunates: A Historical Inquiry Into the Influence of Eugenics, Educational Efficiency as well as Mental Hygiene Upon the Vancouver School System and Its Special Classes, 1910-1969*. PhD Diss., University of British Columbia, 1999.

Thomson, G. E., "'Not an Attempt to Coddle Children': Dr. Charles Hegler Gundry and the Mental Hygiene Division of the Vancouver School Board, 1939-1969." *Historical Studies in Education / Revue d'histoire de l'éducation* 14, no. 2 (2002).

Tisshaw, K. S., "'Ultra-Modern Village School': Newest Forest Hill Unit has Complete Facilities for Intercommunication." *Civic Administration* (February 1950).

Tomkins, G. S., *A Common Countenance: Stability and Change in the Canadian Curriculum*. Scarborough: Prentice-Hall, 1986.

Weinstein, H., *A Father, a Son and the CIA*. Toronto: James Lortimer & Co, 1988.

Williams, S., "Sympathy for the Devil," *Toronto Life Magazine*, September 1979.

Wright, D., and Saucier, R. "Madness in the Archives: Anonymity, Ethics, and Mental Health History Research." *Journal of the Canadian Historical Association / Revue de la Société historique du Canada* 23, no. 2 (2012): 65-90.

Wright, M. J., and Myers, C. R, eds., *History of Academic Psychology in Canada*. Toronto: C. J. Hogrefe Press, 1982.

Zaretsky, E., "'Charisma or Rationalization?' Domesticity and Psychoanalysis in the United States in the 1950s." *Critical Inquiry* (Winter 2000).

# Index

Adams, Mary Louise
  *The Trouble with Normal*, 136
Adler, Alfred, 48
Aichorn, August, 159, 164
Alan, Gary
  *Second Chicago School? The Development of Postwar American Sociology*, 69
Allen, Woody
  *Zelig*, 67
*The Americanization of the Unconscious*, 80, 235–249
Annau, Catherine
  *Eager Eugenicists*, 46
Anschluss, 158, 160, 168
Anti-Semitism, 88, 100–102, 120–121, 123, 125, 127–128, 132, 149, 155, 169, 178, 183, 202, 206, 220–221
Anxiety, 3, 6, 76–77, 83, 102, 110, 123, 167, 170–172, 182–187, 211, 236, 235, 238-239
Aufreiter, Johann, 154
Auschwitz, 103, 127, 179
Bagnell, Kenneth, 32
  *The Little Immigrants*, 28
Bagshaw, Elizabeth, 46
Basic Books, 190–192, 200, 202
Bell, Norm, 108–109
Bellamy, Mathew
  *Profiting the Crown*, 237
Bentley, George Firman, 225, 237–239
Bettleheim, Bruno, 67–75, 102, 112, 171, 177–179, 181, 184, 213
  *Love is not Enough*, 73–74
  *The Professional Soldier: A Social and Political Portrait*, 70
  *Social Change and Prejudice*, 71
  *Symbolic Wounds: Puberty Rites and the Envious Male*, 74
Bialystok, Franklin
  *Delayed Impact*, 126, 221
Bion, Wilfred, 95
Bissell, Claude, 230
Blacker, Carlos Paton, 95–96

Blair, Frederick Charles, 34
Blatz, William, 44, 48–50, 113, 116, 120, 195, 198 – 199, 219
Bledsoe, Jim, 231
Bloom, Allan, 67, 74
Bott, Edward, 44, 48–49
Boulanger, Jean-Baptiste, 96
Bowlby, John, 95
Brandeis University, 5, 218, 229
Breines, Wini, 135–136, 180,
British Eugenics Society, 95
British Immigration and Colonization Association (B. I. C. A.), 32–34, 36
Brown, Norman O., 217 Browne, R.W., 54
Bullis, Edmund, 112–113
Cameron, Ewan, 84–85, 96
Cameron, G.D.W., 89–91
Camp I (Fort Lennox), 166–168
Canadian Art Therapy Association, 169
Canadian Commonwealth Federation (CCF), 87, 189
Canadian Institute of Psychoanalysis, 149
Canadian Jewish Congress, 121, 126, 128, 133
Canadian Mental Health Association (CMHA), 4, 76, 86, 120, 177, 186, 213, 233
Canadian National Committee on Mental Hygiene (CNCMH), 41–43, 45, 47–50, 53, 81–83, 85–89, 91–94, 99–100, 148,
Canadian Psychoanalytic Society, 96, 155
Canadian Psychological Association (CPA), 52–53
Carver, H.S.M., 39–40
Center for the Study of Democratic Institutions, 229
Central Intelligence Agency (CIA), 96
Chisolm, Brock, 41, 44, 50–55, 59–61, 65, 83, 89
Christie Pits Riots, 121
Churchill, Winston, 95
Civilian Advisory Committee, 57–60, 62–63
Clarke Institute of Psychiatry, 3, 95

Clarke, Charles K., 41–42, 47–48, 50, 93–94, 149
Coates, Donald
 *John Seeley: Poet and Revolutionary*, 233
Coates, Lila Frances (Maltby), 105, 107, 109–110, 198, 227
Cohen, Sol, 44
Cold War, 41, 59, 83, 119, 224
*Community Chest: A Case Study in Philanthropy*, 1888
Concentration, 183–186
Coontz, Stephanie
 *The Way We Never Were*, 136
Copp, T. and B. McAndrew, 51, 54
 *Battle Exhaustion: Soldiers and Psychiatrists in the Canadian Army*, 40
Court, John, 8
*Crestwood Heights*, 5–7, 68, 75–78, 80, 93, 107, 118–119, 122, 125, 127, 131–133, 135–137, 139, 154, 178, 180–187, 188–192, 193 – 211, 213, 215, 217-221, 231–235
Dachau, 69, 160-161, 237
Dassin, Jules
 *The Naked City*, 135
Deracination, 183
Dewey, John, 64
Diefenbaker, John 223
Dionne Quintuplets, 48–49, 219
Directors Personnel Advisory Committee (DPAC), 230–231
Doan, Mary, 122–123, 193, 195–196
Douglas, Tommy, 42
Dowbiggin, Ian, 50, 94
 *Keeping America Sane*, 42
Dreams, 152, 159, 174, 240
Duffin, Jacalyn
 *Langstaff: A Nineteenth Century Medical Life*, 157
Duhl, Leonard, 5, 231
Earl, R.O., 228
Eichmann, Adolf, 129
Eppinger, Hans, 161
Epstein, Nathan B., 155
Eugenics Society of Canada (ESC), 48, 52–53
Eugenics, 41–50, 52–53, 59–60, 65, 94–97, 99, 120, 157, 160, 232–233
Farquharson, Ray, 227–228
Farrar, C.B., 47–48, 94–95, 149
Feinberg, A.L., 128–131, 133, 204
Fenwick, C.P., 57
Film Noir, 134–135, 146
Fischer, Beatrice, 8, 11–12, 24, 120, 147, 152–155, 158, 160–161, 164, 168

Fischer, Erica, 154, 155, 160, 162, 163, 169, 170
Fischer, Martin, 11–12, 14, 17, 20–21, 23, 32, 57, 69, 71–72, 102, 121, 146–178, 180, 181, 188, 211–214, 219, 221, 222, 227, 234, 237,
*Flash*, 127–128, 133, 220
Forest Hill Village Project, 4–5, 7, 9, 44, 50, 60, 62, 76, 81, 83, 85, 87–88, 93–94, 96, 98–101, 103–106, 108, 110–113, 117–118, 122, 125, 127, 129–130, 133, 136, 138, 140–141, 146, 171–172, 188–190, 192, 198, 207, 211, 213–215, 221, 222, 226, 230
 and Adult Seminars, 117–119, 122–124
 and Child Guidance Clinic, 83, 105, 107–110, 148, 183
 and Human Relations Classes, 112–114, 116, 118, 131-133, 183, 215, 233
Foucault, Michel, 87, 180
 *Discipline and Punish*, 113–114
 *Mental Illness and Psychology*, 180
Frayn, Douglas, 95, 149, 159
Freud, Anna, 4, 9, 159
Freud, Sigmund, 3, 12, 17, 27, 47–48, 61, 65–66, 68–69, 74, 95, 110, 118, 151, 154, 158–159, 177, 186, 192, 216, 217–219, 224, 239
Friedeberg, Emil Emmanuel, 14–15, 17–19, 23–24
Friedeberg, Frank, 14, 18, 20, 22–25, 27, 30, 62, 71, 102, 152, 154, 172–175, 221, 227
Friedeberg-Seeley, Lilly, 14–31, 35, 62–63, 71, 154, 172–174, 220
Fromm, Erich, 66–69, 157, 192, 202, 219
 *Escape from Freedom and Man from Himself*, 68
Frost, Leslie M., 87
Gadamer, Hans-Georg, 229
Gerstein, Reva, 49, 120, 177, 213
Gleason, Mona, 48
*Globe and Mail*, 7–8, 23, 224–225, 229
Goffman, Erving
 *Asylums*, 180, 187
Goldberg, Adara
 *Holocaust Survivors in Canada*, 130
Government of Canada, 36, 49–50, 59, 88–93, 101, 120, 162, 182, 198, 219, 224, 237
 and Directorate of Personnel Selection (DPS), 39–40, 54
 and Department of National Defense (DND), 39–41, 52–55, 57

Graham, Don, 86–87, 127, 133, 191, 196, 198, 211–212
Grant, George
  *Lament for a Nation*, 9, 223
Greenland, Cyril, 8, 50
Griffin, John, 41, 44–47, 50, 53–57, 59, 65, 82–83, 85–87, 92, 99, 102, 105, 112–116, 195, 213
Group Psychotherapy, 151, 233
Habermas, Jurgen, 290
Herberg, Will, 120
  *Protestant, Catholic and Jew*, 119
Hincks, Clarence, 41–45, 47–50, 54, 59–60, 65, 82–83, 85, 87, 91–92, 94, 99, 102, 112–113, 213
Holding Therapy, 179
Holocaust, 7, 43, 88, 100–101, 125–127, 129–132, 134, 157–158, 160, 165, 169, 183, 237
Holy Blossom Temple, 124–125, 128–130
Home Children, 36, 42, 57, 120
Home Office, 15–17, 19, 28–29
Hughes, Everett, 68, 180
Hunter, Robyn, 149
Huxley, Aldous
  *Brave New World*, 68
Irving, Alan, 51–52
Jackson, R.W.B., 229–230
Jeanneret, Marsh, 68, 202, 203
Josie, Gordon H., 90–91
Jung, Carl, 3, 95, 151
Kafka, Franz, 174
Kesey, Ken
  *One Flew Over the Cuckoo's Nest*, 180
Keynes, John Maynard, 27, 95
Kidd, Roby, 231
King, Allan
  *Warrendale*, 151, 169, 178–179
King, Margery, 86, 213
Kitchener Camp, 163–164
Koch, Eric
  *Deemed Suspect*, 163
Kohut, Heinz, 3
Kraeplin, Emil, 47, 95
Kristallnacht, 163
Letson, Harry, 51–52
Levine, David
  *The Dawn of Modernity*, 4, 8, 236–237
Levitt, Cyril
  *The Riot at Christie Pits*, 236
Lewis, Aubrey, 95–96
Line, William, 39–41, 44, 49–50, 53–55, 57–58, 64–65, 83, 86–87, 94, 99, 102, 113–116

Lipinski, Jack,
  *Imposing Their Will: An Organizational History of Jewish Toronto*, 121
Loosley, Elizabeth, 78, 122, 188–191, 193, 199–200, 210
  *Memoires of the Loosley's and Magee's: Two Canadian Pioneer Families*, 189
Low, Brian J., 7
Lynd, Robert
  *Middletown*, 6–7
Mackenzie-King, William Lyon, 140
MacMurty, Helen, 170
Mallinson, Thomas, 76, 112–113, 116, 132, 233
Marshall, Hillary, 205–207, 210
Martin, Paul, 64, 92–93
Massachusetts Institute of Technology, 229
Maudsley Hospital, 95–96
McGill University, 3, 84, 96
McLaren, 48
  *Our Own Master Race: Eugenics in Canada*, 44, 120
McPhail, Agnes, 42
Mengele, Josef, 103–104, 179
Mesmer, Franz Anton, 49, 150
Misgeld, Dieter, 229–231
Nietzsche, Friedrich, 67–69
Ontario Institute for Studies in Education (OISE), 4, 7–8, 229–231
Orthogenic School in Chicago, 73–74, 177
Orwell, George
  *1984*, 68, 85
Owram, Doug, 134
Packard, Vance
  *The Hidden Persuaders*, 236
Parkin, Alan, 154
Pernkopf, Eduard, 160
Phillips, Eric, 223
Plato, 61, 135, 216, 221, 236
Pötzl, Otto, 159
Psychoanalysis, 3–4, 6, 9, 11, 41, 44, 46, 60, 64–66, 68–69, 73–74, 95–96, 102, 111–114, 116, 121, 135, 146–157, 158–159, 169–170, 171, 173, 175, 177–181, 186, 186, 188, 214, 216–217, 233, 235, 239
Queen's University, 106, 149
Radcliffe, G., 52–53
Ralston, James, 53
Regal Road School Project, 50, 86, 113
Riesman, David, 5–7, 67–69, 70, 72, 75, 77, 80, 102, 112, 118, 120, 133, 136, 140, 157, 171, 185, 192, 199–204, 213, 219, 237
  *The Lonely Crowd*, 5–6, 67–68, 74, 140

Rosenthal, Arthur, 192, 200, 202
Ross, Murray, 38, 72, 154, 176, 214-215,
   221–231, 232–234
   *Memoirs*, 227
Rossman, Michael, 234
Ruby, Clayton, 5, 154, 216- 221
Rudin, Ernst, 47
Sable, Martin, 133
Sachs, Hans, 66
Sachsenhausen, 164
Sadism, 103, 180-181, 235, 236
Salome, Lou Andreas, 159
Salutin, Rick, 154, 217–218
Saywell, John T., 225–226
Schiffer, Irvine, 154
Schwartz, Morris, 5, 108
Searle, G.R.
   *Eugenics and Politics in Britain*, 120
Seeley, John R.,
   and interviews with author, 8–12, 37, 55,
      71, 81, 115, 173, 196
   and anxiety, 6, 76–77, 102, 167, 171–172,
      2011
   and biblical David, 8 and Christianity, 11,
      69, 236
   and Martin Fischer, 11–12, 14, 17, 20,
      23, 32, 57, 69, 71–72, 102, 121,
      146–157, 169–178, 182, 213–214
   and Forest Hill Village Collegiate, 87–88,
      100, 108, 128, 131–132, 138,
      193, 214
   and Immigration, 28–32
   and Canadian military, 39–65
   and Riesman, 5–7, 66, 68–69, 72, 75, 77,
      80, 102, 112, 118, 120, 133, 136,
      170, 171, 185, 192, 199–204, 213,
      219, 237
   and Bettleheim, 67–75, 102, 112, 171,
      177–179, 181, 184, 213
   and Everett Hughes, 75–80, 88, 98, 180
   and Aldwyn Stokes, 95–98, 99, 102, 112,
      148, 149, 154, 190-198, 203–204,
      212–215, 231
   and Clayton Ruby, 5, 154, 216- 221
   and Tom Mallinson, 76, 116
   and William Line, 39, 49, 55, 64–65,
      115–116, 214
   and Alex Sim, 76, 78, 93, 122,188–189,
      194–202, 209–212
   and Murray Ross, 38, 72, 154 176,
      214-215, 221–231, 232–234
Seeley, Margaret, 38, 66, 70, 154, 174–177
Shakespeare, William, 120

Sim, Alexander, 76, 78, 93, 107, 110, 122,
   124–125, 188–189, 194–202,
   *Robert Sim II: His Life and Work,
      1876–1956*, 189
Simmons, Harvey, 89
Smith, Sydney, 64, 222-225
Sociology, 4–8, 64–71, 75, 78, 81, 94, 98, 110,
   112, 119-120, 134–136, 183-187,
   193-196, 217–218
Socrates, 71, 219, 233
Spock, Benjamin, 9–10
Stanton, Alfred, 108–109
Stodghill, Charles, 89–91
Stokes, Aldwyn, 47, 94–100, 102, 108, 112,
   120–121, 148–149, 154,190-198,
   203-204, 212–215, 231
*Strange Journey*, 8, 35
Strong-Boag, Veronica
   *Home Dreams*, 135
Suicide, 55–57, 161, 175
Teicher, Morton, 148
Thompson, Peter, 95–96
Thomson, G.E., 44, 154
*Toronto Daily Star*, 127–128, 130, 207, 208,
   220
Toronto Psychiatric Hospital, 47, 94, 107–108,
   148–149
Toronto Psychoanalytic Study Circle, 154
*Toronto Star*, 98, 139, 142, 170, 206, 211, 218,
   223–224
*Toronto Telegram*, 206
Trilling, Lionel, 6
Troper, Harold and Irving Abella
   *None is Too Many*, 120, 237
Trott, Vernon, 86–88, 191, 198
Trudeau, Justin, 233–234
Trudeau, Pierre, 224, 233
University of California, 5, 230
University of Chicago, 6, 25, 37, 39, 65–67,
   69–70, 73, 75, 78–79, 81, 99, 102, 180
   188, 193, 215
University of Toronto, 39, 49–50, 63, 86,
   92, 101, 105–108, 148–149, 55, 159,
   168–169, 188, 190, 196, 202, 205, 214,
   215, 229–231, 233, 235
   and Jewish Quotas, 148
   and Department of Psychiatry, 4, 41,
      47–48, 88, 91–92, 94–98, 105,
      145, 148–149, 159, 169, 177, 192,
      196, 212–214, 214, 233
   and University of Toronto Press, 68, 78,
      188, 190, 202, 205–206
University of Vienna, 158–161, 163

Veblen, Thorstein, 119
Wagner-Jauregg, Julius, 159
Watson, Gordon, 196–197
Weber, Max, 68
   *Protestant Ethic and the Spirit of Capitalism*, 6
Whyte, William H. Jr.
   *The Organization Man*, 5
Wilder, Billy
   *Double Indemnity*, 135
World War I, 14–15, 29, 32, 39, 44, 49, 51, 95, 158, 160
World War II, 32, 40–41, 43, 47, 51, 53–54, 56, 59, 62, 82, 100, 160, 166, 189, 237
York University, 38, 176, 216, 219, 222–228, 229, 234